Praise for *Wild on Purpose*

"The most exciting environmental idea of the twenty-first century is a massive private-lands effort to recreate our lost American Serengeti, and Sean Gerrity is the Muir-like visionary who launched it. *Wild On Purpose* is Sean's story of how this globally-famous idea came to be. I wager Americans will still be reading this book a century from now."

—DAN FLORES, *Wild New World*

"Wild places are dying and disappearing from agricultural over-use and under acres of asphalt. Gerrity's *Wild on Purpose* is part memoir, part conservation narrative, part origin story, and a much needed call-to-action to reimagine, protect, and revitalize the wild spaces of the Western prairie. Beautifully written, compelling, and a reminder that action is needed now more than ever."

—REBECCA LEBER-GOTTBERG, Rediscovered Books

"*Wild on Purpose* challenges the notion that our greatest nature conservation successes are behind us. Sean Gerrity's story demonstrates that the most ambitious and exciting work is yet to come, and rewilding is at the heart of it."

—KRIS TOMPKINS, President & Co-Founder of Tompkins Conservation and former CEO of Patagonia

"Gerrity is an impressive leader and an inspiring conservationist who can teach us all a thing or two about turning magnificent dreams into glorious reality. I've had the privilege of hiking and paddling through part of the American Prairie project area with him while filming BBC's The America's documentary series, and I was blown away by his vision, commitment and achievements. The effort of prairie rewilding is an astonishing, bold idea. Read *Wild on Purpose,* learn more about thinking big, creating change, helping improve our planet."

—SIMON REEVE, *Journeys to Impossible Places*

"A book about the future of conservation couldn't have come at a better time. Amidst so much uncertainty, the story of the American Prairie Reserve stands as a guiding light, showing how large-scale conservation efforts can create space for the biodiversity and humanity that nature intended. It's a powerful reminder that the impossible becomes possible when your vision is clear. *Wild on Purpose* is a powerful story of how a visionary made the impossible possible."

—KATRINA MENDREY, Chapter One Bookstore

"*Wild on Purpose* is the deeply personal, inside account of a great experiment in large landscape conservation. We need more Sean Gerritys!"

—BETSY GAINES QUAMMEN, *True West* and *American Zion*

WILD ON PURPOSE

WILD on Purpose

The American Prairie Story and the Art of Thinking Bigger

Sean Gerrity

TORREY HOUSE PRESS

Salt Lake City • Torrey

First Torrey House Press Edition, November 2025
Copyright © 2025 by Sean Gerrity

All rights reserved. No part of this book may be reproduced or retransmitted in any form or by any means without the written consent of the publisher.

NO AI TRAINING: Without in any way limiting the author's (and publisher's) exclusive rights under copyright, any use of this publication to "train" generative artificial intelligence (AI) technologies to generate text is expressly prohibited. The author reserves all rights to license uses of this work for generative AI training and development of machine learning language models.

Published by Torrey House Press
Salt Lake City, Utah
www.torreyhouse.org

International Standard Book Number: 979-8-89092-034-8
E-book ISBN: 979-8-89092-035-5
Library of Congress Control Number: 2024952448

Cover design by Kathleen Metcalf
Interior design by Lark Washburn
Illustrations by Eryon Shondíín Greenburg
Distributed to the trade by Consortium Book Sales and Distribution

Torrey House Press offices in Salt Lake City sit on the homelands of Ute, Goshute, Shoshone, and Paiute nations. Offices in Torrey are on the homelands of Southern Paiute, Ute, and Navajo nations.

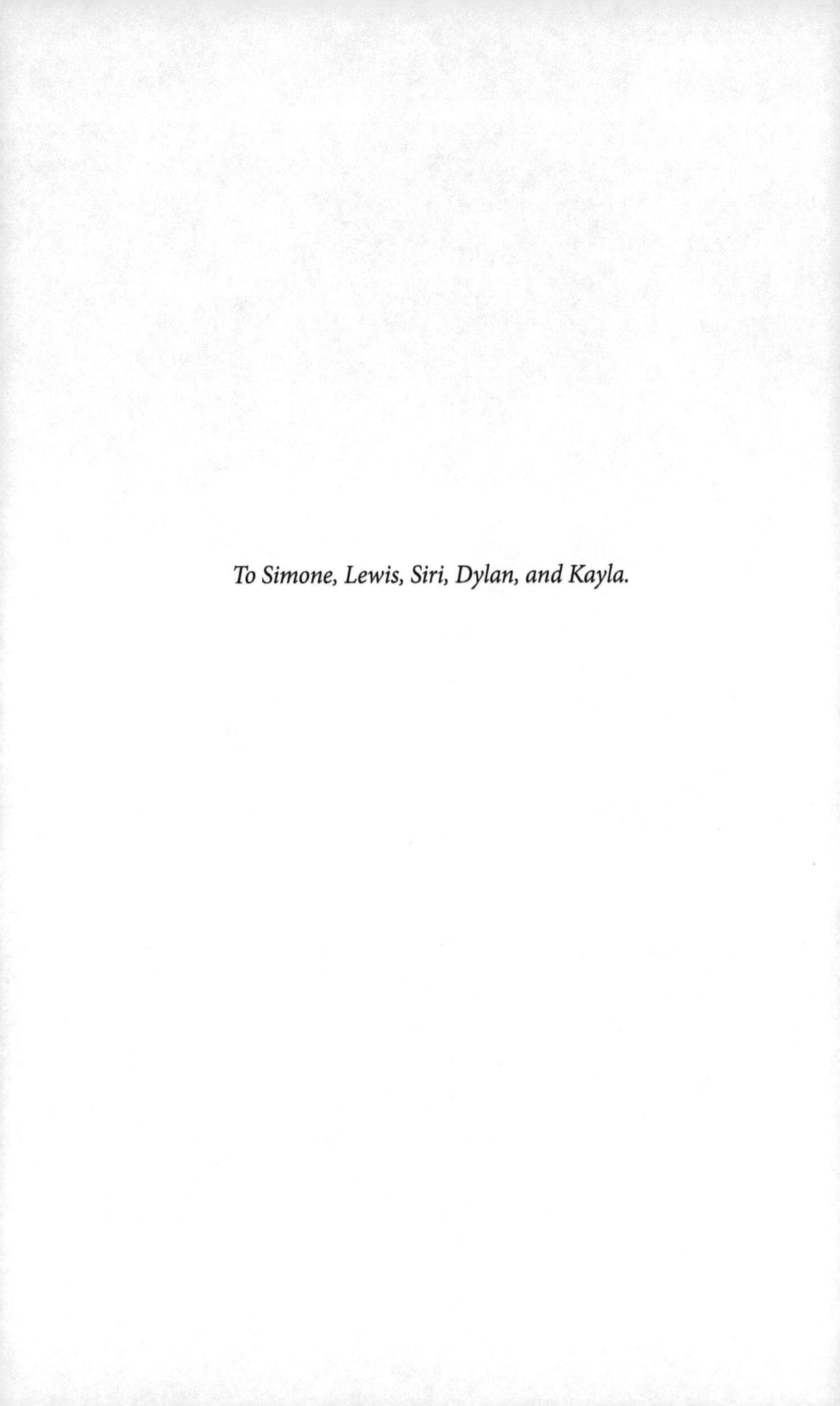

To Simone, Lewis, Siri, Dylan, and Kayla.

CONTENTS

Foreword by Ken Burns — i
Prelude: Homecoming — 1

Chapter 1 — Baselines — 11
Chapter 2 — A New Way of Seeing — 67
Chapter 3 — No Looking Back — 79
Chapter 4 — Adapting Nonstop — 91
Chapter 5 — Welcome to American Prairie — 101
Chapter 6 — The Art of Momentum — 119
Chapter 7 — Making Change — 151
Chapter 8 — Semi-Relaxing into Level Flight — 167
Chapter 9 — New Endings, New Beginnings — 189
Chapter 10 — Wayfinding — 197
Chapter 11 — Purpose and Values — 217
Chapter 12 — Vision and Alignment — 231
Chapter 13 — Embracing and Navigating Transitions — 247
Chapter 14 — Doubts and Risks — 257
Chapter 15 — Optimism and Hope — 273
Chapter 16 — Trendlines — 283
Chapter 17 — Feeding the World's Humans — 295
Chapter 18 — Onward — 303

Afterword by George Horse Capture Jr. — 309
Acknowledgments — 311
Suggested Further Resources — 313

"The best time to plant a tree was thirty years ago.
The second-best time is now."

—*Origin Unknown*

Foreword

KEN BURNS

The American Prairie story is nothing short of historic. Almost unbelievable in this day and age where it can seem overwhelming to move large, visionary projects forward, American Prairie is working steadily toward its goal of connecting 3.2 million acres to create the largest wildlife reserve ever established in the Lower 48 states.

I've always believed that one of the many factors that contribute to America's uniqueness is our long history of people pursuing exciting, inspiring and lofty ideas, and then, through ingenuity and perseverance, bringing them to fruition in ways that strengthen us as a nation. In this captivating and compelling story, Sean Gerrity describes the circumstances and events in which he and his team took a stunningly big idea—one that had existed for a very long time—and made it a reality.

Sean grew up in a middle-class environment, mostly in Montana, without a prestigious network of people to draw upon or access to significant financial resources. But during his first forty years of life, he accumulated the kinds of experiences and skills that led to his being perfectly suited for launching and effectively stewarding the nascent American Prairie effort from the early 2000s through 2017. Sean recognized that the opportunity to lead American Prairie intersected with a particular phase of his life where his purpose, values, and vision aligned ideally with the needs of the fledgling project. He then carefully assembled an excellent staff and board of directors that year by year racked up nonstop, incremental successes and built ever stronger momentum on American Prairie's way to creating what now can be described as a "movement."

Sean Gerrity is a person who was able to step in and play a critical role at the right time, which included setting out a workable path toward the vision, coalescing the right team for the early and middle phases of the project, and keeping the effort on a highly productive track for the first decade and a half. The collective hero of this story ends up being the staff, board of directors, and the thousands of supporters who together have helped move this extraordinary endeavor toward completion.

Sean's example is one for all of us. He didn't start out as a conservationist and knew little about the field, but during his seventeen years as American Prairie's leader, his views evolved regarding why conservation is so important and why it's our job to preserve nature and biodiversity on our fragile planet. Sean describes how the remarkable achievements of American Prairie should not be viewed as an anomaly. Much of what American Prairie has accomplished can be replicated in various biomes around the world where nature sorely needs our help. Sean also believes that many facets of his own personal journey may be emulated by others.

America's complex past includes countless achievements that have significantly improved our country. But this history also involves many things that have hurt rather than helped us as a country. Still, the United States has always been, and remains, a nation in which there exist endless possibilities of improving our interactions with each other and the natural world. Sean Gerrity has given us a book that challenges all of us to think about how we might move forward to make some of our bold, seemingly impossible dreams come true.

Homecoming

If any of those things get on my property, I'm going to shoot them."

I'm talking with a seventy-year-old rancher named Ray Shores as we are both filing into a community meeting. A tall bear of a man in worn coveralls, he raises a finger and points at me as we stand at arm's length in the doorway and says, "You need to be responsible for those things!" I reply that if our bison somehow got on his property, we ask that he give us twenty-four hours to get there to ensure there is no damage done and move them back to our place. I said if we can't make it right in twenty-four hours, he would be welcome to shoot them. A bit surprised at that, he replies, "Well … I suppose that works alright for me," and continues on into the room to find a seat in the big circle of folding metal chairs.

It's 2005, on a warm Tuesday afternoon and we're inside Second Creek Hall, a small arena about the size of a basketball court roughly a hundred miles south of the Canadian border, where Curt Freese, Kyran Kunkel, and I are meeting with fifty or so local cattle ranchers at their request. I'd learned that if ranchers bother to gather on a weekday afternoon, versus a weekend social gathering, it usually involves a less-than-positive topic. Sometimes it is to discuss new regulations regarding water rights or rumored changes to federal guidelines and fees related to their leased government lands. Today, however, they are here to grill me and my colleagues about our long-term plans.

A few weeks ago, word got out that American Prairie had purchased twenty-two thousand acres of former grazing land where, among other rewilding initiatives, we intended to reintroduce bison, which had been absent from the Montana prairie for more than 120 years. Bison are the largest land animals in North America, with males often growing to six feet tall at the shoulder and weighing as much as two thousand pounds. An estimated thirty million or more of these beautiful creatures with shaggy brown fur, short black horns, and tufts of goatee-like hair under their chins once roamed in vast herds across the grasslands of what is now the United States, Canada, and Mexico. But largely due to extensive commercial hunting in the late 1800s, their numbers plummeted to fewer than one thousand by the turn of the twentieth century.

We planned to reintroduce these animals as part of American Prairie's mission, which is to carry out the largest privately funded restoration of a fully inact and wild prairie ecosystem in North America. One acre at a time, we are rebuilding essentially an American Serengeti, complete with pronghorn, prairie dogs, pollinators, grassland birds, cougars, swift fox, bison, black-footed ferrets, and countless other species that have in the recent past been wholly eradicated or reduced to miniscule populations and replaced with agricultural operations.

But first we have to introduce ourselves to our neighbors. We are seated in a circle of fifty in the community hall.

"I've heard that bison are the most destructive animals on the planet," claims one rancher. "They'll bust through every fence and infect all my cattle with disease," warns another.

And another, one of our direct neighbors in his eighties, muses about our larger plans. "A lot of these animals you want to bring back have no value. When Lewis and Clark came through on their expedition, they never wrote anything in their journals about eating prairie dog stew! So why do you want to bring back prairie dogs? What good are they?"

While it's true that bison can catapult their muscular bodies to speeds of more than thirty miles per hour, they're grazing animals that subsist mainly on grasses. They don't tend to bother other species or destroy property. Furthermore, as I'd said to Ray on our way in, I emphasized that if any of our bison escape, we will fetch them immediately. And if we can't within twenty-four hours, I explain that they are welcome to shoot the animals—provided that they deem it necessary. What's more, we promise to disease-test them regularly and provide written animal health reports to anyone who asks.

Some ranchers seem to regard us with some level of openness, others grumble and dab sweat off their faces. One rancher leaning against the wall and listening to the proceedings says, "Let's just cut to the chase. How many of these bison are you trying to bring here with this first round? Five hundred? A thousand?"

I clear my throat. "Actually, eight."

"*Eight?!*" He says incredulously. Then what the hell are we all doing here? Sheesh!" Others around the circle interject that, once those eight were on the ground, many more would come later, which we confirm. But by this time, we have answered most of the questions, and the ranchers begin filtering out. We offer that we will be writing up a Memorandum of Understanding (MOU) for their consideration outlining our intentions on how we would operate with disease testing and, if needed, the retrieving of any bison that wander away from our property. The completed five-year MOU, which covers all details of our bison management philosophy and practices and includes an open invitation to come tour our operations at any time, was later sent to all property owners who were part of the local Ranchers Stewardship Alliance (RSA). There are 2.6 million cattle in Montana—that's three for every man, woman, and child—so there's only so much fuss you can kick up over eight bison. Some of the ranchers shake hands with

Curt, Kyran, and me. Some just nod on their way by; a few glower at us and shake their heads. Many are clearly not wild about their future neighbors, but we've cleared our first hurdle. And while we intend to steadily bring more than eight bison to Montana—and eventually build to thousands—that's a topic for another day.

Two weeks later I'm at Wind Cave National Park in South Dakota with my friend and colleague Curt. A biologist and former chief scientist at World Wildlife Fund (WWF), Curt cofounded American Prairie, and without him, my long journey to build an American Serengeti would still be a pipe dream. Together with some of our fledgling staffs from American Prairie and WWF, we are preparing for one of the more important days in American Prairie's short existence. Nestled between Black Hills National Forest and Badlands National Park, Wind Cave shelters a wild bison population that at the time was believed to be one of the least genetically compromised, semi-free-roaming bison herds in North America. Wind Cave has a maximum carrying capacity of 450 bison given its limited available habitat. Each year they must round up excess animals and transfer them to other reserves and tribal reservations. Thanks to Curt and his team, after months of negotiations with the National Park Service and navigation of a mountain of paperwork, we've been approved to purchase and transport twice the number of bison we'd originally requested and now will have sixteen bison for our reserve.

In those days, rounding up the bison at Wind Cave was an exercise in controlled chaos. A park service helicopter glides a few dozen feet over the treetops. Its booming blades are like a giant leaf blower in the sky, scaring the bison into openings in the trees. They sprint away, but the chopper nimbly changes direction and cuts them off. The animals and the machine continue this strange dance for thirty minutes or so, the bison charging and reversing direction like an NFL halfback and the helicopter slowly gliding to and fro in response. The bison begin to tire and are steadily driven toward a giant complex set of corrals about an acre in diameter. The helicopter eases them into a winged chute that spirals inward, gradually narrowing until the agitated animals trot in single file into the inner pen. At long last, the bison are contained. The helicopter flies off to get another batch of bison, and the prairie is quiet and still once more.

Just a little while longer, I want to tell them, *then you'll be free again.* The land they will soon be roaming in Montana is nearly 30 percent bigger than Wind Cave National Park; if all goes to our initial plans, it could grow to hundreds of thousands of acres or more within their lifetimes.

One by one the bison are led into a squeeze shoot, a contraption that immobilizes the animal for thirty seconds or so and allows rangers to draw blood for disease testing and to inspect their teeth, which helps determine a bison's age.

There are five other organizations receiving bison from the Park Service today, including several Native American Tribes. For thousands of years Native Americans depended on bison for meat as well as for the animals' bone and hair to build tools and make clothing, which is partly why the mass slaughter of bison by European settlers throughout the 1800s coincided with the calamitous decline in Native American populations. Tribal leaders tell me they are bringing breeding bulls back to their lands in hopes of rebuilding their ancestral herds, and it makes me proud to bear witness to such an important moment.

"American Prairie!" Yells a park ranger. A shoot opens and a handsome young bull sprints down an alleyway and into our holding pen. He's strong and wild and unsettled. I share a glance with Curt and the others. I think of all the work it took to get to this moment: many semi-sleepless nights, the endless fundraising trips, the early roadblocks that threatened to derail our vision at every turn, etc. Yet somehow, some way, with tenacious teamwork between the two organizations, we seem to be slowly turning the dream into reality.

Thirty minutes later the ranger again yells "American Prairie!" and our second bison, an older shaggy-haired female, charges into the pen.

Hours later, we have sixteen bison in a holding corral assigned to American Prairie where they'll spend the night. The next afternoon after waiting many hours for blood test results from the state veterinarian, we are cleared to depart for Montana. We load the animals up ramps into the heavy-duty, gooseneck trailers that are hitched to two diesel trucks capable of towing eight bison—or around ten to twelve thousand pounds—each. Now it's a five-hundred-mile race against time, as the bison can't eat or drink while squeezed shoulder to shoulder and nose to tail into the trailers. After all the delays, we finally pull away from Wind Cave National Park in the late afternoon, two of us in the cab of one truck and two in the other. As the diesels roar to life, I glance at the trailer in the rearview mirror. I'm overtaken with excitement.

We are about to tow our starter herd of sixteen bison into Montana. We drive for five hours from South Dakota to Billings, Montana, stop for a quick hamburger and get back on the road. We push on through the darkness, knowing the health of the bison is deteriorating with every hour they are crammed into the trailer. Having been born wild and never transported, the bison had never experienced such a loud, stressful, and hot environment. At our dinner stop, we switch drivers. Now Curt is driving one rig and I'm driving the other. It is a tough balance of keeping up our pace to get to our destination as soon as possible while trying to go easy on the animals. We are acutely aware that every pothole, every bump, every turn is causing them more anxiety.

We've begun to feel a few raindrops as we gas up in Billings. The radio tells us there's a low-pressure front moving in, delivering steady rain through the night. In three more hours, we will be leaving the pavement to start traversing fifty miles of wide open, seemingly endless prairie, first on gravel and later on slippery mud roads. Getting stuck in the mud with sixteen bison in the middle of the night and no help around just isn't an option. They can't spend the entire night in those trailers having had no food and water for a long while, and we can't let them out to graze and drink as we'd have no way to contain them or load them back in.

We continue north on highway 87, one of the more desolate stretches of road in the country. We are surrounded by flat, inky blackness. By the time we cross the Missouri River just after midnight, light drizzle has turned to steady rain. Curt and I turn the rigs east off Highway 191 onto the gravel-surfaced Dry Fork Road. We stop for a moment to check the animals. Rain patters on the aluminum trailer as I listen for the bison, but they remain eerily still. On a sunny afternoon one might drive a maximum of forty-five miles per hour down this road, but on a dark, soggy night pulling heavy trailers, thirty-five miles per hour is all we can muster.

After forty-five miles the gravel gives way to a rutted dirt road, and we pull over to check on the bison again. They are holding still, wide eyed and stressed from rocks loudly bouncing off the trailer bottoms. Next, I inspect the road ahead. In this region the dirt is mostly bentonite, a volcanic ash that when mixed with water turns into the slickest and stickiest mud you can imagine. On the prairie it's called "gumbo"— once slathered over your tires it's nearly impossible to get off. If you aren't careful, in very wet sections the gumbo can swallow your truck to its axles; you'll need some sizeable machinery to pull it out. Meriwether Lewis discovered gumbo for the first time when journeying along the Missouri River through what is now Montana, writing in his diary: "I attempted to walk on Shore[.] Soon found it very laborious as the mud stuck to my mockersons and was very slippery." I've been stuck in gumbo many times, but with roughly seven tons of live bison in those trailers, the stakes were higher than ever before.

It's close to one in the morning, and now the rain is coming down steadily, making the roads softer and greasier. Curt and I discuss our options over the two-way radios as we keep moving along. We only have five miles left, but it is on the very worst section of mud, so we slow to fifteen mph to avoid flipping a trailer. The trailers are beginning to fishtail behind us as the four-wheel drive truck and trailer rigs undulate, eel-like, from one side of the slimy road to the other. We press on. The transfer case on my truck whines as the low-range gears struggle to overcome the thick mud as we climb one hill after another and then use the low gear and engine as breaks as we slide to and fro on the downhill sections. I'm a few hundred feet ahead of Curt; my spinning tires are creating deep gumbo ruts that he struggles to avoid.

Curt and I are talking nonstop on the radio and adjusting plans. At the same moment, we both decide we need to increase our speed. In normal off-road conditions, you want to crawl as slow as possible. In gumbo, however, you need to do the opposite: to create strong forward momentum to avoid getting stuck. I stomp on the accelerator and the truck careens down the road, the gooseneck groaning as the trailer fishtails behind me. Fifteen long minutes later, I see dim lights up ahead through the mist and rain—the American Prairie and WWF staff, waiting for us in the middle of a very wet, dark field.

"The gumbo is deep by the corral," someone says over the radio to the four of us in the trucks. "Drive fast if you can! If you sink before you reach the corral, the bison will have to stay in the trailers till daybreak." The diesels roar as we pick up speed and slide around the outer perimeter of the corral, brake to a stop, shift to reverse in quick motion, and let the clutch out and back crazily into the corral before our rigs sink into the prairie. I drift to a stop and cut the engine. Curt comes up with his rig right alongside mine. I sit there in silence listening to the steady *tick ticking* of the hot motor as wet gumbo oozes down the windshield. There is no sound at all coming from the trailer behind me.

Someone closes the gates behind us as I look around with a flashlight at the enclosure we've created. Our staff spent weeks stacking one-ton round hay bales twelve feet high into a makeshift pen about an acre in size. The animals will spend ten days here acclimating to their new surroundings and being released into progressively larger areas over the next month. It is astounding to me that we are actually here, standing in the rain and about to let these animals out. After conferring with the staff, we all decide it is time. I unshackle the trailer door and brace as I swing it open, half-expecting the bison to launch into the corral like bucking horses.

Nothing happens. The trailer remains dead silent.

I peer through the trailer's narrow side openings. The bison have squished themselves together as far back into the trailer as they can, clearly anxious about what awaits them. We open Curt's trailer to find the other eight bison in the same state. We wait; I stand silently in the rain alongside Curt and our staff, the headlights of other trucks softly lighting the arena which glows in the silvery mist. Perhaps five minutes later, an older female steps gingerly onto the top of the ramp and gazes out at the prairie. Bison are matriarchal by nature, so the females tend to lead. She swings her massive head left and then right. Then, apparently making up her mind, she trots down the ramp and onto the dewy grass. For the first time in nearly 130 years, wild bison have arrived back in Montana.

Suddenly there is a rumbling, and the rest of the bison are bursting out of the two trailers like sparrows. Once on the ground, they slow down immediately; some trot a few times around the corral, others standing still, looking around at the strange lights and their enclosure. The same female who was the first to leave the trailer wanders over to a water trough at the center of the corral and drinks. For the first time I get a close look at her. She's older than the rest, maybe fifteen to eighteen or so. While most bison adult's horns curve upward like a Viking helmet, her left horn juts straight out, almost parallel to the ground. The matriarch quietly drinking at the trough seems to calm the others down, and they watch her closely. She passes up a pile of hay before strolling further into the pasture and instead starts grazing peacefully on the native grass. It's almost as if she said, *It's okay. We're home.* One by one, the other fifteen bison drink from the trough and join her. At long last they are at peace in their new home.

It's beyond late but no one is tired. Someone runs into the ranch house and grabs bottles of whiskey and coffee cups. Curt and I recount the harrowing drive to about a dozen staff and volunteers as we sit quietly, sipping Jameson and watching the bison graze. As the night progresses, I take repeated walks around the hay bale enclosure's perimeter and look in at the bison from various viewing holes. Later fatigue overtakes us, and we slip and slide through the mud back to the small house. There are only three beds, so most of us sleep on the floor. When I wake up around six in the morning, the house is empty again. The sun has peeked over the eastern horizon and is spilling into the pasture. I pour myself coffee and walk outside to find everyone back with the bison. They are watching them mostly in silence—a few whispers here and there—all caught up in the beauty and implications of the moment. My staff is scruffy and weary, running on roughly two hours of sleep and caffeine, but they're all grinning. The rain is gone, the sky is blue, and the dew is evaporating. It's a new morning in northern Montana. American Prairie is still in its infancy, but we have sixteen healthy bison and a grand plan.

I sip my coffee and think: *This might really work out.*

CHAPTER ONE

Baselines

Back in the early 2000s, more than a few people told me I was a bit nuts to quit my steady, established career to help launch what some saw as a naive new venture in Bozeman, Montana. But as of today, things have worked out better than many expected. Now, after twenty-five years of being steeped in the world of rewilding, I'm more optimistic than ever about the potential to restore and preserve far more nature and biodiversity than many people believe is possible—not out of continuing naivete, but because I have seen firsthand that it can be done.

American Prairie, the organization I launched and led for seventeen years, remains focused on creating the largest wildlife reserve ever established in the Lower 48. As a founder, I got to be a part of a team that from the very beginning was—and still is—doing the seemingly impossible. In 2001, our tiny crew was made up of regular people of modest means, and only a few with backgrounds in conservation biology. We first created and then fell in love with an extraordinary vision and made it our jobs to do whatever it took to figure out how to bring it into reality.

I was motivated to write this book for a variety of reasons. One reason is that I hope readers will come to understand that there are not only endless opportunities for American Prairie's approach to be replicated in the American West but also around the world. Over these past decades, I've read a great deal about nature preservation and studied countless other rewilding projects. Learning about them has confirmed for me that American Prairie is not an isolated bright spot in an ocean of bad news about the state of our planet. As more people start and join such causes, we have much potential to do more than merely save what's left of nature; we can bring back much of what we have lost.

I also hope that readers will realize that we don't have to wait

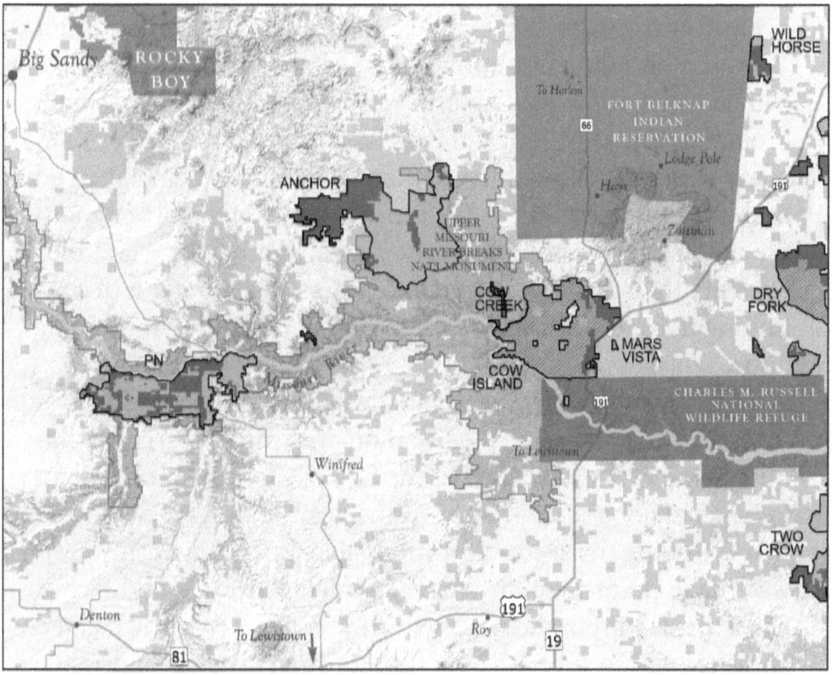

AMERICAN PRAIRIE | Land Map

This map shows American Prairie's forty-eight property acquisitions to date, including private and public leased acres. As of late 2025, American Prairie has assembled 600,017 acres; equal to 964 square miles.

for governments or large NGOs to dramatically improve conditions in our natural world—small groups of regular people can also come together and soon start making outsized positive impacts on our environment. The key is to build organizations that will endure. American Prairie is more capable, powerful, and productive now than at any time in its twenty-five-year history. I was a founder and an effective leader during my time there, but its continued strength building upon strength—long after my departure—is anything but accidental. Since our beginnings, it has required a core group of people who will

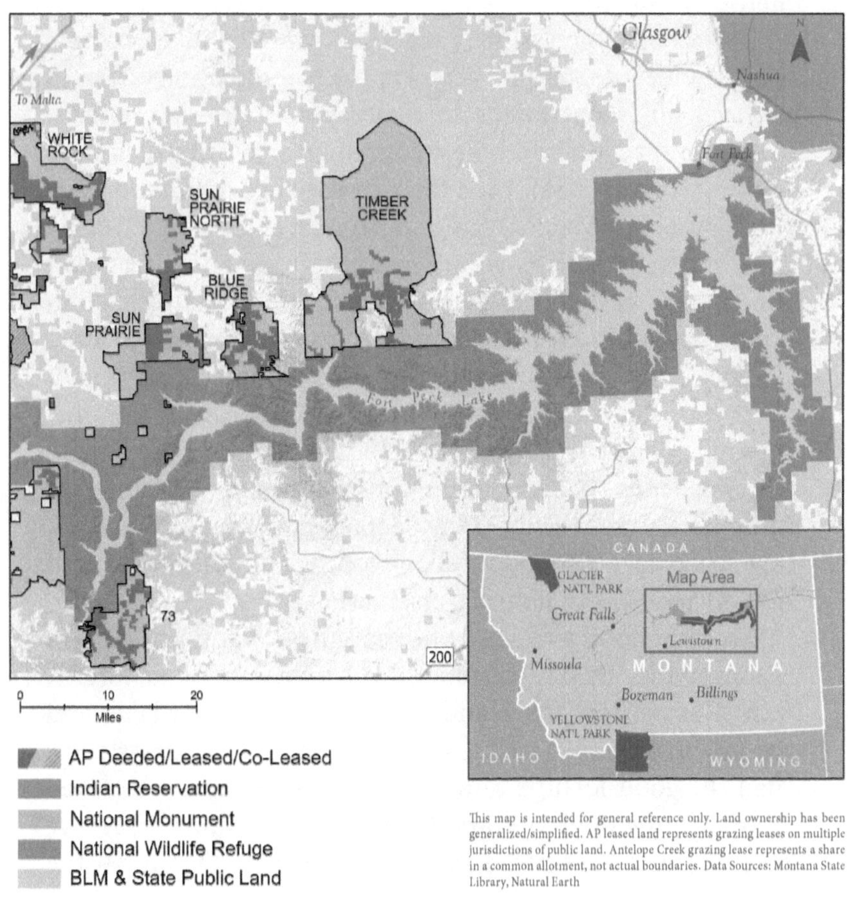

This map is intended for general reference only. Land ownership has been generalized/simplified. AP leased land represents grazing leases on multiple jurisdictions of public land. Antelope Creek grazing lease represents a share in a common allotment, not actual boundaries. Data Sources: Montana State Library, Natural Earth

stay aligned and enthusiastic through the good times—and who always find a way to stay motivated (and to motivate each other) when frustration, confusion, or exhaustion inevitably set in. Even though individuals have come and gone over time, we succeeded in building an effective, lasting organization by carefully shaping an organizational culture that matches the specific needs of this audacious, long-term project. After a long career in a different industry, I had to learn to reshape myself as a leader for the demands of this project, as did some of my colleagues, but whatever challenges or difficulties we faced were—at least for me—far outweighed by frequent feelings of intense satisfaction.

I also want to reassure readers that you don't have to possess advanced degrees or deep experience in conservation to be a valuable contributor to American Prairie-like efforts. Conservation didn't become a conscious area of focus for me until my early thirties. Even then, it would be another decade before I was inspired to transition from an enthusiast to taking some real action. Discovering meaningful, fascinating interests—even a new chosen field—later in life is relatively common. I left behind a rewarding fifteen-year career co-leading a Silicon-Valley-based organization development consultant business to launch American Prairie. As it turned out, my upbringing and my later career helping organizations be more effective, ended up being useful for what would be required of me at American Prairie. Many people I have met in the rewilding space have also followed unexpected, circuitous paths to their current role in nature conservation.

My childhood was filled with countless nights camping in national parks like Yellowstone and Glacier, in national forests, in the Rocky Mountains, and alongside picturesque lakes and free-flowing rivers as well as on Montana's eastern grasslands. I had the good fortune of being raised by parents who loved spending time outdoors, and the wide-open natural areas we so often visited seemed as vast as the Pacific Ocean. In the

1960s, Montana's ninety-six million acres—150,000 square miles—were home to fewer than seven hundred thousand people; I never stopped to consider how so few humans could, over time, have an outsized impact on so much space.

My grandfather, Thomas Gerrity, lived two thousand miles away in Long Island, New York. On my seventh birthday, he sent me an annual membership to the Wild Mustang & Burros Society. It came with a cool, official-looking certificate sporting my name in large letters, which I promptly hung on my bedroom wall. Every few months, I received *The Mustanger* newsletter, which told of the ongoing plight of what were then considered wild mustangs and burros and what the Society was doing about it. It was my first experience seeing people organizing and advocating for another species.

When I was a teenager, the environmental movement, which I learned about in public school, focused national attention on the dangers of acid rain, smog, and water pollution. But, as with the wild horses and burros, it all seemed very far away from my own world. It wasn't until I was on my own in the mid-1970s that I read and traveled more widely and began to slowly develop my own understanding about the plight of nature.

In 1981, my girlfriend, Kayla, and I took fall semester off from Montana State University to spend three months exploring the south of the Mexico-United States border. We hitchhiked—riding on mostly long-haul trucks—some two thousand miles east and caught a cheap one-way flight from Washington, DC, to Mexico's Yucatán Peninsula. Guided by advice from other ultra-low budget travelers we'd met, we made our way to the-then tiny fishing village of Playa del Carmen. In this town of a hundred or so residents, we erected our two-person backpacking tent in a rustic campground owned by a man named Hugo. The palm-tree-covered grounds spilled out onto what was to us the most stunning beach and peaceful aqua-blue ocean scene anywhere in the world. Nearby, a little tienda kept us well stocked with beans, rice, fresh corn torti-llas, beer, and Mezcal.

One day we went snorkeling on the nearby coral reef. Using Hugo's directions drawn with a stick in the sand, we walked a mile up the beach just past an old, abandoned fishing boat lying on its side, and from there we swam out from shore. The crystal clear water was only about ten feet deep over a white sand bottom. Three hundred yards out, we came upon the reef: spectacular colors, a wide variety of corals in every direction, and a mind-boggling array of marine life almost too abundant to comprehend.

Later back at camp, Hugo lent Kayla a tattered and stained book on Caribbean reef fish and corals. She read every word as we lounged under the palm trees and, day after day, taught me the names of damselfish: blue tangs, parrotfish, squids, and wrasses. As we sat outside our small tent sipping Mezcal and watching the evening sea turn shades of orange and peach, we learned how the plants, fish, corals, currents, and wave action all worked together as a complex, interdependent system. We snorkeled the reef twice a day for the next week.

Hugo explained that the preservation of the reef was at risk: Fishermen were operating nearby—illegally—and catching too many fish. He speculated that the Mexican police turned a blind eye to the issue or were bribed to not interfere. Later, as we rode slow local buses through other parts of Mexico to Guatemala, I began thinking that the locals might need to take some kind of action if this reef were to be saved for future gen-erations, but, being twenty-one years old at the time, I didn't really know what those actions might be.

Fifteen years later in 1998, Kayla and I returned to Mexico with our five-year-old daughter, Siri, and eight-year-old son, Dylan. We pulled them out of their public school classes for a month-long chicken bus trip through Quintana Roo and Yucatán, including a visit to Playa del Carmen. The town's human population had exploded from about one hundred people to nearly one hundred fifty thousand. (Today, it's more than three hundred thousand.) Hugo's campground was gone. But, directly in front of the string of fifteen or so resorts now lining the beach, the water was still that same gorgeous aqua hue. We swam with the kids out to the reef—now marketed as a snorkeler's paradise—and found it changed. The once stunningly bright colors were a bit more muted, and grayish patches of dead or dying coral dotted the ocean floor. The still-active part of the reef seemed smaller, maybe 80 percent of the size that we had seen in 1981. The years of overfishing and tour boat anchors breaking off pieces of the coral had steadily taken their toll.

Siri and Dylan loved it. It was their first experience snorkeling, and they couldn't believe the amount of marine life moving about the reef or the fascinating array of colors in the corals. There was no sense of loss, only childlike wonder. They had never seen the reef as it used to be.

That memorable experience was one of my first lessons on how fast and dramatically nature can change in the hands of human beings. At the time, I did not know exactly what I wanted to do about it, but conservation was suddenly very personal. Over such a short time, what I'd so much wanted my own children to see had noticeably diminished.

I would eventually learn the name for this phenomenon: shifting baseline syndrome. Each human generation tends to perceive the natural environment's condition based on what they experience during their own lifetime without knowing about or considering historical changes. For the past three hundred years—during which time the earth's total human population has grown from roughly seven hundred million to over eight billion—this shift has almost invariably involved the gradual lowering of expectations about what constitutes healthy, fully functioning, and intact natural systems.

A few years after our family trip, that Playa del Carmen experience was still fresh in my mind when I sat down with

Dr. Curt Freese of WWF for the first time. We were meeting to discuss the still-emerging yet intriguing idea of building a big new wildlife reserve. Curt noted that the gradual lowering of expectations about what constitutes a functioning and intact natural system on Montana's grasslands had been underway for the last six human generations. As I listened to his vision for what might one day become American Prairie, he explained that moving today's baseline back in the direction of what used to be would require reassembling the native habitat and creating the conditions that allow for all native species to return in spectacular abundance. We would need to do it in such a way that every local community—including Indigenous Tribes, and those relative newcomers, the cattle ranchers of mostly European decent—would one day cherish the reserve and help protect it forever.

Over the following months, as we repeatedly discussed Curt's high-level description of this idea, it felt exciting to think that—after so much discussion about the importance of restoring a portion of the Northern Great Plains—that just regular folks like us could possibly do it. Maybe, we mused, in twenty-five or thirty-five years, this natural grassland biome would indeed become significantly larger, and wilder.

—

It wasn't that long ago that the US government routinely created new parks, reserves, and refuges. There are compelling reasons that the National Park System has sometimes been referred to as one of "America's best ideas," though many parks indeed came at the expense of displaced Native people. Yellowstone National Park was created in 1872. In the decades that followed, the US established Grand Canyon National Park, Yosemite, and Zion. The Everglades, Glacier, Denali, and many others would follow. In the 1950s, however, the creation of large, iconic national parks had slowed to a trickle.

America is still making some modest national parks today, but far less frequently. These newer reserves are generally quite small compared to the spectacular giants that were boldly established in the heyday of US park building. Worse, they are usually too small to support an intact ecosystem.

Today, the Bureau of Land Management oversees 245 million acres of public land—one eighth of the country's total land mass—and the US Forest Service oversees an additional 193 million acres. That's close to half a billion acres of largely available public land. Yellowstone National Park, in all its glory, is just 2.2 million acres. With nearly half a billion acres already under management between just these two federal agencies, the untapped potential for establishing big new parks seems almost limitless. If we wanted to, that is. As an American society, that's a big if.

As baselines for nature and for our own imaginations keep shifting downward, our belief about exciting possibilities slips further out of reach. In two generations, the idea of establishing new, large-scale parks and reserves went from routine and broadly celebrated to almost unimaginable. We didn't run out of space, so why the abrupt slowdown in building new parks? The shift toward preserving less nature was intentional. Beginning in the late 1950s, well-organized pushbacks came from powerful private industries like mining, timber, and agriculture. Industries that would reap significant profits from leasing the public lands invested heavily to ensure that park building became contentious, and this sometimes-fierce resistance caused politicians—even those who would have liked to see more parks established—to become squeamish about pushing too hard to designate new big ones.

As still happens today, they feared that doing so might jeopardize their reelection prospects, and the trend of regularly establishing and protecting expansive new national parks quickly began to fade.

But now things may be changing. We used to be a country

of doing really bold things, from building the Brooklyn Bridge to laying the first transatlantic cable and putting the first astronauts on the moon. The American innovation of protecting large, iconic natural areas has inspired many other countries to follow suit: National parks now exist in Africa, Asia, Europe, and Oceana, and in North, Central, and South America. But I believe that we are gradually starting the transition out of an environmental Dark Ages. The public land to do so is there. The techniques for raising more than enough food to feed all the world's humans—while using far less space to do it than we do currently—exist and are already being successfully deployed. I believe this transition is accelerating around the globe and may achieve critical mass as soon as the next fifteen to twenty years. From my experience of starting and helping to build American Prairie, I believe we can absolutely emerge from what has been a relatively quiet fifty-year period of creating big new protected areas. I believe we are primed for a rewilding renaissance.

The speed of the transition I am describing depends upon how many people—how many more people—decide to get meaningfully involved and help move the renaissance forward instead of sitting back, watching and worrying and waiting.

Based on the type of projects I have learned about from around the globe, it seems likely that many future conservation initiatives will be started and led by private citizens. Sometimes their efforts will evolve into collaborations with local and national institutions, and sometime with one or more of the existing large, global environmental organizations. I predict that these long-term initiatives will be geared toward not just saving what little we have left; instead, they will help regain a good deal of what we have lost. Along the way I think some projects will help dramatically shift our current approaches to agriculture. And in the US, these efforts will likely repurpose at least a portion of the hundreds of millions of acres of public lands currently leased to for-profit industries. They might once again become exceedingly rich areas of biodiversity that also offer people improved access to nature.

Impacts of Our Species' Continued Expansion

From the time when the first human beings appeared around three hundred thousand years ago until the Middle Ages, Earth's human population grew at a relatively slow pace. In the latter 1500s when Shakespeare was writing plays, the total global human population was estimated to be four hundred million to five hundred million. Since then, we have grown to an estimated eight-plus billion people in 2025. Looking ahead, we are now on track for our fastest growth spurt yet, likely adding yet another billion humans by 2030. It's nearly impossible to overstate the negative impact we have wrought on all of the world's other species in this brief span of time. Humans are driving what many scientists refer to as the sixth extinction of wild species, and the first one to be largely human created. It is clear that this is the time to think big about restoring and conserving land and wild habitats in order to have the best possible chance of protecting the wild species and helping them thrive on it.

My own sense of urgency regarding the need to save existing wild spaces and to help rewild as much habitat and species as we can increased as I learned about the world's remaining grasslands. There are, science tells us, only four places left on earth with the room and appropriate conditions to restore large-scale, fully functioning grassland ecosystems: the Northern Great Plains and the Kazakh, Mongolian, and Patagonian Steppes.

But each year, these remaining four places are shrinking; they are all continuing to be converted from rich, complex native grasslands to single species crops to grow more food for humans and our livestock.

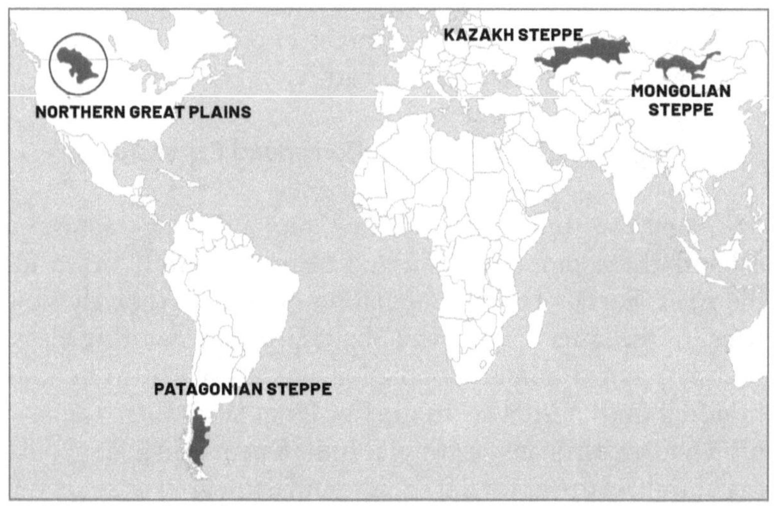

The American Prairie project is located in the Northern Great Plains, a 180-million-acre grassland that encompasses much of five western US states and two provinces of Canada. Reports show that in 2020 alone, 1.8 million more acres of native prairie were plowed up to plant monoculture crops in the plains of Canada, the United States, and Mexico—and the destruction of wild habitat continues. Removing complex grassland habitats is like cutting a rainforest. While not impossible, it is exceedingly difficult and expensive to bring it back to its natural condition where it can once again support hundreds of different birds, aquatic species, reptiles, rodents, ungulates and predators. The basic components of this story are being replicated in nearly every biome in the world, including wetlands, deserts, forests, and oceans.

A Case for Optimism

As alarming and depressing as these trends are, I believe they are neither intractable nor inevitable. If you look hard enough, there is much good news happening around the world that helps paint a more balanced story. For instance, not long after my family saw those degraded reef conditions in 1996 along the Mexico, Belize, and Honduran coastlines, things began to change. Today, more than forty-seven marine protected areas have been established along that coast, the Mesoamerican Reef Restoration Network is operating there, and numerous reef restoration projects are underway using electrolysis and other innovative techniques to help bring reefs back to thriving conditions. As a macro-level example, for the first time in three hundred thousand years, the world's human population is predicted to actually stop growing, to level off at about ten or so billion, and then gradually but steadily decline. Those extraordinary events are predicted to happen within my grandchildren's lifetime. And as just one example of a species level success which I learned about while in Southeast Asia in winter 2025, after more than a century of steady decline in Thailand's tiger population due to habitat loss, in just the past fifteen years the tiger population there has increased by an estimated 250 percent. The sustained conservation efforts by numerous private organizations and Thai authorities have led to Thailand being the only Southeast Asian country where tiger populations are increasing.

There already exist many well-known, well-proven ways to manage agriculture more effectively that could not just reduce humanity's negative impact on nature but actually reverse many of the trends of deforestation and monoculture agriculture. These are not far-off-in-the-future solutions akin to powering our vehicles with hydrogen. They are out in the world now and are being used by thousands of innovative, everyday people. For instance, the Netherland's Wageningen University, one of the top-ranked agricultural-focused universities in the world, specializes in life sciences and leading-edge agricultural techniques. Its students learn how to grow abundant food for humans on a fraction of the land than is typically used today. These techniques have led to the Netherlands becoming the second largest exporter of food, as measured by value, in the entire world, second only to the United States—a country with more than *270 times the Netherlands land mass*. Can we even *begin* to imagine what it would take to transform American agriculture this dramatically?

Absolutely. Not only do we understand what must be done, the knowledge and technology we need already exist. As was the case way back when we started American Prairie, we could do it *simply by deciding to do it*.

There are countless other high-impact initiatives just waiting to be staffed and funded properly, bold ideas whose time will come if only enough people take a chance and make it their vocation for some portion of their working lives; or—if not their vocation—to make it one of their main areas of philanthropy over the long term, which is another powerful way to add important fuel to these exciting projects.

It sometimes feels we are being taught to lower our expectations, to compromise and accept what is, to aspire only where success is likely or—even better—only minimally disruptive, to play defense exclusively and forgo offense. With regards to restoring natural areas, we've been conditioned to be "realistic," to prioritize only the plausible—given today's constraints and politics—over the possible, to live with small-scale dreams that often feel overwhelmed by the anxieties and perceived dangers of the twenty-first-century world we've created.

I consider myself a *possibilist* verses a blind optimist. I know when I talk about the possibility of millions more people one day choosing conservation as a path, some people will say, "Sean, you're thinking too big again. It's simply impractical." I've been criticized for thinking too big before, but we've proved our doubters wrong. In a world where the baselines have shifted to the point where conditions in the natural world are sorely out of balance—and our own collective imaginations have diminished so much—*somebody* has to think big about these things.

In the following pages, I will do my best to explain how

we got this initiative up and running, and why—twenty-four years later—the momentum toward the big vision remains strong. I'll touch on the key things I believe we got right in the beginning that are still being done right twenty-five years in, and which still drive the movement forward today. And maybe most importantly, I'll explain why I see more than enough reasons and solid evidence out there to suggest that this is the best time ever to consider starting all manner of things that could one day make the world a better place, one that we will be proud to pass on to future generations.

Stepping Stones to Nature Conservation

Looking back on it now, I'd say there were upsides and downsides to living in eighteen different houses, seven states, and one Canadian province by the time I'd graduated high school.

On one hand, particularly when I was younger, it was difficult not knowing when the next move would happen, in which case I'd have to make new friends all over again. On the other hand, I learned at least a rough version of the Buddhist concept of nonattachment by becoming adept at not becoming overly committed to places and people, a skill that helped me to risk moving on to rewarding new experiences later in life. Regardless, our family's nomadic lifestyle seemed normal to me.

The reason for all the moving was my dad's career. He'd already held many jobs by the time I was born, including tracking the whereabouts of Southern Pacific Railway's boxcars along the eastern seaboard, and working as a grip on a crew shooting television commercials. Eventually, around my first birthday, he decided he wanted a more predictable income, so he took an entry-level job sweeping floors in the Boeing Company's warehouses, eventually working his way up to supervisor. The early 1960s work culture at Boeing agreed with him, and he accepted the periodic requirement to move as new projects arose across the US and Canada.

Four moves after leaving Long Island, New York, in the fall of 1961, we landed in Great Falls, Montana. Our first home was in a trailer court adjacent to Malmstrom Air Force Base. The sixty-foot-long, single-wide trailer was cramped for a family of five plus our two black Labradors, but I was happy. There were lots of kids my age in the trailer park and, for the first time in my short life, I began to feel a sense of place and a connection to a group of people beyond my immediate family. My parents loved Montana as well, with its mountains, grasslands, rivers, wildlife, and endless camping opportunities.

Shortly after arriving in Montana, my parents equipped my two older sisters and me with inexpensive outdoor gear from the local Army/Navy surplus store so we could all go camping almost every weekend from May to late October. My mother was obsessively curious about the natural world. Whenever she could steal some time, she would take me on circuitous, no-destination walks to find flowers, birds, insects, and trees, carrying *Peterson Field Guide to Birds of North America* in one hand and *Peterson Field Guide to Wildflowers* in the other. She walked slowly, looking closely, hunting for the next interesting thing. Years later, my friends coined the term "land snorkeling," which aptly described her style of exploring.

My dad found joy in the outdoors just by being out in the wild beauty, marveling at the enormous Montana vistas and the practice of going "just a little further." He taught us that if you take a little more time to go around that next bend or to crest that next ridge, you might be rewarded with delights, like a rare encounter with wildlife, a surprisingly beautiful scene, or a previously unknown stream.

By the mid-1960s, both my parents had embraced fishing and big-game hunting. In late summer, we set up hunting camps on national forest lands in the Highwood Mountains and the Rocky Mountain's Front Range. Come autumn, we searched for whitetail, mule deer, and elk. Trailing after my parents year after year, I learned to track animals, to spot weather patterns, and not just when wildlife moved about, but why and how. My parents' dedication to getting us outdoors whenever possible helped increase my feelings of competence in nature. It felt as though I fit there.

Unfortunately for me, the opposite was happening at school, where my grade school report cards highlighted my penchant for fidgeting, talking out of turn, and daydreaming. At the end of each year in grades one through five, I sat down with my teacher, the principal, and my mom as they discussed whether or not to flunk me. They determined that my starting school at four years old instead of the normal five may have contributed to my inability to concentrate, which in turn influenced my behavior. Attention deficit hyperactivity disorder (ADHD), with which I was not diagnosed until I was a much older adult, may have contributed as well. Between poor grades and demeaning yearly meetings to decide if I'd flunk out or squeak by to the next grade level, I started to assume I just wasn't very smart. So it always came as a particular surprise when I'd scored repeatedly in the ninety-fifth percentile in reading comprehension on those required national aptitude tests. How could a dumb person like me be in the ninety-fifth percentile of anything? I didn't know it then, but that one proficiency eventually helped change my self-image into something much more positive than it had been in my earlier years.

While my parents were growing up in the 1930s and 1940s, the only topic that adults discussed even less than sex was finances. Neither of them had learned much about the making, handling, or saving of money. Luckily, as a couple, they had similar ideas about how much income and possessions were sufficient for an enjoyable life. After living in Montana for a time, their modest goals included a small used aluminum fishing boat with a thirty-five-horsepower motor, a dependable four-wheel-drive pickup truck, and, later, a small family-constructed cabin built on the cheap, using mainly discounted or discarded materials. But they did need to somehow generate some extra cash to acquire such things.

My first lessons in sales came when I was only four. I watched my dad walk out the door after dinner on weeknights to spend a few hours hawking silverware door to door in our neighborhood. It continued in later years; I watched both parents during evening gatherings in our living room with twelve or so invited guests. My dad poured stiff drinks as my mom guided potential customers toward placing a hefty product order at the end of the night, initially for Avon products and later Tupperware and Amway.

Later, my parents told me that my proto-hustle culture childhood was driven by their desire to avoid the stress of living paycheck to paycheck. It was a formative, early lesson: Experimentation, persistence, and constant teamwork tend to pay off.

Discovering Unexpected Interests and Abilities, Then Converging on an Idea

Toward the end of high school, most of my friends seemed to already know what they would be doing after graduation. Some were heading directly to college, others lining up local jobs in the building trades, training to become firefighters, or pursuing other vocations that didn't require a college degree. I had no such plans nor much money. I'd read somewhere that only about 35 percent of Americans were cut out for the rigors of higher education. Given my marginal performance as a student, I figured I was solidly in the other 65 percent.

Thus, after graduation, I found a job with the Boeing Company, helping manage a large parts and supply store in Great Falls. The pay was an hourly rate of $5.20—a king's ransom compared to my last job during high school as a Holiday Inn desk clerk at $2.25 per hour. Later I joined the field team as a weapon system mechanic, where our six-person crew spent our days in remote areas of Montana, deep inside Minuteman missile silos, upgrading computers and flight guidance systems for warheads that, if ever launched, could have meant the beginning of the end of the world.

My parents lived a few miles away on the other side of town. I got along well with my mom and calmly tolerated her gentle but repeated inquiries about whether I was considering college. (My dad had only attended one semester of college before deciding it wasn't for him and therefore applied no such pressure.) I repeatedly pointed out that I was making good money and was blissfully free of stress since leaving school, where she knew I'd struggled.

But about a year and a half into my job, the sixty-six thousand-member International Association of Machinists and Aerospace Workers went on strike. Our union leaders claimed they had enough cash reserves to pay all workers for at least four months, yet barely a month later the fund was empty, and my income was zero. I'd gone from feeling like my financial destiny was squarely in my hands to realizing it was in the hands of union bosses I'd never met, seven hundred miles away in Seattle. I began to reconsider my mom's encouragement to try college. As it turned out, having heard about the strike, she had requested an application for Montana State University. "Just in case," she said. Mostly to appease her, I filled it out and sent it in, assuming my mediocre grades would guarantee a rejection.

The welcome letter that arrived a few weeks later stated that I could start that winter quarter. With no end to the strike in sight and my checking account down to less than five hundred dollars, I decided to accept the offer and, in January 1978, with no small amount of trepidation, traveled south to Bozeman in my 1968 Camaro that was packed to the ceiling with all my worldly possessions. I pulled up to the curb in front of North Hedges dorm watching hundreds of students streaming in and out of the imposing twelve-story-tall building, feeling I was at the precipice of self-esteem-crushing mistake. But I reminded myself of what mom had said: "If it didn't work out after a few quarters, Boeing would still be there, and no hiring manager would fault you for having left in the middle of a prolonged strike."

My first quarter was surprising in many ways. My classes were quite interesting, not just because of the subject matter but also because of the energy of the professors and the caliber of students. On the downside, I grossly misjudged how much time I needed to devote to studying. At quarter's end, my transcript showed only Cs and Ds. During the second quarter, I did a little better, studying more and trying to stick to Friday and Saturday nights only for beer, weed, and staying up late. The result in May was no Ds.

Thanks to the compassionate help of a superb university guidance counselor, I found my place firmly on the general studies track. For the first time in my life, school became fascinating, and I discovered I was not dumb after all. Although I took a broad range of classes, my interests repeatedly drew me back toward psychology, in which I got a bachelor's degree in 1983.

My interest in how small groups of individuals worked together increased while spending one college summer with a group called Wilderness Odyssey, or W.O. as it was known. W.O. was one of many programs run by a small Virginia-based outfit called Growing Edge that worked with various for-profit and nonprofit organizations to help them improve effectiveness in regard to leadership, teamwork, and organization alignment. Because of my outdoors background, I was hired as a guide to lead summer trips with teens and adults. From late May through August, I co-led multiday river, rock climbing, and camping trips in the semi-remote mountain areas of Virginia and West Virginia.

Like Outward Bound and other similar organizations, W.O. used these trips not so much to teach city people outdoor skills but to develop leadership expertise by using outdoor problem-solving challenges and general adversity as metaphors for life. As trip leaders, we were trained in models around group development, conflict resolution, and leadership establishment in a group.

Each group of twelve participants, depending on the trip, stayed together on a combined rock climbing, orienteering, and whitewater adventure schedule for up to eighteen straight days. Everyone had to sleep on the ground under clear plastic tarps, cook all their own meals, and, with no access to showers, bathe in rivers whenever possible. There was no need to create artificial tension and conflict between them for discussion's sake. It arose naturally.

Early on each trip, we introduced something called Kolb's experiential learning cycle. Some refer to it as the world's simplest continuous improvement process. In the evenings, after a day of helping each other navigate their canoes or manage to walk ten miles through the woods with no trail using only topographic maps and compasses, they would go through this four-step progression:

1. Recall the day's experience in general.

2. Talk about what you experienced today in working with each other. Analyze what you observed happening throughout the day.

3. Make some generalizations about what knowledge you can take away about the relative quality of your interactions. What is going well? What could be improved with your group interactions?

4. From this discussion, what do you want to try tomorrow to work better together?

By summer's end, I couldn't say I wanted to make a career out of being a backcountry trip leader, but lasting seeds had been planted. I was fascinated with how groups of people could form, move through predictable stages of group development, and solve challenging problems together. I also discovered that I enjoyed teaching ideas and facilitating discussions about models and theories on the topic.

Back at school in Montana, I continued to take additional psych courses but with a new, stepped-up interest in learning how I might apply what I was learning to some future job. But as graduation approached, I was not only still unsure how I wanted to apply my fascination with psychology to my life, I also had no idea what I wanted my working life to be. I decided to spend more time trying to understand that and myself in general before settling into any long-term career.

So, after graduating college in 1983, instead of finding a job, my then-girlfriend, Kayla, and I went on a six-month, slow-paced adventure through seven countries of Southeast Asia. We'd had previous journeys of this sort, but this trip offered an opportunity to ponder some important life questions: What were my real interests at this stage of my life? What kind of career might best match my values and interests? And was this person I was traveling with the one I wanted to marry and spent my life with? Little things like that.

Partial answers arose in various ways. A few days before departing the US for Singapore, a friend who knew of my interest in psychology mailed me a magazine article; in a hurry to finish my packing, I put it in the bottom of my backpack to read later. The article remained in my pack for many months, often under some damp, unwashed T-shirts molding in the equatorial heat. During a weeklong stopover in the small, quiet fishing village of Pangandaran, on Java's central southern coast, I rediscovered it and gave it a thorough read. The story cited numerous new studies focusing on people with different backgrounds, races, intelligence levels, and economic classes who were nonetheless alike in that they seem to experience a minimum of psychological suffering, no matter what kind of resources they had or what traumas they'd endured in their earlier lives. Some commonalities included generally optimistic outlooks, a strong focus on continuous improvement, a sense of purpose, and an inclination to find satisfaction in accomplishments of all sorts. Many of these people also added noticeable value when they were a part of groups.

The article offered no suggestions for how to start a career in this emerging field of focusing on such people, but my brain lit up with possibilities. I couldn't visualize what a specific job might look like, but it had something to do with helping people who were attempting to achieve something important, who were looking for ways to become more aligned with others and together create sustainable momentum toward some future vision.

I must have read that inspiring article ten times as we crisscrossed Indonesia, Burma, Thailand, Malaysia, Singapore, Hong Kong, and Taiwan. During an extended stay on the small, quiet Thai island of Ko Samet, an idea emerged: I wanted to start a business that focused on helping organizations that wanted to improve their overall effectiveness.

A Decent Start Disrupted by an Unexpected Opportunity

In the early winter of 1984, just back from Southeast Asia, Kayla and I relocated to Seattle with the goal of trying to start that business together. We had no business contacts or friends there, but given the city's size, potential customer base, and (back then) low cost of living, it seemed like a good place to try to launch the concept.

While searching for a cheap place to live, Kayla noticed a tiny advertisement in the newspaper's help-wanted section looking for assistant managers for a 265-unit apartment complex. The job, which we secured after touring the five-building facility with the manager, came with an unfurnished apartment and a $150 per month stipend. We spent part of each morning painting recently vacated apartments, fixing toilets, sweeping stairwells, and breaking up arguments between hotheaded tenants.

Our afternoons were devoted to working on our business plan. Soon we registered as a business in Washington, created some basic marketing materials, and compiled lists of organizations we hoped to pitch. Moving the business along took more time and was much harder than we'd anticipated. But we were together, living on our own, and working on the early phases of a dream.

We read voraciously on how to get a new business off the ground, books like Paul Hawken's *Growing a Business*, *Honest Business* by Sally Raspberry and Michael Phillips, and other books of that era describing a new type of organizational culture that was more inclusive, innovative, high-energy, and productive. We were moving forward inch by inch but also struggling with how to prioritize. We kept at it and remained hopeful that we would soon achieve some much-needed traction.

Early one drizzly Seattle evening, after nine months of diligently refining our business idea and working like crazy to find pathways to our first clients, I received an unexpected call from my friend Bill Underwood in Virginia, one of the cofounders of Growing Edge whom I had gotten to know during my time with Wilderness Odyssey. Bill had just spoken with the head of the executive programs at Boston University School of Management, who had asked him if he would consider leaving Growing Edge to help run a new California-based Boston University annex. Bill had declined the offer since Growing Edge was becoming successful after some challenging start-up years, but he recommended me.

The position description was intriguing. Some years back, BU had developed a new approach to teaching leadership skills to their MBA students. Later, as graduates landed jobs in the private industry, they quickly acquired reputations for being unusually effective young leaders. Companies who had hired them then wanted to send their managers to BU to take portions of those same leadership courses. Now BU was attempting to create a West Coast annex in Santa Cruz so they could directly market their leadership course offerings in Silicon Valley.

The head of the business school called me a few days later. He was highly complimentary of Kayla's and my effort to try to start our own business in the emerging world of organizational development. We talked about the California position, and he offered me a plane ticket and a few nights in a hotel to meet with the new director. Two weeks later I flew to San Jose, rented a car, and drove over the mountains to Santa Cruz to meet with Bill Herkelrath, who had been hired to launch the new annex, along with his assistant Donna, the only other employee. By the end of the first day, it was clear that BU's agenda was very similar to the business we were trying to create in Seattle. However, there was only one position available. But if I took this job, I could gain experience in building this type of business from scratch while pulling a dependable salary from Boston University.

Bill Herkelrath seemed anxious to get started building his team. Being from academia, he was hesitant about my lack of a master's degree in industrial psychology, but he liked my drive and optimism. By the end of our two days together, he'd decided I could probably learn the role quickly. The position started at $21,000 per year and came with a health plan, a roughly five-fold improvement in our financial situation. Still, I felt weird abandoning nine months of effort to start our own business in Seattle. Uncertain as to how Kayla might react, or how enthusiastically I should even pitch the idea, I called and caught her walking out the door to paint yet another recently vacated apartment.

"What have you learned? And what's it like down there?" she asked.

"Well, there are palm trees everywhere. The views of the ocean from all over town are beautiful. It's sunny and about seventy degrees. It's hard not to like." Then I told her about the job description, the salary, and healthcare package, and asked, "What do you think?" I waited, visualizing her standing there in her painting clothes, holding a paint tray and roller, the incessant cold, gray Seattle rain hissing softly in the background.

"Take it," she said.

More Surprises

Less than a month later, we were rolling down Interstate 5 toward northern California, hauling our belongings in U-Haul's smallest rental truck, towing our 1971 Datsun pickup. We moved into a 550-square-foot house just south of Santa Cruz, and within a week, Kayla (who knew very little about boats) landed a full-time position making six dollars per hour in the wholesale division of a supply store called West Marine Products at the local sailboat harbor. Our combined wages made us feel more financially flush than we'd ever been, and best of all, we loved Santa Cruz with its ideal weather, stunning ocean vistas, and eclectic people.

My first task at BU's West Coast outpost was to build an extensive, experiential high ropes course to be used as one of the teaching tools in our management education programs. Thanks to my many previous building and remodel jobs, I already knew how to construct things that were strong, safe, and durable. Still, in 1984, ropes courses were uncommon. Bill Herkelrath specified that he wanted this course to be the most impressive ever built.

Occasionally I would ring up Bill Underwood at Growing Edge for advice. I mentioned that Herkelrath was now looking for an overall program manager and that he would be ideal for the position. A month later, Bill decided to seize the opportunity and moved out to Santa Cruz to join our team. I'd only seen him occasionally while I was working at Growing Edge, but I always admired his high energy, creative mind, sense of humor, and ambitious work ethic. While Bill Herkelrath's role would end up being that of an administrator of sorts and a liaison to BU's business school, Bill's role would be an actual practitioner with paying clients (once we actually had some), which meant he and I would be working together most of the time.

In the early spring of 1985, after being in California for just five months, we learned that the head of the school, who'd developed and led the scheme to have a BU outpost in California, had resigned from the university to take a job in private industry. His replacement began a top-to-bottom analysis of all the programs and initiatives he'd inherited. A month later, he came to visit our fledgling operation. A week after he returned to Boston, we found out that Bill Herkelrath had been ousted, leaving Bill, Donna, and myself as the only employees. Herkelrath had been drawing a high salary compared to the rest of us, so we hoped Boston University was just cutting costs. The question in the back of our minds, of course, was: Were we next? We figured that securing some paying work soon might be our only salvation.

Later that same week, a call came in from Debbie Ward, VP of Human Resources at AT&T. Debbie said that she'd heard about us from a colleague and wanted to know if we would be interested in presenting to her twelve-member HR manager team. We accepted gladly, and a date was set for the following week. Bill and I were excited. If we were able to convince this HR team that we knew what we were doing and got even one paying gig, it would boost our local reputation, provide us some financial breathing room, and show BU that we were already beginning to make money for the School of Management.

On the day of the meeting, we milled about our office anxiously waiting until it was time to head out for AT&T. Just as we were backing out in the car, Donna ran out and waved us down. "Boston U. is on the phone," she shouted. "They need to talk with all three of us, together. Right now." Whatever was going on, we hoped it would be quick.

It was. Donna, Underwood, and I stood in a half circle around the speakerphone as the new head of the business school explained that they'd completed an analysis and decided that the California annex no longer fit their plans. Nothing personal, he assured us, but this call was notice of our termination. Two weeks from today, we'd have nothing—no salaries, no health benefits, no severance.

Donna hung up the call, looked at Bill and me, and asked, "Should I cancel your AT&T meeting?"

Bill and I pondered what to do next. We decided that, given all the work we had done over the past five months building the ropes course, networking, marketing, and hoping for our first shot at paying business, we might as well go for it. On the two-hour drive from Santa Cruz, we discussed what we might do if the meeting went well. Start our own business? Politely decline and go home to Virginia and Seattle? We left all options open and decided to focus on doing the best presentation possible and adapt from there.

As it happened, the session went better than we'd hoped. By the time we finished presenting and taking questions, Debbie and her group were discussing which teams throughout AT&T could benefit by spending a full day or two with Bill and me. However, when her team filed out of the room for a break, and just the three of us remained, it was time to tell her that we had just been laid off earlier that same day. Bill added nervously, "Of course we don't know how you would feel about working with Sean and me if we're no longer affiliated with Boston U."

To our relief, Debbie didn't care. She said she would be hiring the two of us, not some institution based three thousand miles away.

Once I returned to the office, I thought about how I would break the whirlwind of news to Kayla. We'd made a significant bet on moving to California, and after only five months, the job had fizzled. I felt like I'd let her down. Furthermore, before

I left Seattle, we had decided to get married. With our wedding coming up in Montana in three months, and me having just lost my job, I was feeling more than a little off balance and wondering what Kayla would be thinking of me now. But when I called and gave her the update, she calmly asked me to pick up some beer on the way home so we could sit on the beach and talk it through.

The remainder of that week I woke up each morning before dawn to go running on the beach while my mind cycled through all kinds of possibilities. We'd now be living on Kayla's six-dollars-per-hour job, and we didn't really know anyone in California except for Bill, and he might be leaving soon.

One evening at the end of the week, Kayla and I had taken some beers down the end of the street where we could lean on a low wooden split rail fence atop a cliff overlooking the beautiful Monterey Bay. We watched the lights of Carmel come up across the water fifty miles to the south, and she asked how I was doing; I admitted that I felt embarrassed, anxious and stressed about bringing so much turmoil into our lives.

"Well," she said, "I think it's all kind of exciting."

"Exciting!?" I asked.

"In Seattle we had nothing. We were just getting going on a business idea and frankly struggling to get it truly going. Five months later, we're in the same situation. We still have nothing, but you've learned a ton about the exact kind of business we were trying to start. And you built an amazing ropes course that's just sitting there in the woods at a beautiful conference center overlooking the ocean. If you decided to start the same kind of business here that we were going to do in Seattle, you probably could still use it. It'll be tight money-wise, but my pay might be enough for rent and groceries for a while. So yes, exciting. I think we should stay here."

—

A Chance to Make Something Stick

Kayla's view of the situation changed everything for me. I stopped ruminating about losing my job and instead began imagining every path forward I could think of: If Bill stayed, form a new business with him and carry on with our business development. If Bill left, move the business forward on my own while Kayla makes enough money to cover our rent and food. Find a new business partner, maybe, or earn just enough with some early paying gigs to allow Kayla to quit her boat supply store job so she and I could be partners again. These plans were disjointed, but they were at least plans.

I called Bill first a few days later to check in. To my relief, he had concluded that we should attempt to form a new company, assuming I was willing. He and I would be the principals; Kayla might be persuaded to quit her job and step in as operations manager. We needed to find some start-up capital through paid client work, or maybe a small loan, and we would give it at least six months. After that, if it didn't work, we would dissolve whatever entity we'd created and go our separate ways. Game on.

Our first problem: Many to-do items on our list required some capital, which we didn't have. Our final Boston University paychecks had to cover our rent and food for the next month, and neither Bill nor Kayla and I had anything to sell that we could convert into cash, and we had nothing of value that would serve as collateral for a small business loan. Yet we had some immediate requirements, such as a place to work from and a few typewriters and some furniture. Bill called his business partners from Growing Edge and asked if they would possibly lend us $30,000 for one year with interest. They were plenty nervous about the idea, but after some weeks they agreed, provided we promised to repay the $30,000 in full in twelve months' time.

We called our best prospect, Debbie Ward, to see if she had

any paying work that might include us in the near future. She did: One of the managers who'd seen our demo session recently mentioned to her that he wanted to hire us to work with his team. Bill called him straightaway to work out the details. That first contract was followed by two more paid engagements with AT&T the next month; all three went really well. We found ourselves in the very early phases of building quite a favorable reputation, at least with AT&T human resources and numerous line managers in the East Bay.

Soon, a few other mid-level managers around the Bay Area began hearing good stories about us from AT&T. Our client list slowly expanded. At just twenty-six years old, I was nervous about the durability of our business, but as good feedback from customers gradually kept validating our worth, my confidence rose. We created a tiny office out of Bill's rented two-bedroom house in Aptos. Kayla became our jack-of-all-trades office manager, setting up our liability insurance, processing payroll, buying and maintaining office equipment, coordinating client work, and even creating desks out of used doors and sawhorses. We eventually splurged on three brand new 1985 Macintosh computers, two additional landline phones, and a daisy wheel printer. We didn't have much, but we felt like we were rolling compared to where we were a few months earlier.

We barely managed to pay back the $30,000 to Growing Edge by the end of that first year. Over the next three years, on the days we weren't working with clients, Bill, Kayla, and I cranked out cold calls, fishing for introductory meetings that could lead to more bookings.

The process was demeaning, but once or twice a week we'd get a hit. It wasn't always smooth sailing. Some months we had to skip drawing a paycheck because the funds weren't there. Yet, by early 1988, our small company, which we had named Catalyst Consulting, had six employees and the months we were profitable had exceeded the months we weren't. Our word-of-mouth reputation continued to improve, allowing us to find work with blue-chip clients like Pacific Gas and Electric, Crocker Bank, and Levi Strauss.

Later that same year, we got a call that brought us to a new level—Lucille Ueltzen, the head of Apple University in Cupertino. Lucille had a new course offering that she felt was exactly what hundreds of mid-level managers needed to learn, but she was disappointed with a mismatch in style between the course's conservative, academic-oriented external instructors and Apple's unique corporate culture. She'd heard our methodology for conveying business concepts was both innovative and effective, so she offered us a chance to do a demo program.

A week after our session, Ueltzen called to tell us that the written feedback evaluations were excellent—no easy trick, as Apple employees were notoriously difficult to please. We soon took over the teaching of the course, and for the next three years it was one of Apple University's highest rated. With Apple's endorsement and our track record for producing good results, we were on a slow but steady upward success spiral.

Achieving Level Flight

By 1990, we had two parallel businesses going. One provided training programs for a dozen or so managers attending a two-, three-, or five-day course on leadership and teamwork. By this time Kayla and our other consultants were traveling around the US and the world conducting these courses for clients like Intel, Cisco Systems, Sun Microsystems, and Weyerhaeuser. The other business was the still-newish world of organization development, formerly known as industrial psychology. In that business, an intact team in an organization would hire me, Bill, or another consultant from Catalyst to work with them a few times per month. Using a combination of existing strategic planning approaches, we devised a unique, user-friendly methodology that we called the Catalyst Vision and Strategy process. Its success across different industries helped further solidify our reputation as experts in achieving a high degree of organizational alignment. The process was a hit and is one of the main reasons Catalyst's services are still in demand today, thirty-nine years after we first began.

By the early 1990s we had grown from our three original team members to more than twenty, including our adjunct consulting staff. We were working in technology, banking, biotech, movies, apparel, forest products, and many other areas. US-based companies sent us around the world to work with their divisions and subsidiaries in places like Singapore, Sweden, Korea, and Mexico.

The most satisfying and rewarding thing for me at this stage was the pace of learning we ourselves were engaged in. When one of us came back from some client engagement, whether it was from just over the mountains in Silicon Valley or from Southeast Asia—like bees who explore far from the hive and later return to tell everyone what they have found, we would share detailed stories of our client experiences. We were working to develop a simplified way of framing an answer to our clients' key question. They all wanted to know how they could become a learning organization, meaning one that continuously improved in terms of strength and resilience—even while employees came and went, or as the industry they were in continued to morph and evolve. Our discussions about the best practices we'd seen and helped to implement while with our clients eventually led to our developing that secret sauce everyone wanted. It was made up of two parts. The first was to create and organize your organization's story in five parts: mission, values, vision, current reality, and strategies. Part two was to implement the critical processes that would always keep those five things highly visible, constantly reviewed and reinforced, and tuned to the highest level possible. Many organizations we taught this to back in the 1990s are still using it today. It is a large part of Catalyst's ongoing reputation for adding clear and lasting value to its clients.

Ten years in, I was feeling pretty good about having achieved an entrepreneurial start-up success. And this was in the San Francisco Bay Area, legendary for its high rate of start-up failures, but Catalyst was ever-expanding, and our fees were matching the larger, more well-known consulting firms of the day like Price Waterhouse and Booze Allen. We used our Vision and Strategy process on ourselves exactly as we did it with clients. We paid our staff significantly higher than average and included everyone in profit sharing. We provided a generous vacation and flexible work policy that was uncommon in those days. It was a long way from my early jobs that included roughnecking on oil rigs in North Dakota and cleaning toilets and painting apartments with Kayla for free rent back in Seattle.

And as we entered our second decade in business, I was finally getting a little more time now and then to step back and reflect on where my life was headed over the longer term. I began to sense a very distant, new awareness barely seeping into my consciousness, though I was unable to pinpoint the subtle yet unsettling emotions stirring within me.

An Unexpected Catalyst for Change

Kayla and I were greatly enjoying California's outdoor recreation opportunities as well as our business success. One beautiful summer weekend, Kayla and I embarked on a kayaking trip with friends along the South Fork of the American River which flowed down the western slopes of the Sierra Nevada Mountains. The early snowmelt had swollen the water level to much higher than normal, so we took it slow and easy. We launched mid-morning, enjoying the sparkling reflections off the water and the excited shouts of other floaters upstream and downstream of us. The morning proved easy going with only a few tip overs. When we reached the more demanding sections, I went on ahead to stand by in case somebody flipped and needed help collecting any equipment or people that floated downstream.

We stayed close together until we reached the precipice of a flat but powerfully churning, one-hundred-foot-wide pool, followed by a long and unusually swift wave train. I traversed the pool first, headed down through the long series of rapids, and continued around a slight bend where the river dropped again, then pulled over alongside some dump-truck-sized rock formations. I slipped out of my kayak and climbed to a high perch to watch upstream for the others.

A few minutes passed. Given the heavy boat traffic that day, I was surprised that no other kayaks or rafts had yet come by. Finally, one raft came around the bend with six people, but no one was celebrating after having conquered that difficult stretch of whitewater. That seemed odd; instead of celebrating, they weren't even smiling. I waved and they all stared at me. The rafting guide on the boat's rear tube said simply, "There's a kayaker in trouble upriver." They rounded the bend below me in silence and floated out of sight. No other boats appeared. Worried, I again looked upriver and noticed a kayak paddle floating toward me—Kayla's. Twenty yards behind it was one of her float bags. I was familiar with this scene: When a kayaker flips in particularly violent water and swims to shore, the equipment flotsam floating downstream is called a "yard sale."

I kept expecting Kayla to float into view, buoyed by her life jacket and clutching her half-swamped kayak. She didn't. I left my boat and jogged up the gravel beach in my wet suit and life jacket, jumping across high boulders along the narrow riverbank until I was high enough to see up the next section of river.

My stomach dropped. My friend Bill Underwood was standing two hundred yards upstream, looking frantically across the river at two house-sized boulders. Pillows of whitewater surged around their edges. Dozens of people were perched around them on high rocks, desperately scanning the crashing water below. Kayla was nowhere in sight. Bill, looking absolutely stricken, had not seen me yet. In a growing panic, I yelled over the roar of the rapids: "Bill! Where is Kayla?!" He spun toward the sound of my voice. He was shaking his head—and then I knew. All I could muster was, "Bill! Not Kayla? *It's not Kayla?!*" He looked at me with more anguish than I'd ever seen in a human being.

"I know, Sean!" was all he could say.

I realized that whatever happened to Kayla had occurred nearly five minutes ago—an eternity when every second of oxygen counts. *If she had been trapped underwater for that long...*I put that thought out of my mind. I had to get to her, and that first meant crossing the river. I pulled my life jacket belt as tight as I could, took one look at the wide stretch of rapids, and chose a line that hopefully would not slam me into—or trap me under—one of the large boulders mid-river. I lunged into the rapids and swam hard as the current swept me downstream. For every ten feet of gain toward the far bank I was being taken downriver fifty feet or more, but I plowed forward.

I dragged myself onto the far bank some three hundred yards downstream from where I'd started and tugged at my wet suit's ankle cuffs to drain out the heavy water. I sprinted upriver along the bank on a narrow trail until, exhausted, I arrived just below the two rocks above which nearly forty guides and tourists gathered. "Is she alive?" I yelled desperately. A woman coming down the path toward me was in tears. She shook her head and quavered, "I don't think so." Another woman behind her did not look up at me as she slowly picked her way down the path past me. She was crying.

As I came up alongside the rocks, I found the guides and tourists sitting motionless as if in a steep, stone amphitheater with all eyes looking down at a stage. The churning pool pressed up against two huge downstream rocks in a heaving, boiling surge. The water pulsated and flowed back over itself, spilling out into the river's main channel. It was not a place even the most capable swimmer would want to be.

Kayla's bright yellow, fourteen-foot hard-plastic kayak was standing almost vertical on its end, nearly submerged with just one foot of the stern sticking up out of the water. It was being crushed against the rock by the enormous pressure of the upstream current. This meant the water there was at least twelve feet deep. I knew Kayla had to be in the boat's cockpit, some five or six feet below the surface.

A rafting guide high up on the rocks was dangling a rescue rope, which undulated uselessly, snake-like in the foaming water. I grabbed the end of the rope, rushed into the water, lost my footing and using the buoyancy of my wet suit and life jacket, floated the last six feet toward her kayak. Fighting the current with all my might, I reached the boat, threaded the rope through the webbing loop at the stern, and tried desperately to tie a bowline knot. As I struggled to tread water, the person holding the end of the rope back on the shore hollered, "Pass back the end!" I turned and flung the end of the rope to the crowd.

The previously paralyzed throng jumped into action, and within a few seconds ten or more of them had hands on the rope and were hauling mightily. The boat and I moved only slightly at first and then a bit more. Finally, the boat tipped over, scraping against the rocks. Once horizontal, it slid backwards—along with me, holding the rope—and careened across the boiling pool toward to the shouts of "pull!" I regained my footing and looked inside the cockpit.

It was empty.

The crowd fell silent again. I instinctively stepped back into the water. My life jacket floated just enough in the churning foam to keep my head above water. The current sped me back across the pool to exactly where the kayak had been. I put my feet up to brace off the wall of rock. They hit stone, and the water, now surging against my back, positioned me on the rock as if I were repelling down a cliff.

I looked down into the water between my legs, struggling

to see through the sunlight flashing in the blinding white foam. Through the blurry swirl, about five feet below, I could make out colors—bright red and lavender—the color of Kayla's paddling helmet and life jacket. Then I saw blond hair swirling crazily. I moved my feet down the rock until the water was at my chin, and then just under my nose. I could see Kayla's limp body moving like a rag in the water, her purple helmet stuck in a rock crevice.

I took a deep breath, reached down, grabbed her life jacket's shoulder pads, and pressed out and up with my legs as hard as I could. Her head came out of the crevice, and I could feel that her body was now free. But I realized I didn't have nearly enough strength to counteract the surging water pressure that was pulling her—and now me—downward. I did not know what to do. But now that I had her in my grip, I did not want to let her go. Holding my breath, I stuck my head under the surface and, way down, saw bright light where a powerful flow of water was going under the two rocks and must, I figured, be coming out, somewhere on the downstream side.

I often say there are two types of difficult decisions. One is when there are a variety of *really* not-good options, and you don't know which to pick. Another is when there is clearly only one option, but you *really* don't want to do it. This situation involved the latter. As my feet began slipping, I made my decision. I lifted and pulled Kayla's body up and as far away from the rock as I could, and then—having no idea where I was sending her—shoved downward on her shoulders as hard as could in the direction of that bright light. My hope was that the powerful current would carry her downward and somehow flush her out on the other side, which I also hoped was relatively calm water in the boulder's downstream eddy.

Once she was gone my face was instantly pinned against the rock. I yelled to the crowd, "She's out! She's coming up on the other side—go get her!" I kept screaming the command over and over. Meanwhile, I was now hanging only by my hands, which gripped narrow, wet ledges above my head. It would only be a minute or so before my arms tired and I'd be pulled under. At that moment, from directly above me, someone yelled, "Take my hand!" Two strong young men had scrambled to the to the top of the rock above me, laid down on their stomachs, and reached for my arms. Together they hauled me up. I thanked them profusely as we all climbed down to the gravel shore on the rock's backside.

When I got downstream of the boulders, twenty or more people were standing in the calm eddy water up to their chests. Three men were cradling Kayla as she floated on her back. One man held her legs while two others gently held up her head. I pushed toward her, looking desperately for signs of life. I held her face close to mine and felt her breathing, ever so faintly. I later learned that one of the guys holding her was a firefighter, well-trained in first aid. The moment she'd floated up from the depths, he and some others had held her still in the water while he gave her two quick mouth-to-mouth breaths. She immediately coughed up water and began breathing. His firefighter training and quick actions saved her life.

Eyes still closed; Kayla began moaning. Her face was stark white and very cold. I added up the amount of time she had been underwater—somewhere nearing eight or nine minutes—and imagined the potential brain damage from the lack of oxygen. As I studied her arm and leg movements, she slowly became more lucid. Her eyes fluttered open. It seemed like she could move her limbs slightly without pain or restriction. She began turning her head slightly from side to side. Her mouth was bleeding from multiple places. Several of her front teeth were broken.

Moments later, still floating on her back, she looked up at me and all the people surrounding her, "What happened? Where are we?" Her eyes darted around the big semicircle of people standing in the eddy, many of them shaking their heads in disbelief. I told her that she had been stuck underwater for a time, but we'd gotten her out and that she was going to be okay. I didn't say that she was trapped so long that many rafting guides—all specifically trained in river rescue—assumed she'd drowned and had given up on her.

My friend, Mark, brought Kayla and me the rest of the way down the canyon in his large raft. An hour later she was helicoptered to UC Davis Medical Center, a few hours' drive west. Bill Underwood and I arrived a few hours later, having driven the distance since there had been no extra room in the helicopter. I walked into her room, where she was surrounded by nurses and a doctor. Her eyes were closed, and she was resting. They listed her injuries: five broken teeth, a likely cracked cheekbone, large bone bruises on both sides of her skull behind her ears, possibly a concussion, and, most worrisome, significant water still in her lungs. The lungs were at risk of infection and pneumonia. She would need to stay in the ICU for several more days under close observation.

The doctors and nurses were surprised to hear that, according to bystanders, Kayla had been underwater for as long as eight or nine minutes, but they said her survival was consistent with a few other horrific stories. Most people drown after a minute and a half underwater, but occasionally the staff had seen other extraordinary cases, including a small boy who was recently found lying at the bottom of a swimming pool for an estimated fifteen minutes. He, too, was brought back to life. The nurse shrugged her shoulders and said, "Your lovely wife got lucky for reasons we'll never know. Today she was just one of those people."

A few months after leaving the hospital, we were sitting on our front porch looking across the train tracks at Monterey Bay. Kayla's front teeth, newly capped with dental plastics, looked completely natural. Her cheekbones, although still sore, had returned to their normal color. Her headaches had mostly subsided.

Kayla had been speaking about her ordeal with a therapist,

who asked her what she remembered about the incident. She said that after the first frightening moments when she gave up struggling and realized her life was over, she felt no fear, but rather a deep sadness. She'd had time for three thoughts. First, she saw, from afar, people gathered for her funeral. Second, she was sad that Sean would be left on his own. Third, she realized she would never get a chance to meet her children. Her body then forced her to take a breath. Water poured into her lungs. Everything went black. The next thing she remembered she was sitting semi-upright in a large raft, riding downriver toward the helicopter.

Insight

Over the coming months, at work and at home, I watched Kayla anxiously. She seemed fine. As was her nature, she was moving forward with life quite well.

But I wasn't.

A steady undercurrent of fear and unease now followed me all the time, driven, I surmised, from the thought that I'd almost lost her. I hoped the feelings would diminish over time. They didn't. My sleep was suffering, and I was having terrible reoccurring dreams. I brought up this issue with a therapist, telling him about one of my nightmares that was always set in a house where I'd lived in my early teens in Great Falls, Montana. In the dream, the house was completely empty, as if my family had moved once more and had left me behind. Meanwhile, a very large beast that seemed like a giant refrigerator-sized angry badger was chasing me down into our dark basement and was on the verge of attacking. It was strangely very upset and seemed about to hurt me—badly. Every time, just when the creature reached me as I was cowering in a corner, I woke up.

My therapist suggested something I believed I'd already understood. Given all the moving I'd had to endure while growing up—nineteen different homes by the time I was eighteen—I'd learned to practice my own kind of nonattachment. I resisted emotional bonding to people and to places, and I was unusually at ease with letting things go. This strategy served me well growing up, and later in life, it actually helped me be more adventuresome and take more risks. But, he suggested, maybe I was now reaching the limits of that strategy. He said I finally had something in life that I cherished unconditionally—Kayla—and I would do anything to hold on to her. Perhaps I now feared that I didn't know how to operate in this new world. Maybe this dream was a wake-up call to a new phase of life where I would now risk becoming deeply attached to important things and people. But I might also be very afraid that I wasn't capable of being good at secure attachments. He said these feelings had likely affected my choices on the type of work I'd engaged in thus far as well. It would take three more sessions to hear and understand that last part about my work. I later realized maybe it was simply something I didn't want to hear or contemplate. At each future session he reminded me these combined realizations might be the greatest unknown I've ever faced, and he found it unsurprising that my dreams were so unsettling, confusing, and scary.

The following year, our son Dylan was born. Our daughter Siri would be born four years later. The more I reflected on my therapist's thoughts on the new risky phase I was entering, the more wisdom I found in his words. I became only slightly more comfortable embracing the total attachment and love I felt for our family of four, while simultaneously trying to mitigate the fear that I could somehow lose one or more of them at any time. I'd heard that wise people can live with such cognitive dissonance. I wasn't feeling wise yet; I was still feeling unsettled and uneasy in this new unstable territory and not feeling at all competent in or comfortable with what I was trying to be.

Processing that river experience and trying to consciously allow myself to get attached to things that I could admit were important to me, forced me to slow down and think much more carefully about what I really wanted. While Kayla and I both felt grateful for just about everything in our lives, we agreed that changes were looming. We revisited the things we'd had in common when we first met. We'd both wanted a life with frequent adventures. We wanted kids. We hoped to create a situation where financial worries were minimized. We also hoped for satisfying, interesting work that felt meaningful, which, thus far, Catalyst largely was. But as I tried to be more honest with myself, I discovered my interest in consulting was slipping. I began a years-long private struggle to figure out why and what, if anything, was missing.

—

I've always loved the movie *Groundhog Day*, but I never thought the phenomenon might apply to my own life. Now, the endless, repetitive tribulations of Bill Murray's cynical weatherman seemed uncomfortably relevant.

I didn't dread my work with Catalyst exactly, but very inherent to consulting that had once energized me—different projects, different clients—had become surprisingly predictable, day after day. When we competed for work with other consulting firms, we usually won the work contracts. And then we delivered what we'd promised. Day after day after day.

The reputation we'd earned—and the word-of-mouth advertising from each new successful project—generated an ever-growing portfolio of work. I saw my path clearly over the next decades: I would gain increasing recognition as a successful entrepreneur and organizational consultant, and I'd do fine financially. I still found our client work personally rewarding; It feels good to help people and to be recognized for being good at it. And because of our commitment to constantly improving our own skills and offerings, I was learning nonstop. But my energy for that future vision was slowly dissipating.

By late 1994 I found myself thinking, *What the heck? I've achieved my goal of building a successful vocation that involves what I consider important work. What is my problem?*

Sorting Through the Nuances of What and Why

Probably some of my malaise was related to a busy work schedule. More and more I resented being pulled away from Siri and Dylan by my work, especially with all the overnight traveling I was doing. My friend Larry Biehl, a financial planner, mentioned that he knew many people who were caught up in their work success and said that most of these people didn't feel "rich" in the typical sense, even if their net worth suggested otherwise. What many people wanted most—even if they didn't realize it—was to be in control of their time, which was Larry's definition of being rich. At Catalyst, we used to joke that at the level we were operating, the consulting business is always on the front burner with the dial set on high. There were no medium or low settings. The control-of-my-time issue had merit, but I sensed there was also more to my fading interest in the consulting lifestyle.

The more I thought about what I learned from therapy regarding attachment, the more closely I looked at why consulting had been such an easy fit for my career. In our approach, I was a coach and facilitator who joined the client group for a time but always eventually left for a new gig. Start a new client engagement, meet new people, succeed per the contract, leave. No risk of getting too attached. Always easy and appropriate to move on. Now, in my late thirties, I wanted attachments, but to what, job-wise, I had no idea.

Permission to Explore a Big Transition

One weekend Kayla and I were camping along the Big Sur coast with Siri and Dylan, then aged two and six. We were sitting on some high rocks watching the kids below play in the tide pools. I'd been reluctant to talk with her much about my confusing feelings—I didn't want her to think I was spinning out into a midlife crisis—but her opinions mattered more to me than anyone's.

Kayla was aware that my increasing interests in somehow making the world a better place wasn't being addressed at Catalyst like it used to be, where our clients were understandably mostly interested in greater efficiencies and productivity to help increase their profits and stock price. More importantly, the constant moving from one project, company, or team to the next was eating away at my satisfaction. I was dreaming about some kind of work situation that wasn't ephemeral, that wouldn't go away in three to six months, that would make me feel good about its contribution to people or our planet. Kayla understood all this and knew that I wanted to spend more time with her and the kids. She made it clear that if I wanted to make a change, she thoroughly understood and was supportive.

Later that week, I sat at our kitchen table thinking about the Bridges Transition Model, a tool from William Bridge's book *Transitions,* something I'd used many times with organizations and individuals to help them work through large-scale changes. The model has three stages: endings, the neutral zone, and new beginnings.

I was starting to accept, reluctantly, that my interest in continuing my full-time, rainmaker role at Catalyst had been, for a few years, fading. It was time to acknowledge that I was subconsciously much further into the neutral zone of a transition than I'd understood.

However, I hadn't yet thought of anything specific regarding my potential next career. I was also feeling confused and at loose ends over losing interest in consulting, which I'd worked so hard to get good at. And I was confounded by the idea of pursuing a transition which involved many disturbing details, like leaving behind my Catalyst colleagues whom I truly valued and enjoyed working with. On the other hand, basic yet faint elements of a new vision were floating around in my brain, kaleidoscope-like, with compelling shapes and colors. My cerebral familiarity with this transition process, coupled with Kayla's typical openness to new adventures and possibilities, helped somewhat lessen my feelings of anxiety and urgency. Creating some significant time to step back and take stock before deciding what might be next as a job seemed like the right move.

Packing for the Neutral Zone

I began pulling out all the stops to clear my mind and become more open to a range of possibilities. I sought advice and calibration with everyone I could. I practiced articulating what I wanted to move *from*, and what I wanted to move *to*. Some people understood and were encouraging; others thought I was crazy to consider walking away from all that I'd helped build at Catalyst.

For a few months, Kayla and I brainstormed details of what a holistic transition, rather than just a job change, might look like. The most tangible first step was relocating from our home of thirteen years—Santa Cruz—back to Montana. We had always planned this move to give the kids easier access to the uncrowded outdoors and nature, and to be closer to their extended family. We also discussed what a less demanding schedule at Catalyst could look like for both of us.

Kayla was working as a part-time Catalyst contractor doing frequent international travel. I was mostly creating new work for our other Catalyst consultants. Rather than waiting until we made the actual move to Montana, Kayla suggested that I change now from working five days (and often more) per week to three. Kayla would stay in her part-time role. The effect was that we would have much more time to figure out our next phase of life.

Back at the office, I explained to my coworkers that I was planning on being less involved. Most of them were dubious; they even started betting on when Kayla's and my Montana fantasy would run its course, and we would return to Santa Cruz. The average guess was three years.

Our daughter, Siri, was three years old and didn't truly understand what was happening. But Dylan, who was seven, did. He was sad about leaving his friends and his ability to play at the beach—a five-minute drive away—anytime he wanted. So, we did what countless parents have done since the dawn of time in such situations: We promised the kids we would get a puppy after settling into our new home in Montana. It worked.

Meanwhile, with some aspects of a plan taking shape, Kayla and I could not wait to return to Montana. We were excited to go camping more often and closer to home with the kids, to have terrific downhill skiing close to our house, and to be nearer to extended family. We planned to rent out our Santa Cruz house for a few years because it was still appreciating, and the rent would cover its mortgage payment. We hoped to sell it and use the proceeds to pay down the mortgage on a much cheaper home in Bozeman. (This also gave us a hedge for a possible return to California in case our Catalyst coworkers had guessed right.)

On a late June afternoon, we pulled out of the driveway and into heavy Bay Area traffic. Siri and I were in a twenty-six-foot moving truck, towing our family minivan packed to the headliner with possessions. Kayla and Dylan followed in our pickup truck, towing a trailer. Our nephew and his girlfriend brought up the rear in a third vehicle, hauling even more stuff. The two-day, thousand-mile drive felt cathartic. We were moving onto the next phase of our life.

The last segment of our trip included an empty two-lane highway that wound northward down the Gallatin River Canyon through a section of Yellowstone National Park. As our headlights pierced the evening darkness, I noticed an enormous, shadowy form standing broadside and statue-like on the road's narrow shoulder. Not wanting to swerve suddenly with a heavily loaded truck and trailer, I held the steering wheel steady and applied soft pressure to the brakes. Siri looked up from her picture book to see what was going on. As we approached the thing, I saw a huge bull bison, six feet tall at the shoulder and likely weighing two thousand pounds. As we passed just a few yards from his enormous head, he calmly eyed our truck. Siri looked at me with wide eyes and said, "What was that?!"

"Well, honey, that was a real Montana experience," I replied. "A big, wild, bull bison. We're passing right through his territory. We've finally arrived in our new home."

—

Back in Montana, enjoying mostly four-day weekends, I was spending more time than ever with family and friends. I tried not to overly focus on what I was going to do next career-wise and instead worked on being patient, reconnecting with my old interests that I'd set on the shelf when I'd been building Catalyst and seeing what new interests might be emerging. I read far more books and magazine articles than I would normally have had time for. I studied mindfulness as much as possible—though I was still struggling to fully practice it. I read poetry, books on visual arts, and anything I could find that related to being more conscious about the kind of life I wanted to lead in my forties and fifties.

This experience of overall spaciousness and time to think—and feel—was sparking new ideas for my future. It also helped me to play around with, and examine more frequently, the two lists I was carrying around in my head and in a pocket journal. One list defined the criteria that my next career would hopefully meet, and the second was a brainstormed list of possible vocations or new businesses.

When I did think about new vocations, for some reason I

imagined most of my business ideas structured as nonprofits, or what were then beginning to be called public benefit corporations. For a time, I was moving several business ideas along simultaneously: Bringing a program from California to Montana called the Fourth R, which had been proven to increase grades and graduation rates in public schools; creating team-based mentoring approaches to improve the effectiveness of Montana's foster care system; developing aquaculture that involved growing fish using sustainable techniques similar to hydroponic vegetables and would help take pressure off wild fish populations in the oceans; and designing a franchise model to combine senior living facilities and child daycare centers. (I imagined that the two facilities would be physically connected by an elaborate, very large commercial greenhouse and plant nursery, allowing the seniors and children to interact and take care of the plants together.) But my favorite idea was something I called *Legacy Magazine*.

About five years prior to moving to Montana, I'd been hired by Time Warner Inc., which had just recently acquired *Sunset Magazine*. The newly installed Sunset CEO, Ron Kovas, wanted my help, as he put it, "to bring the Sunset organization out of the 1950s and into the 1990s." A magazine junkie myself, I jumped at the chance.

Over the next year, I met at least once per month with Ron and his executive team at Sunset's bucolic corporate headquarters in Menlo Park. As I learned more about the magazine business in general, I privately started fantasizing about creating and running a magazine myself. I even knew the magazine I wanted to do. For years I'd been drawn to news stories featuring successful businesspeople who, mid-career, quit their jobs as vice president of whatever and went on to do something completely new.

That "something" always involved trying to help make the world a better place. They figured out how to build schools and libraries in war-torn areas. They started clean water projects in remote villages. They created mentoring and financial support programs for youth. They launched inspiring wildlife and habitat protection projects.

My fantasy was to profile three or four of these social and environmental entrepreneurs in each issue of my magazine. We would tell their individual stories: Why they quit their lucrative for-profit positions, how they found, settled on, and succeeded at helping a cause that matched their interests. I hoped that in addition to creating some hope and optimism in general, some *Legacy* readers might be inspired by these stories enough to embark on similar projects themselves.

A Surprisingly Wild Addition to the List

One autumn weekend in 1999, about three years after moving to Montana and taking the time to think about what next, including the above scenarios, I road-tripped to the Canadian border with an old friend from college and two of his buddies. Four days later, on the long drive home to Bozeman, we traveled in a crew-cab pickup truck through one of the most remote sections of grasslands in all of Montana, downing coffee and water trying to recover from the previous late evening out.

One of the people on the trip was Steve Forrest, a wildlife biologist and one of two staff members with World Wildlife Fund US (WWF) Northern Great Plains office. As we stood in the knee-high sagebrush gazing across a huge prairie vista, Steve noted that we were standing in what had become a controversial landscape.

For decades, he explained, it had been the focus of reviving a very old idea for an exceedingly large wildlife restoration project. The first known suggestion for this concept came from the artist George Catlin, who had made six trips to the area between 1830 and 1840 to paint and chronicle the lifestyle of the Plains Indians. Stunned by the area's wildlife abundance, he appealed to Congress in 1836, suggesting it be saved as a "nations park." This was forty years prior to the establishment of the US Park Service. Catlin's suggestions went unheeded.

In the mid-1980s, Deborah and Frank Popper, two demography researchers and professors at Rutgers University, published a paper predicting two key things. First was that the steady, decades-long human outmigration across North America's Great Plains that had started in the 1920s would continue indefinitely. Second, that eventually there would be so much land available as a result—millions upon millions of prairie acres—that at least parts of the region could theoretically be repopulated by all the wildlife that used to be there prior to European settlement in the 1800s. They concocted the term Buffalo Commons in their paper to create an image of a vast landscape returned to the wildlife marvel that had been there for thousands of years.

Then, in the early 1980s, Robert "Bob" Scott, a rare book dealer from Missoula, conceptualized and tirelessly promoted what he called the "Big Open," a five-million-acre wildlife sanctuary that would have fulfilled Catlin's wishes and provided an impressive demonstration project to validate the Poppers' ideas. Bob's widespread support from US college audiences, to whom he spoke frequently, was counterbalanced by vehement, non-enthusiastic responses from local cattle and sheep ranchers. The headwinds from livestock organizations such as the politically powerful Montana Stockgrowers Association, ultimately proved too vexing. After nearly twenty years of effort, he left the project in the early 2000s and returned to his rare book business.

Back when Bob was still toiling to get the Big Open off the ground, The Nature Conservancy produced an important scientific report identifying ten priority areas on the Northern Great Plains that could be suitable for a multi-million-acre wildlife restoration project. Steve explained that landscape we were driving through sat near the top of their list. And, just a year before, a small group of entrepreneurial thinkers within WWF had picked up the idea and committed to finding some way to help implement the big reserve idea. It was for this effort that Steve, a lawyer and biologist by training, had recently been contracted by WWF to help.

With hours to spare before we reached our destination, Steve expounded further on the detailed history of the effort. In the late 1700s, French fur trappers from the Hudson's Bay Company had noted the unusual abundance of wildlife in this area in their travel journals, as did Lewis and Clark during their 1803 trip through the region on their exploratory journey to the Pacific Ocean. It occurred to me while listening to Steve that I had gone to public school in Great Falls, Montana in the 1960s, and while we'd been taught about the bravery and tenacity of Lewis and Clark as explorers—ad nauseam in my opinion—we'd not been taught that while traveling through what would later become northeastern Montana, they had corroborated in their detailed journals daily observations of an astounding variety and numbers of wild animals in this exact region of the plains. This now surprising omission in my schooling seemed second only to the lack of history regarding the abysmal treatment—to put it mildly—of Montana's Native peoples who'd lived on these plains for thousands of years.

The bottom line: The idea to create a large, protected area in this special spot had been passed along from explorers, artists, would-be entrepreneurs, and conservation organizations for more than 150 years. But in all that time, no one had ever figured out how to translate the dream into reality. Now, Steve explained, the WWF-US hoped to be the catalyst for creating a workable long-range plan and then somehow figure out an approach to executing well against that plan.

As I listened, I realized that Bob Scott's Big Open concept, assembled in the mid-1980s, very closely described what WWF was now promoting more than a decade later. Bob had envisioned a five-million-acre wildlife park bisected by the

Missouri River as it flowed east across the prairie toward St. Louis and down to New Orleans. WWF had identified a smaller but still huge 3.25-million-acre protected area which would geographically overlay quite closely on Bob's original project maps.

WWF's role began in 1999. Dr. Eric Dinerstein, then-chief scientist of the WWF-US, had traveled from Washington, DC, to Montana on the invitation of Defenders of Wildlife's Minette Johnson and the Predator Conservation Alliance's Jonathan Proctor. The meeting's purpose was to explore how to get numerous conservation groups to join forces to create a large habitat for prairie dogs and black-footed ferrets in northeastern Montana. Eric, an out-of-the box thinker, listened patiently to the scheme, but, true to his nature, immediately began thinking of something bigger—much bigger.

During this period WWF-US was beginning to think about organizing their work in enormous ecoregions, as they would be called, in the Chihuahuan Desert, the Bering Sea, the Klamath Siskiyou Forest, and the Northern Great Plains. Eric began to think that a multi-million-acre prairie reserve could be a first-out-of-the-gate anchor or flagship project, demonstrating from the start that WWF knew how to initiate big, meaningful ideas. As Eric kept shaping this concept, he and his DC-based colleagues determined that any flagship ecoregion project should strive to restore all native flora and fauna of that region and not just focus on a few species.

Some months later, Eric returned to Montana with two DC colleagues and together with Johnson and Proctor, drove the seven hours to the proposed reserve site in northeastern Montana. Later, in a letter to his colleagues, Eric described his breathtaking experience standing on a ridge on the prairie looking over this landscape for the first time in his life, declaring this a place that could match the Serengeti in size and wildlife numbers, and that he could easily imagine the completely restored flora and fauna that had once flourished here for thousands of years.

Eric's post-trip report, coupled with his relentless evangelizing, created a small, isolated movement within WWF to establish a flagship project in each ecoregion, and to get started on the Northern Great Plains. Eric soon befriended a WWF donor named Elizabeth Ruml, who tentatively pledged a significant financial gift to help set the project up, *if it ever got going.*

According to Steve, the WWF's first tangible move to get the plan rolling was to ask a retired WWF associate, Dr. Curt Freese, to relinquish his serene lifestyle that consisted of writing books in the beautiful Bridger Mountains north of Bozeman, and have him return as a full-time WWF employee, based in Bozeman. Curt's main role was to be an on-the-ground local operative who would help figure out how WWF could be an effective catalyst for launching the overall project and remain as some kind of player/partner once it was underway.

Still in the truck as the miles toward Bozeman clicked off, Steve and I sat in the back seat discussing the whys and hows of the yet-to-be-launched project. Like most Montanans by this time, I knew that the US government had brutally taken the northeast corner of the state away from the Indigenous peoples who, by the 1860s, were being forced to live on reservations. The vast area that used to be their homeland was populated by white European settlers who soon transformed it into their own money-making cattle and sheep operations. Prior to that, I, like many others, had assumed it was composed largely of empty grasslands. But Steve described something I'd never been taught in Montana public schools or anywhere else: a scene with hundreds of thousands of bison, countless bird species, and huge populations of elk, bighorn sheep, deer, pronghorn, cougars, wolves, and grizzly bears. (Up until that conversation it had never occurred to me that grizzlies were originally a plains animal.) For many hundreds and thousands of years, all this wildlife was enabled by a rich and complex grassland ecosystem, and where we were currently driving was one of the last remaining large-scale bits of intact prairie, not just in the Great Plains, but anywhere in the world.

Looking out the truck's window, I started viewing the place differently than I had since first experiencing it as a kid in the 1960s. I later learned that this was a classic example of the shifting baselines syndrome, where someone like me assumed that what they had grown up with, such as these plains being largely devoid of wildlife, was how it had always been.

Nonetheless, I expressed my many misgivings about such an audacious project, starting with the predictable and fierce resistance from local ranchers. Steve countered, citing demographic evidence that showed a nine-decade-long trend of steady population decline beginning in the early 1920s. Ranching was the main industry in the area and, like so many other businesses, decade by decade it required fewer and fewer people to run its operations as new approaches and technology improved efficiency. He said that the slow, steady drop in employment associated with more efficient production forced locals to join the exodus seeking work elsewhere. In particular, since the 1930s there had been a measurable, steadily diminishing presence of the archetypical American cowboy. For nearly a hundred years—like so many other similar rural regions around the world—towns had been shrinking, rural schools consolidating, tax bases atrophying, capital investments of almost any kind evaporating. This meant that, for the next few decades at least, it was likely that plenty of property would be up for sale. On the assumption that adequate funding could be found, those acquired properties could gradually add to the Reserve's habitat base.

I had other concerns, such as how the federal Bureau of Land Management and the Montana Department of Fish, Wildlife and Parks would feel about a private organization making plans for huge increases in wildlife populations in a five-thousand-square-mile area. And, not least of all, where would all the funds come from? Steve said that as best they could estimate at the moment, it might cost as much as $450 million to $500 million from start to finish. Five hundred million dollars!

After hours of discussion, Steve and I took a break from talking and both sat quietly watching the wide-open landscape roll by. I thought about the project's immense financial costs, the time needed to complete it, the likely very stiff resistance it would encounter, and the critical challenge of building the right kind of organization to run it long term. I turned to Steve and said, "The vision is compelling for sure. I really like it. But as with any start up, entrepreneurial idea, the devil is in the details. At the moment, I think there are too many negative, or at least exceedingly difficult, forces to overcome with this scheme."

I thought for a few moments more before speaking again.

"I don't think it's going to work."

CHAPTER TWO

A New Way of Seeing

As we arrived back to Bozeman, Steve suggested that if I was interested, maybe I could talk with his boss, Curt Freese. Over the past few years, I'd been meeting with many people I normally wouldn't, nearly always coming away having learned something interesting that altered my view of things in general—and at times discovering something that added to my thinking about my future. I figured it couldn't hurt to talk with this fellow Curt and hear how he was wrestling with this unusually big and seemingly far-fetched idea.

Some weeks later I met with Curt at his home office: a small, stuffy attic on the third floor of his ninety-year-old house on Wilson Avenue. Steve had told Curt that, given my background in consulting to businesses including many early start-ups, I might have some useful ideas about how this prairie project could be structured and executed. Seated across from him I found him to be thoughtful, gracious, and very experienced in the world of conservation biology. He also had a knack for explaining things in a way that acknowledged that the thornier details would be hard to solve, but not so hard that they made the project a nonstarter. For more than an hour he explained how this region might be one of the best hopes in the Lower 48 to bring back a large-scale grassland ecosystem and protect it along the lines of a national park. He also convinced me that many of the difficult and separate pieces of the puzzle for this project had been largely solved in areas he'd worked around the world, and that many of those solutions might be borrowed and applied to this project in Montana. That idea of usable, borrowable solutions existing elsewhere piqued my interest. As I listened to the content of his thinking and observed the way he delivered his thoughts and beliefs, I thought about the list of criteria I wanted my next career to meet. One item was being around quality people whose thinking and values I admired. Curt certainly exuded those characteristics.

Curt had been travelling the state for six months asking folks from the world of conservation for advice and testing their interest in becoming involved. He also talked to them about the challenges of designing and launching a suitable organization to run the project. When he learned more about my previous job with Catalyst, where we often helped people launch new organizations, he invited me to join some of these exploratory trips.

One fall day in 1999, we attended a meeting of conservationists who were gathering to discuss possible approaches to creating a prairie wildlife preserve. The gathering included representatives from National Wildlife Federation; American Lands, a real estate company; Predator Conservation Alliance; Off the Beaten Path, a Montana-based adventure travel company; WWF (represented by Curt); and a few others. Curt noted that many of these people had deep Montana roots and had been working in the land and wildlife conservation world for decades.

We met at the National Wildlife Federation's Missoula offices, where Curt introduced me as someone with a background in helping new enterprises get off the ground. I mostly listened but as the afternoon wore on, I found a few openings to ask questions. "If the project might cost as much as $500 million, what is the fundraising strategy?" The somewhat testy answer from a few of the people I'd just met was that large conservation organizations always raise a lot of money; if a group of conservation organizations like theirs worked together, they would simply pool their fundraising efforts. This seemed simplistic, as did the fact that they seemed to have few ideas, or even much concern, about what kind of staff was required to operate such an undertaking over such a long period of time. Mostly they seemed to be focusing on the local and national political challenges the project might incite. At the end of the four-hour meeting, it was still not clear to me who would actually run the proposed project day to day.

By late afternoon, Curt and I were on the road heading back to Bozeman. It was a warm day and Curt's little truck had no air conditioning. Humming along at seventy miles per hour with the windows down, we shouted at each other over the wind noise. I asked Curt for his impressions of the meeting: He thought the proposed starting structure seemed cumbersome—it involved many conservation groups in sort of a United Nations format overseeing things—but hoped it might smooth out once the basic components of the plan took shape. He didn't sound convincing. Sensing my skepticism, he asked, "Well, Mr. Consultant, you must have seen a lot of meetings like this one. What did you think?"

I replied that a project anchored by such an aggressive and audacious vision probably wouldn't proceed very effectively if it was mostly run by a part-time consortium or committee whose members all held demanding day jobs with other organizations. There also seemed to be significant—and maybe insurmountable—differences in opinions within the group as to the project's top priorities for the next five to ten years. I felt a better structural approach might be to find a leader—essentially a CEO—willing to make this undertaking a full-time job. She or he needed to be an innovative, hard-charging, entrepreneur who was good at assembling a strong team from scratch and who would view this project as their own next big thing. Perhaps most importantly, this person would need to be able to act with minimal interference or bureaucratic oversight. Curt was skeptical, as what I was suggesting, from what he told me, was an uncommon model in large-scale nature conservation, but he was interested in talking about it further.

In the following weeks Curt and I met regularly to visualize and kick around from various angles the organization model I'd described. The idea looked good on paper, but my experience told me that in practice, success or failure usually hung on the individuals charged with moving things forward week by week. Who would be running things was a critical but still undetermined factor.

—

Shortly after settling in Montana, I had taken the visionary goals I'd articulated for myself six months before leaving Santa Cruz and plugged them into the Catalyst Vision and Strategy template. I was in the habit of frequently reviewing the hard copy version I kept on my home-office desk.

So far, my updated purpose and values were holding steady: My simple purpose for the next five years still boiled down to being the kind of father and husband that I'd found too challenging to pull off while working full-time with Catalyst. It also included settling into a career that allowed for the lifestyle Kayla dreamed of, while also making me feel like I had a decent shot at leaving the world a better place.

My values hadn't changed in the past four years. The vision criteria had evolved and expanded slightly from my original list a year ago, but the basics were the same. The actions aspect of the template still specified exploring new people, new ideas, new experiences with our kids, and living at a much slower pace than we had in the previous fifteen years. My *Legacy Magazine* idea matched most of my plan's criteria well and remained the clear front runner in my long list of possibilities. But now, this prairie reserve concept, coming completely out of left field, was increasingly occupying my thoughts.

One winter day in 2001, Curt told me that he and his WWF colleagues had become interested in moving in the direction of the freestanding organization I had described earlier. If the idea went forward, WWF's first order of business would be to create a new, stand-alone 501(c)(3) nonprofit. Second, because a Montana-based nonprofit must have at least a three-person board of directors, he asked if I would be willing to join. I'd never served on a nonprofit board before, but it sounded interesting and not overly demanding time-wise. Importantly, it wouldn't interfere too much with my evolving plans for *Legacy Magazine*.

Next up, the board would have to find an executive director for the newly formed nonprofit. I mentioned that, except for working with a few large hospitals systems and universities, my sixteen years with Catalyst had been focused entirely on for-profit businesses. But the more Curt explained how nonprofits were set up and the rules they had to live by, the more I realized how much they had in common with for-profit businesses, especially regarding leadership skills. The CEO needed to be able to attract quality employees, have experience in aligning people around a vision, be adept at making the constant adjustments required to keep the organization moving forward, and have a penchant for continuous improvement.

This newly formed independent organization, Curt suggested, would initially exist to build the Reserve. Key to that would be acquiring hundreds of thousands of private acres and slowly stitching them together to create a fully functioning grassland ecosystem. Later, the new entity would also be responsible for creating and maintaining productive relationships with the other local constituencies including the Nakoda and Aaniiih Nations, the US Fish and Wildlife Service, the Bureau of Land Management, and Montana Fish, Wildlife and Parks. This organization would also design and implement a public access and visitation model while maintaining a symbiotic relationship with surrounding agricultural-based communities. WWF, meanwhile, would address the large and complex task of biodiversity restoration on three million-plus acres and, whenever possible, help to steer money toward the project.

One day, out of the blue, Curt asked if I would consider taking on the role of the nonprofit's interim executive director. His thinking was that I would learn firsthand precisely what kind of executive would be needed, and then, based on my assessment, we (the board) could start a nationwide search for a permanent leader of the staff organization. Once that person materialized, which Curt speculated might take about six to nine months, I would go back to being just a board member.

This unexpected concept both intrigued and worried me. I agreed to think about it, despite knowing it would require a great deal of time and energy. For one, I couldn't take on this responsibility and be involved with Catalyst at the same time, even at three days per week. There was no way around the fact that this concept was a start-up, an entrepreneurial effort that I knew from experience would require tremendous focus and persistence to launch effectively. I knew I'd have to discuss it thoroughly with Kayla because it would certainly impact our family, even if it only lasted half a year. In the meantime, if I agreed to do it, I would need time to transition out of Catalyst. Curt offered to list himself as the temporary director and oversee the basics, like getting the entity legally registered in Montana, establishing an office, stringing in some landline phones, and so on.

If I became temporary executive director of this new organization, I'd be back to working five days per week. I'd have to take a sabbatical from Catalyst, or, maybe more realistically, leave for good. I'd have to put my *Legacy Magazine* business idea on the shelf for a while. I was only working two-thirds of the time with Catalyst, but it paid well, was comfortable, and, frankly, was easy. The world of large-scale rewilding, nonprofit fundraising, and marketing was all new. If I decided to take on the role, *comfortable and easy* would not describe my experience anytime soon.

Convergence

Kayla and I began a series of rolling discussions about this scheme. Curt and I had not talked about compensation directly, but we had talked conceptually about a search and what a permanent nonprofit leader in this situation might be paid. Kayla noted that my compensation would likely be less than half of what I was making at Catalyst working part-time, but for nearly two decades we'd been diligent about living well below our means, had saved almost enough for our kids' college education, and were only a year or so away from paying off our home mortgage. So, she was fine with the change in income.

During one talk she said, "Frankly, it seems as though the more you are thinking about this idea, the more excited you are getting about it. If you somehow end up liking the role, I can't see you giving it up to someone else. That's fine with me. I'm just pointing that out for you to be aware of."

Her comments were spot on. I'm not sure I'd fully realized it, but I had already been thinking that if the position was fulfilling, I might not want to give it up right away. It could be intriguing to run it, for a while at least. Kayla's major pieces of advice were to take it slow, seek counsel from others, and not rush into a decision.

Over the next month I pondered this situation on my late afternoon walks with Silas, our black Labrador, as we meandered from the Catalyst downtown office to my home south of town. While Silas searched the sagebrush for Hungarian partridges, I would sit on a park bench situated high above our town, with 360-degree views of four different mountain ranges. On one particularly beautiful, cool late afternoon, I sat on the bench reading in my pocket journal the list of other job options I'd been contemplating, including *Legacy Magazine*, and tried to assess the feelings that accompanied each comparison. Now, after nearly four spacious years of exploring ideas and at the precipice of an actual decision, the exercise took on new urgency. I was actually attempting what I had taught so many clients to do over the years: Take the time to ask yourself what you really want. Once again, I thought over the content of my purpose, values, and vision.

I remained happy with what I had put together on paper regarding what I wanted in this next phase of life, but I was feeling some trepidation. The main concern, or maybe outright fear, was "What if this prairie thing fails?" The people from various conservation groups associated with it would still have their salaried jobs with benefits at their organizations. But as a leader of the new nonprofit, I would have tanked a start-up and, having left Catalyst, would be out of work, as would whatever staff members I'd assembled. I could recover job-wise, even if it meant rejoining Catalyst, but it would still be after an investment of possibly a number of years and a failure of not only the Reserve, but also of attaining my dream of becoming deeply involved in an important and lasting endeavor. I was surprised to find myself thinking back to the time with my therapist after Kayla's kayaking accident six years earlier. Sure enough, my old habitual fears of risking getting attached to something I cared about, and could possibly lose, were kind of bubbling up again.

While at Catalyst I'd coached many executives as they considered a strategic business decision or a personal career change. After they had done much analysis and settled on what they felt was probably the right decision, I would prompt deeper thought: "Take a moment to imagine yourself moving on this opportunity. Notice what feelings begin to emerge." Then I would ask, "As you imagine it, does your energy go up, stay about the same, or go down?" That simple exercise almost always resulted in unexpected insights, no matter the answer. Now I asked myself that same question. As I considered *Legacy Magazine*, my energy went up. But, in comparison when I imagined the prairie reserve idea, my energy rose considerably further. But I wasn't really clear why. So, which to choose?

An idea struck me while I was sitting there on that bench: *Legacy Magazine's* purpose was to put a spotlight on innovative, interesting people who had traded a life of achievement and comfort for one of substantial personal risk and trying to make a difference in the world. But in the role of magazine publisher, I would not be one of those people. It was similar to consulting. If one of the social entrepreneurs I featured in the magazine failed, it wouldn't be my fault, and I would just move on to other interesting stories. I was now realizing that I wanted to be one of those people who actually stuck their neck out on a new venture, helped something meaningful take off, and might one day be profiled in *Legacy*, instead of being the guy who published and printed the magazine. I thought back again to that insight I'd had with my therapist years earlier, after Kayla's accident. I was realizing that this was what I'd wanted in my next vocation: to take a risk on something I really cared about that, nonetheless, might fail. On the other hand, if it succeeded, it might add amazing richness to my life and end up having long lasting value to both wildlife and people.

In Carlos Castaneda's *Journey to Ixtlan*, the mystic Don Juan said that the trick in life is to practice being awake because opportunities are constantly floating around just outside your peripheral vision—but every so often they float directly across your field of view. If you're awake, you have a shot at seizing what he called that one "cubic centimeter of chance." It occurred to me at that moment, sitting on that bench in the quiet, crystal clear air, that what I wanted to do next might indeed be floating right in front of me.

—

As the afternoon was turning into early evening, I gathered up Silas and walked home to talk about it once again with Kayla. She had to be an equal partner in this decision. Checking my gut as I neared our house, I felt that if she was not keen on the idea, I'd keep looking.

After I told her how well this Prairie Reserve idea seemed to fit the criteria I'd been turning over for the past few years, she responded with many questions, partly to hear the content of my answers, but also to slow me down to give herself time to think, which is what she always does when evaluating one of my new ideas.

Then she asked, "What does Gib think?" meaning Gib Myers, a longtime friend and a highly successful, thirty-five-year veteran of the venture capital business in California. I told her that I'd talked to Gib repeatedly and that he liked the idea, but he also worried that a million things could go wrong. However, if I decided to do it, he would join as an advisor, which not only gave me great comfort but gave the same to Kayla. She knew that Gib was skeptical and demanding when it came to advice on starting and building new ventures.

Kayla also asked about Dakota Meeks, the twenty-five-year-old part-time assistant I'd hired a few years earlier to help manage my remote Catalyst Consulting office. Kayla liked Dakota a great deal and admired and appreciated her ability to keep me focused and organized. I told Kayla that if I decided to go the prairie route, I would tell Dakota she was free to stay at Catalyst or she could join me at the start-up. Kayla was adamant that my chances for success would rise considerably if Dakota was involved.

As daylight gave way to twilight, Kayla got quiet, sipping her wine and gazing out our back window at the quaking aspen trees.

"It sounds exciting and definitely worthwhile—if it survives," she said. "But I agree with Gib. It'll likely be way harder than you are making it out to be."

She set her wine glass down and turned to me.

"But down the road," she added, "you'll be kicking yourself if you hadn't given it a try."

She was in.

CHAPTER THREE

No Looking Back

My mind was spinning with excitement. After nearly four years of exploring, I'd finally decided what my next career might be—assuming I could build it into something that would last. I gave myself four to five months for the complete transition: from late summer 2001 to January 2002. Over that time, I would work simultaneously for both organizations. My role at Catalyst would be slowly winding down while American Prairie was ramping up.

I'd been with Catalyst for sixteen years. I cared for the organization and my colleagues, so I wanted to allow enough time for everyone to feel good about my departure. I was also elated that Dakota had decided to join me. As Kayla said upon hearing that news, with Dakota on board, our chances of success had increased substantially.

It was now time to let my good friend and Catalyst cofounder Bill Underwood know that it would soon be time for me to leave our company for good. Over the years, Bill had always been supportive of my plan to one day return to Montana, but there wasn't much I could do or say to make either of us feel better about that reality now that this next step was upon us. Most significant transitions come with a sense of loss. This was no exception. We were both sad knowing that although we would stay in touch, our relationship would never be the same after we ended a sixteen-year partnership.

Curt and I had worked out an arrangement between our new entity, American Prairie, and WWF-US. The then small, two-person team at the new WWF Northern Great Plains (NGP) ecoregion would focus on helping save grassland habitats in five US states—Nebraska, North and South Dakota, Wyoming, and Montana, and two Canadian provinces, Alberta and Saskatchewan. Additionally, WWF NGP would take the lead in planning the early flora and fauna restoration aspect of the Montana-based American Prairie project. Importantly, they would also provide us with some initial start-up funding, mostly for Dakota's salary and overhead costs of our small two-person office. And, most important to me, they offered to help with fundraising when possible. Our yet-to-be-formed American Prairie organization would buy and manage land while creating and maintaining key relationships with local Indigenous leaders, all relevant government agencies, and other interested parties in the local area, including ranchers.

We had our work cut out for us. WWF's direct financial support was limited and finite; our nonprofit, with its own independent board and staff, would soon need to be self-sufficient financially and in all other ways. We required millions of dollars not only to buy enormous amounts of land but also to maintain it. The initial, very rough project cost estimates assembled by WWF before I arrived on the scene suggested we would need $450-plus million for land purchases, twenty to twenty-five years of operational costs, and an endowment to cover all annual costs for reserve management. Everyone knew, since no one had ever attempted such a project, that those numbers were a best-guess placeholder and would need to be revised—probably multiple times—after some years of actual experience on the ground. (Today, twenty-four years later, that revised figure is closer to one billion dollars.) No matter what, we had to start raising money—fast.

During the last eight weeks of my transition from Catalyst—December 2001 and January 2002—Curt and Steve would manage the formal registration process with the state of Montana for the new nonprofit entity. Until I completed my departure from Catalyst, Curt would keep the executive director's chair warm, working with Dakota on basic administrative tasks such as setting up bank accounts, changing the lease on my Catalyst office to the new entity, and dealing with myriad other details. Importantly, Curt communicated with the many conservation groups and individuals such as National Wildlife Federation, Predator Conservation Alliance, and others that he'd met with over the past year. Most had expected our nonprofit would end up being directed by a committee of sorts, comprising representatives from each organization. While some were fine with our new approach—an independent organization led by me—others were less so.

My weeks during this period were split between Catalyst and the new organization. Dakota's and my first order of business was to develop our goals for the first two years, including establishing a skeleton crew to staff the Bozeman office. Kayla agreed to work part time with us to set up critical business processes such as finding bookkeeping software, securing liability insurance and health insurance for Dakota and me, and recruiting future employees. One aspect of my job was to figure out how to complete our first land acquisition, something I wanted to happen by the end of year two, even though I didn't yet have any idea how we would finance it.

The latter part of 2001 was an incredibly busy time. Each day, Dakota and I would meet in front of an eight-foot-wide whiteboard and attempt to tackle her elaborate and ever-evolving to-do list. There were two sections on her board: The first was to prepare the new organization for its official launch in February 2002; the second was to steadily wind me out of Catalyst after my sixteen years there.

Curt, who had been working as a WWF contractor out of his home's third-floor attic for a year or so, decided that it was finally time for a real office. Dakota suggested that, at least for a while, he share mine downtown, on Main Street, so both orga-nizations could save money. Dakota's and my total monthly office rent was $280, part of which, with Curt moving in with me, would be paid for by WWF NGP. Every little bit helped.

But my 1960s-era orange-shag-carpeted space, at a mere two hundred square feet, quickly felt crowded. Curt and I lasted less than two weeks in the same room. Prone to introversion, Curt required abundant quiet time. My frequent calls to Cata-lyst colleagues, clients, and potential donors got on his nerves—to say nothing of my incessant questions directed toward him about rewilding. Meanwhile, his periodic questions about how I was doing with my early plans for fundraising grated on me. Mercifully, Dakota discovered that additional space was becoming available on our floor. Curt grabbed the lease and moved into his own small two-room office a few hundred feet down the hall. Our relationship immediately improved.

During these early months, Steve Forrest, Curt, and I often met for beers after work to talk about the future. One late after-noon, just across the street at the Rocking R Bar, we were once again kicking around names for the new enterprise since we needed to list something on the official forms for starting a Montana nonprofit. One contribution from Steve was "The Prairie Foundation." He felt its elegantly simple name implied we would be accumulating a pot of money for a singular pur-pose: to build one big prairie reserve. We discussed the pros and cons lightly, and briefly, then looked at each other, smiled, raised our beers, and said, "To The Prairie Foundation. Done!" This company name only lasted a few years, but it was one more thing to check off the early to-do lists.

Now it was time to fret about finding the needed funds to keep our enterprise humming while also figuring out how to build a land-acquisition fund. One morning, Curt and I were sitting in his office brainstorming on that topic when he sug-gested we approach the Hewlett Foundation, the Gordon and

Betty Moore Foundation, and the David and Lucile Packard Foundation. Coincidentally, three of the leaders at the Packard Foundation—Chief Operating Officer Carol Larson, CEO Dick Schlosberg, and Chairman of the Board Susan Packard Orr—had each, over three separate years, attended an American Leadership Forum Silicon Valley (ALF) multi-session class that I'd taught while at Catalyst. During that time, we'd gotten to know each other well and had stayed in touch. Additionally, a former colleague of Curt's directed us to Jeanne Sedgwick, head of the Foundation's conservation programs. Given our combined contacts to use as references, with just one call to Jeanne we were able to secure a meeting the following week. We booked flights to California and scrambled to develop some kind of presentation about our plans.

Sitting in Jeanne's office at the Foundation's headquarters in Los Altos, California, we explained that we only had five months' worth of cash, and we were just getting started with fundraising. I took out a folded paper road map of Montana—the kind you used to get at a gas station—on which Curt had circled the roughly five-thousand-square-mile project area in orange highlighter. (That was the total extent of our marketing materials for our visit to a foundation with a sixteen-billion-dollar endowment. Twenty-four years later, I still have that map.)

Jeanne studied the map as Curt explained that we were talking about eventually assembling a contiguous landscape similar in size to the Serengeti, roughly five thousand square miles with an astounding variety and abundance of wildlife. And, he added, it would eventually provide many economic benefits to local Indigenous communities and others living in the surrounding area. Aware of Curt's long history as a well-regarded scientist advising conservationists around the world on wildlife projects, Jeanne wanted to know if there were similar projects like this anywhere in the world. "And how will you fund such a large effort?" she added.

"It's totally unique," Curt said and mentioned that it could end up becoming a new model for large-scale habitat conservation around the world. For now, we'd be relying on conventional philanthropy from individuals and a few foundations.

She asked me about my background. I explained the nature of Catalyst and that we specialized in helping new business entities—either independent start-ups or new teams being launched inside much larger organizations—to get up, run, and achieve success faster than would normally be expected. I mentioned that more than 50 percent of our long-term clients who knew me well were located within a thirty-mile radius of where we were sitting in Los Altos.

After another half hour of conversation about our big ideas, Jeanne leaned back in her chair and gazed at each of us, back and forth, again and again. The moment stretched to the point of awkwardness.

"Well, what do you think?" Curt asked.

Still quiet, Jeanne leaned forward, grabbed her blouse with both hands and pulled it in and out a few times as if to cool herself off. "I'm sweating!" she cried.

"Is that a good thing?" Curt asked.

"I am so excited this is happening!" she said, adding that this was one of the most innovative projects she had ever seen, particularly our approach to start a new independent entity, the unusual combination of backgrounds and skills between Curt and me, and our partnership with an established organization like WWF NGP on the science. Jeanne then explained that she was open to the idea of providing the project with some first-year general operation funds and suggested that we send her a three-page proposal asking for $80,000. She made no promises, but she would take the request to the board meeting in a few months' time.

Sure enough, two months later, we received a letter from Jeanne awarding us an $80,000 general support grant. The foundation gave money to WWF in DC nearly every year for various projects. To make it logistically easy, the money would be run through WWF NGP, but it would be directed toward start-up funding for American Prairie in our first year. This gave American Prairie an additional six to nine months of financial breathing room to get our own fundraising up to speed. More importantly, it indicated to me that—as had happened with Catalyst—if we could just get in front of the right people with the right story, we could probably raise all the money we needed.

However, the first of my many mistakes as leader of American Prairie was assuming that my sales experience pitching Catalyst's services would easily transfer to fundraising. That first autumn I made call after call to people I knew in California to tell our story and ask for modest support. I received mostly cool responses, partly because the 2002 tech crash was in full swing. But Bob Irvin, one of American Prairie's first three board members and a veteran of working in nonprofits, explained that sales involved an obvious quid pro quo of a business exchange linking products or services with some defined need, but with fundraising, you also need to offer something in return—but it was far less tangible. To do so, I would need to learn my donors' values and interests over multiple calls and in-person visits as part of the cultivation. With luck, some of them might decide that this project was somehow going to improve their lives. At that point, I might be positioned to make a modest, first-time ask for support. If I performed well with their initial contributions, Bob said, I could ask for more later.

These revelations were new to me, and I did not like them one bit. Clearly, I needed to learn a different way of interacting with people when attempting to win their enthusiasm for our effort. I wasn't sure I could do it: It didn't fit my personality or my many years of experience selling and securing countless projects for Catalyst. And I feared we didn't have time for these protracted cultivation phases.

I also realized that just because I was acquainted with some relatively high-earning, high-net-worth people from my Catalyst days, it didn't mean I actually knew a lot of philanthropists. (And I was surprised to realize there was a difference.) Essentially all in-person meetings now meant getting on a plane to leave Montana, not just driving over Route 17 from Santa Cruz into the Bay Area. This fundraising thing was turning out to require much, much more time than I'd first anticipated. And, I had a lot of learning to do. In darker moments I found myself thinking that we simply didn't have the time; we needed money now or the project would fail. Ever so slightly, I privately began to panic.

We were facing other issues beyond fundraising. For one, the animosity expressed toward our plans by a small contingent of local townspeople and cattle ranchers was loud—and even louder in local newspaper editorials. They claimed our plans would negatively affect the local economy compared to cattle ranching by reducing revenue and therefore tax income for the already struggling area. Our response, that we paid the same property taxes as a cattle ranch and that our employees paid the same state and federal income taxes as anyone else, did not mollify them.

They also believed that bringing back large numbers of wildlife like elk, pronghorn, bison, wolves, and grizzly bears was inappropriate, since the area had long since transitioned into agriculture, and that many of those wildlife species no longer belonged in this region at all. Critiques even surfaced from prominent nature conservation groups that disagreed with our model, such as our intent to buy land outright versus protecting some of its conservation values through conservation easements while continuing to optimize the land for livestock production.

Meanwhile, certain Montana politicians seeking rural votes saw us as a convenient campaign foil, framing us as outsiders bent on destroying both the agricultural industry and the ranching way of life.

Keeping the Faith and Perspective

Despite all this fundraising stress and outside criticism, which I'd been warned about repeatedly before we started, I was still happy I'd taken this job. It was aligned with my purpose for this phase of my life, and it felt deeply meaningful. And, truthfully, there were many locals who felt our idea had merit and should be given a chance, and I was convinced their numbers would grow over time.

In order to stay energized and optimistic amid these difficulties, I endlessly revisited, refined, and refocused on our long-term vision. To help with that, both Curt and I found it restorative to frequently venture out into the vast area where the Reserve would one day be located, even though we had no land of our own yet. We would take a rented 4x4 vehicle and spend a few days touring the landscape and talking about what the terrain would look like with less livestock grazing and all the wildlife back.

Many times on each trip, we would stop at a random high point where we could see far beyond fifty miles. We would leave the truck and walk away with our binoculars—sometimes with each other and sometimes heading in opposite directions—and just wander the prairie for a bit. Our purpose was always to get a feel for the landscape by just being quiet, listening, smelling, and seeing. The slower you go and the closer you look, the more likely you are to discover new things: Some fascinating, like the tiny insects roaming the ground between complex plant systems, and some downright beautiful, like delicate sky-blue asters or prairie violets, or far off rocky escarpments poking into a cerulean sky filled with pillowy cumulus clouds. The sublime aesthetics of the sprawling, quiet prairie complemented the excitement about our project.

Stopping to notice subtle things, to breathe the clear, unpolluted air, and look closely at the gorgeous land and landscapes, always helped me regain perspective.

At those times when I might feel a little worn down working on this long project, I would think about a quote from Franz Kafka: "Anyone who keeps the ability to see beauty never grows old." Our dream was that this idea of beauty would permeate every aspect of the eventual reserve, from the wide-open, fence-free landscape to the clear, unpolluted air, the incredibly complex plant community, and the variety of wildlife—from tiny creatures hardly big enough to see, to flying ones, to those that pounded across the ground making the earth shake as they ran.

Curt, a marvelous teacher, described the complex interactions between grassland species in ways I'd never experienced. I could ask him anything about the region's reptiles, birds, spiders, nematodes, ungulates, and predators, and his answers were always rich and interesting. When he would tire of talking, he would suggest books and articles that would help move me along my steep learning curve. This track of constant learning, combined with a focus on such a compelling long-term vision, fed my enthusiasm in ways I'd never experienced in any previous job.

By the end of my third year at American Prairie, I'd accumulated hundreds of hours talking with Curt, Steve, and many others about the nature of fully functioning and intact grassland ecosystems. I also read a book or two every month about animals like pronghorns, about naturalists such as Rachel Carson and Aldo Leopold, or about modern humans' destructive impacts on wildlife, particularly on the grasslands. My previous, narrow understanding of individual terrestrial species as disconnected parts was changing. I was constantly having to let go of a lot of what I thought I knew, having grown up spending so much time outdoors, about nature and wildlife. Other aspects of myself were changing too.

Many writers who have chronicled the life of Aldo Leopold, the author of *A Sand County Almanac*, note how his views evolved significantly over time. In 1920, while working with the US Forest Service, he promoted the idea of wolves and cougars as unwanted varmints needing to be eradicated from sportsman's favorite deer hunting grounds in New Mexico. But just ten years later, after much self-education and contemplation of the emerging study of whole systems ecology, he was touting the importance of restoring and protecting functioning ecosystems, including all the top predators. Later in life he became an outspoken champion for robust populations of wolves having an important role to play in ecosystems.

Perhaps due to my evolving understanding of wildlife ecology, learning more about what we have done recently as Western Europeans to all but destroy it for profit and sport, and my growing passion for protecting wild species on the prairie, my desire to hunt animals, as game—something I'd been raised to enjoy—was unexpectedly diminishing. It felt akin to the mid-1990s when my interest in continuing in the consulting business was declining—this interest too was fading. This time I didn't need a therapist to understand why.

More than a decade later, I still enjoy hunting in the wild and am fortunate to be able to do it frequently, but now I use only a camera and my five senses. I bring home photos of wild species—including plants—or often just landscapes, and a memory of what the air, temperature, aroma, and light was like while I was there. Later, with images that particularly move me—either ones I've taken myself or those from friends or colleagues—I try to recreate my experiences in watercolor or oil paints. I indeed had a lot of fun hunting with guns in past times. A big part of it was being out of doors for days on end with my parents or good friends and, at times, walking behind enthusiastic dogs who were keen to help us find upland birds.

The way I hunt now is different, and these days, for me, is more pleasurable. Generally, the wildlife is just as challenging to find and get close to as when I carried a firearm. I still get to spend a lot of time outdoors in the wild—alone or with friends—and still love looking for a wide variety of species. Now when I head home, I like leaving the wildlife behind—alive—for others to discover and enjoy. It simply fits better with my personal purpose during this phase of my life. It is different than it was, but this style of hunting is something I imagine myself enjoying until my last few days on earth.

CHAPTER FOUR

Adapting, Nonstop

These many trips across the prairie with Curt were welcome respites from the realities of running a fledgling nonprofit. Each month it seemed we faced a new challenge. In early 2002, Dakota was trying to secure business credit cards and found that every bank in town stipulated that we needed personal collateral, since American Prairie had no meaningful assets. I'd been in this situation sixteen years earlier when we'd started Catalyst when Kayla and I had no credit history. Bill Underwood, a little older than us, did, however. So, we used his personal credit to back our company credit for the first year or so. Here I was again, starting another company, but with much higher personal stakes.

In 2002, the country was about a year into the dot-com recession; by October, the value of tech stocks had declined nearly 80 percent from their peak in 2000. The rest of the stock market followed suit. Consequently, many people I'd already asked for donations asked me to check back later. I doubted they would be interested in using their personal credit to back our fledgling start-up. We also considered WWF as a possible guarantor, but as much as they were in support of our project, they were not in the habit of backstopping new, unproven organizations in this way.

By this time, we had three board members, but it didn't

feel right to ask them to risk their personal credit to help us. Out of ideas, Kayla and I reluctantly began using our personal credit card to help fund American Prairie's monthly operations, which included utility bills, airline tickets, hotels, rental vehicles, and so forth. American Prairie paid us back monthly, provided sufficient donations had come in.

Dakota eventually convinced a local bank to provide us with business credit cards, but they still required Kayla and me to provide personal collateral in case American Prairie could not handle its business card payments. We didn't know then that Kayla's and my personal financial backing would be required in this way for eight more years. This episode, along with countless others, sometimes made me envious of Steve and Curt living in another world down the other end of the hall. Their operational expenses were largely covered by WWF-US, a forty-year-old organization whose thirty-person fundraising staff raised over $80 million per year.

My staff of four and me, now that WWF had mostly ended its direct, early operations support, were running an independent nonprofit start-up that in the early years generally held just three to four months of operating cash. If we couldn't raise more money *right now*, we were toast. I sometimes reminisced about my positions with institutions like Boeing, Boston University, or Catalyst, with their steady salaries, health care, and other forms of stability. Still, on most days, I was glad that we were running an entrepreneurial business in control of its own destiny.

Navigating Unfamiliar Territory

One afternoon toward the end of our second year, Curt and I were sitting, sullen and deflated, in a rental car on an upscale residential street in San Francisco, having just emerged from a meeting in a stately row house. We'd traveled from Montana just for this one donation pitch with a well-respected supporter of WWF. While we had tea and English-style cookies in her marvelously appointed home, she listened and responded enthusiastically to our story. A fundraiser from WWF also attended the meeting. Young, smart, and scrupulously prepared, she had warned us ahead of time that WWF was soon going to ask the woman for $150,000 to support a project in the Congo. Therefore, this interaction was to be one of those cultivation meetings where Curt and I could introduce our project, but we could not solicit a gift until the Congo ask had been made and, probably weeks or months later, the subsequent gift was in the bag.

Sitting with Curt in the car post-meeting, I felt that if we had been allowed to ask for a $10,000 to $15,000 gift, this donor would have agreed without cannibalizing the Congo ask. Curt concurred, but, as we'd experienced in previous meetings, we were at the mercy of WWF's fundraising team.

Although my confidence in WWF as a predictable contributor to American Prairie's fundraising efforts was waning, the WWF fundraisers were not at fault. Their job was to balance all the competing conservation priorities within the WWF family, where each ecoregion's needs felt important. Yet it was becoming clear that American Prairie's timeline was not going to be a good match with WWF's. As I grimly tried to adjust my outlook, I knew we would have to speed up the design and implementation of our own customized, long-term approach, create an organization capable of our own fundraising, and somehow build out our own reliable donor network. It was not lost on me that I had never done any of those things before.

Luckily, unanticipated help sometimes comes out of the woodwork, and often just in time. About a year after we'd received the $80,000 from the David and Lucile Packard Foundation, I received a call from Dick Schlosberg, the CEO then. He and the Board Chair, Susan Packard Orr, wanted my help navigating a difficult restructuring within the foundation. In the wake of the recent tech crash, the Foundation's sixteen-billion-dollar endowment—invested entirely in Hewlett Packard Corporation stock—had sunk to six billion. Like so many struggling organizations and industries at the time, they had no choice but to dramatically consolidate their programs and lay off hundreds of employees. Knowing that I'd assisted with many challenging organization transitions while at Catalyst, Dick said he would pay my full consulting rate, plus travel expenses, if I would meet with the foundation's board of directors in Los Altos for an engagement that was expected to last a year. I would see them two days every month to help lead the transition. I agreed, but only if Dick would convert my fees to a direct contribution to American Prairie.

He agreed. I hung up the phone, did some quick arithmetic, and figured the income would cover nearly a third of American Prairie's monthly operating expenses for the next year, assuming our cash burn rate stayed relatively flat. Importantly, it would buy us much-needed time to try to get our fundraising productivity moving in the right direction.

About two months later, at Curt's suggestion, I booked a relationship-building trip to WWF in DC to become acquainted with a variety of senior executives. One meeting was with Diane Wood, VP of Research and Development, who was curious about my work with innovation labs during my time consulting with Apple, Amdahl, and other tech companies. Such experimental labs, sometimes called "skunk works," had gained popularity in the 1980s.

In a skunk works, small groups within a larger organization work together on completely new innovations outside of the normal protocols of corporate strategic planning, budget approval, or critiques by nonparticipating colleagues. Each group is given a budget and expected to get a working prototype of their idea out the door in an unusually short timeline without studies, focus groups, coordination with marketing, or any need to make the concept fit into the company's current suite of products or services.

Diane asked me if I could help her create and test a small skunk works-like environment inside her organization at WWF DC. I consented and, like Dick Schlosberg, she agreed to pay me a daily consulting fee plus travel expenses. It was a shorter contract but it, too, would help cover some of American Prairie's monthly expenses and buy me more time to get better at fundraising.

These two moonlighting gigs, a temporary balm for my money anxiety, were a useful tool to help us through incredibly lean financial times. Now that both engagements were underway, I was happy to chug along doing something I was already good at while endeavoring to get better at something I wasn't.

A Shared Journey:
Taking the Long View on Neighbor Relations

While growing up in Great Falls, Montana, most of my Indigenous friends from grade school and junior high came from the Blackfeet Nation. They had come to Great Falls either because their families had moved there from the Blackfeet Indian Reservation, or they had been sent to live with relatives in Great Falls for a time. One of eight Tribal communities in Montana, the present-day Blackfeet Nation is located approximately 150 miles northwest of Great Falls and adjacent to Glacier National Park. This relatively close proximity to Great Falls, (at least in terms of Montana's great expanse,) facilitated a greater interaction between Indigenous and non-Indigenous peoples compared to some other regions of the state.

When I was young, in the mid-1960s, I sometimes tagged along with my mom who, as a case worker for the county welfare department, routinely visited families in their homes and connected them with resources to help them cope with the challenges and stressors typical of poorer communities. For the first time, I saw firsthand the effects of systemic racism and generational poverty. Montana holds a long and tumultuous history of severe marginalization and isolation of the Indigenous peoples who for thousands of years inhabited vast territories across the Great Plains. While my mom did not use today's terms, she tried to help me understand that—to her constant frustration—the concept of diversity, equity, and inclusion in regard to Indigenous people in Montana society was, at that time, not at the top of our state's list of priorities.

From the very beginning of American Prairie in 2001, I wanted to ensure that we approached our rewilding project in a way that surrounding local communities would appreciate. I also saw that, in particular, the local Indigenous cultural and community values of living at one with all wildlife, and actually viewing wild species as one's relatives, strongly overlapped with American Prairie's mission of recreating a vast and seamless intact ecosystem.

While trying to figure out how American Prairie might get off on the right foot, I recalled countless stories about well-meaning government and nonprofit-led programs designed to make a difference in Indigenous communities. A high percentage had fizzled within a few years. These outcomes were often due to cultural mismatches in approaches and values, insufficient long-term funding, erratic execution, or the diminished resilience of those trying to help, given the often-remote locations of the work and other factors.

I wanted American Prairie to be an anomaly in these statistics. I wanted us to demonstrate unusual success in becoming valued, long-term neighbors and friends with the local Indigenous communities, and particularly our geographically closest neighbors, the Aaniiih and Nakoda Nations within the Fort Belknap and Fort Peck Indian Communities.

I was unsure of how to approach this effectively and not at all confident that I could figure out the best ways forward on my own. I looked for advice and ideas from books and articles, and I asked seasoned professionals to introduce me to key leaders in the Indigenous communities. I was fortunate to eventually meet, among others, George Horse Capture Jr. who graciously joined American Prairie's National Council in 2006 and, along with many other Tribal members, has been a stalwart advisor, friend, and advocate ever since.

Gathering sage advice is critical in the early years of any venture, but putting those teachings into practice is sometimes not easy. Dakota Meeks turned out to be our organization's most helpful guide to Indigenous outreach during our first ten or so years. Although not of Indigenous heritage herself, Dakota grew up on and around several of Montana's Tribal Nations, including the Aaniiih and Nakoda communities. And since both of Dakota's parents had remarried into Indigenous societies, she acquired a unique understanding of their priorities and values.

Dakota asked me thoughtful questions about what I felt success with the Tribes might look like. Three things, I responded. First, I wanted the Indigenous communities to view the American Prairie as a respectful and valued neighbor. Second, I hoped that our rewilding efforts would in many ways complement the Indigenous cultural values of being an integral part, rather than the overseer, of the natural world. Third, I wanted Indigenous peoples to have full access to our private lands. I also wanted them to feel welcome as citizens (versus visitors) and as owners of American Prairie's leased public lands (primarily those under the federal Bureau of Land Management [BLM] whose grazing privileges are leased to private landowners such as cattle ranchers and American Prairie) and of the more than five million additional acres of public BLM lands in the region.

This last point was particularly important. Since my arrival in Montana in the early 1960s, I've seen an increasing number of fences and KEEP OUT signs erected on private property, many of them intentionally located such that they block public access to public lands. I hoped that one day Indigenous people would appreciate American Prairie's efforts to help undo centuries of forced isolation, degradation, and prejudice (as best we could in the local area). I figured that as an eventual large private landowner, with hundreds of thousands of leased public acres, helping Indigenous people to feel welcome as owners of that public land, as any member of the public should, was certainly within our sphere of influence.

Dakota encouraged me to visit Indigenous leaders in person as often as possible—rather than rely on phone calls and email to try to keep in touch—and urged me to be completely transparent, since these communities have a long and complicated history of deceit and abandonment by "outsiders." Her ongoing advice to me in this regard was invaluable in the years ahead. I met and now have had a long-time association with Terry Brockie, a revered leader in the Aaniiih Tribe. The frequency of our interactions with George Horse Capture Jr., Terry Brockie, and many others of the Aaniiih and Nakoda communities increased steadily along with a sense of familiarity and mutual trust.

—

By the middle of our second year, we were realizing modest but somewhat steadily growing financial support. We'd begun sending out bimonthly, bulk mail newsletters, and donation requests containing photos of the prairie's landscape and wildlife. The resulting contributions were mostly $25, some $100, and a few were as much as $500. More important than the dollar totals were the increases in the volume of responses, and that a growing percentage came from outside Montana, which indicated increasing national support. Sometimes we would receive a handwritten note along with the donation. The comments had a repeating theme: "Thank you for what you are doing," or "I have been dreaming about one day seeing a project like this. I am so excited!" And surprisingly often, "I hope I get to come see the prairie project in my lifetime, but even if I never do, I am very glad it is happening." I became increasingly confident that we would continue to attract more and more supporters. At the same time, I realized it was time to hire more people to primarily focus on fundraising.

I'd first met Gib Myers in the early 1990s as a participant in the same American Leadership Forum classes where I'd met the Packard Foundation executives. We stayed friends over the years, and I asked him to be an advisor to our project. Gib, an accomplished and respected Bay Area venture capitalist, had funded hundreds of start-up companies since the late 1960s, and I was hungry for his advice.

When I told him I was trying hard to build out our nascent fundraising operation, he mentioned that his twenty-two-year-old daughter, Sarah, was looking to work at a nonprofit while she applied to graduate school. I interviewed Sarah by phone and found her smart, engaging, and full of ideas on how she could help grow our support base. She moved to Bozeman a few months later, began reporting to Dakota, and immediately started to improve our donor outreach. It is a rare event that something ends up being far easier than you expected. This was one of those moments and I was grateful for it.

Susan and Gib Myers came to Montana to visit Sarah later that year, which gave me multiple opportunities to talk with them about the American Prairie. Even though Gib was already an advisor to me, they became increasingly enamored with our vision and our unusual, privately funded approach to achieving it. More than that, they were both captivated by the rewilding vision and, in particular, the idea of bringing back bison.

Eventually, they both agreed to join our board of directors. Not long afterward, they provided us with a $10,000 general support donation, which was huge for us at the time. Susan's nonstop enthusiasm and her never-ending support was soul-nourishing for me. Given his background in launching so many business start-ups, Gib's presence on the board in its early beginnings gave our project much-needed credibility. I had no idea then that the two of them would evolve into some of our most tireless, helpful, and valued advocates, and they would stay closely and enthusiastically involved with the effort for the next twenty years.

CHAPTER FIVE

Welcome to American Prairie

One morning Curt and I were driving east on Dry Fork Road, a fifty-mile stretch of gravel that led to a property for sale on Telegraph Creek. For nearly a year we'd been dreaming about acquiring it, if only we could secure the funds. We had no appointment with the owners. We just wanted to drive the perimeter of the 20,000 acres and become better acquainted with the topography and its potential for wildlife habitat.

As we rolled along, the gravel noisily pelting the bottom of our pickup and the bright sun shimmering on sage and yellow grasses, we noticed a pronghorn buck running straight toward us from a quarter mile away on our right side. We stopped our conversation and marveled at how fast he was closing on us. These exotically beautiful creatures have the unparalleled ability to achieve top speeds of fifty to sixty miles per hour. The buck, now less than 150 feet away, swung parallel and sped effortlessly across the prairie alongside us while glancing toward our direction every few seconds. Curt held the truck steady at about thirty-five miles per hour. A moment later Curt gently increased our speed to forty-five. The buck, unfazed, kept pace and continued watching us. He didn't appear even slightly winded. As we watched him, looking more as though he were flying like a bird rather than running across the ground, the buck suddenly lowered his head nearly level with his back and pulled ahead of us, as if bored with our pace. In just a few seconds he was a hundred yards out in front and still accelerating.

Finally, the buck veered left like a fighter plane, cut diagonally across the road in front of us, and resumed his position and speed, now on our left side. After another minute the buck pulled up, stopped, and turned broadside to watch as we passed. His face was calm, his mouth closed. His expression seemed to say, "I am so obviously faster, smarter, and better looking than you two. Come find me if you ever want to race again."

How Values Inform Actions and Outcomes

For quite a while, I'd been telling Curt that I wanted to find a way to bring potential donors to the prairie. I wanted them to experience moments like we'd just had. I wanted them to feel the openness and savor the extraordinary quiet and darkness and the starry night skies. I was convinced the trips could help accelerate our progress. Curt liked the idea, so we began to work through the details of a pilot program. We didn't own any land where we could hold such an event, but we were driving through an area of more than three million acres under the jurisdiction of the federal Bureau of Land Management (BLM)—all readily accessible public land where camping was free.

Hosting a group trip would be a financial risk as we didn't really know if we would do it more than once. We would require ten or more large canvas wall tents, cots, sleeping bags, pillows, a large weather-proof pull-behind equipment trailer, safety equipment, and food and water storage infrastructure. We hopped out of the truck and spread out a large map showing the region's BLM acres on the hood of the pickup. We located a spot just five miles east of us that seemed promising for our purposes. We drove to the place and our hunch was confirmed: The slightly elevated location offered spectacular views in all directions, including nearly fifty miles to the south. At night, with no ambient light, it would offer nothing but the moon, the stars, and the Milky Way, and for background noise, the howls of coyotes as they sang out their positions to others of their kind.

I'd led enough outdoor trips to know that people experience their days and nights differently when they are immersed in beautiful scenery, enormous skies, and the aromas of nature—here that meant pungent sage, the tang of broad-leafed forbs, and earthy smell of the bentonite soils. And the silence: no traffic, leaf blowers, or aircraft overhead, and no cell service at the time, meant no ringing phones or dinging texts. I was confident that if we could bring prospective donors to these excursions, the grandeur and appeal of the project would captivate them.

We decided to refer to the outings as *safaris* to create a sense of romance and adventure, as well as to suggest something more comfortable than a mere camping trip: tents with unexpectedly comfortable bedding, good food, drinks, and most important, interpretive guides who could make each moment a learning experience about the deep geological and human history, the native plant and animal species, and the future potential of the land.

After four months of detailed planning and struggling to find a full contingent of interested people to attend, we picked up our first group of eight guests at the airport in Great Falls. From there we drove to the Grand Union Hotel in the small enclave of Fort Benton, Montana. During cocktails we presented a brief slideshow to orient everyone to our project's vision, our route, the place we intended to camp, and the special guests who would provide interpretation throughout the three days.

As soon as the presentation was over, a nervous-looking Dakota pulled me aside. Apparently, our advance team 150 miles east was being hit with unexpected driving rain and high winds. Steve Forrest and Cortland Barnes, a contracted WWF financial modeling specialist, had been planning to set up the camp before we arrived with the guests; now, they were calling from a payphone in Lewistown wanting to know our plan B, given the next day's possibility of many miles of impassable muddy roads. After a few hours of studying topographic maps and many back-and-forth calls long after the guests had gone to bed, we decided to set up camp the next day on a gently sloping hillside of National Forest land in the foothills of the Little Rocky Mountains. None of us had been there before, but we would have our back to the mountains, putting us in somewhat a wind and rain shadow, hopefully saving us from at least some of the forceful, howling western winds that often accompany big prairie storm systems. I tried not to show it, but I was becoming increasingly fearful that after so many months of planning, we might be giving our donor prospects more of an endurance experience than an inspiring one.

Early the next morning, reports of all-night drenching rains and gusting winds confirmed plan B was our best option. Our driving caravan headed east for three hours under still-ominous skies. We took numerous breaks so our guests could look out from the highest viewpoints and become familiar with the topography's scattered buttes, isolated mountain ranges, cliffs, and prairies. At each stop, as the group huddled gamely in the blustery breeze, we told them about the millions of years of geology as well as the prairie's flora, fauna, and human evolution over the past twelve to fourteen thousand years. And like nearly every visitor we have brought to the prairie since, they were surprised, if not astounded, at how far one can see in this country. Most people assume that twenty miles is about as far as one can see before the earth's curvature hides what lies beyond. But that assumes a flat topography as when on an ocean. Visitors expect the prairie to be similarly flat, but it turns out to be anything but in the Northern Great Plains, where small rises in the undulating topography can easily boost the view out to seventy to one hundred miles.

We later wound our way up the foothills of the Little Rockies to the Plan B site, where I was greatly relieved to see that the advance team of Steve and Cortland had already sited the camp, pitching eleven large white canvas wall tents along the timber line. Our guests piled out of the cars and marveled at the views sprawling sixty miles to the east, the wild, swirling clouds above, the wonderful scent of dinner emanating from the cook tent.

That night our guests stayed up late, sitting around the fire as the rain clouds dissipated, allowing a patchy look at the dark heavens and the millions of stars stretching from horizon to horizon. The next morning dawned damp and cool but cirrus clouds against a cobalt sky replaced the previous day's grayness. Our first morning walk with our interpretive guides completely captivated the guests. The mood was upbeat, and the enthusiasm continued throughout the day into the second evening and the third day's breakfast.

The American Prairie and WWF staffs had worked together seamlessly to keep the visitors spirits up and their hunger and thirst satisfied. Curt, Steve, and famed conservation biologist Dan Janzen, who had joined us from Costa Rica with his wife Winnie, continued to provide nonstop interpretive stories about the region and expounded on the exciting potential to rewild it per our long-term vision.

The kudos we received in the following weeks were uplifting. The participating supporters, now more fully understanding why such a project was needed and how it would function, were impressed with our success in assembling such high-quality people on our teams and how well we worked together in the face of adversity. This was exactly what I was hoping for. Our guests would tell their friends that the project was underway, that it was more than just possible, and that the people undertaking the task were credible, determined, and consummate problem solvers. And, based on the number of donation checks we received, modest as most of them were, we decided to hold a safari in the spring and the fall each year. We didn't then realize that this practice of hosting spring and autumn mostly tent-based safaris would endure for twelve more years. It became one of the most effective ways to coax high-level donors to come see the potential for our vision and then continue—and often increase—their financial help.

This early win with the safari idea came at a good time. At this stage, I found our small fundraising staff, including me, sometimes losing confidence about our ability to raise enough money to drive the project effectively. None of us came from wealthy backgrounds, and we were often perplexed about how best to steward a potential donor's interest to the point where they might contribute funds. Mostly due to our lack of experience, we sometimes felt like we had very little control over that process since it involved the donor's own emotions and motivations. It was their money after all, and we couldn't force them to give it to us! The realization (or, at the time, the assumption) that we had such little control over such an important thing was sometimes unsettling and frightening.

I found it particularly challenging to be an inspiring leader on this topic since my confidence about fundraising sometimes wavered as well. So, I chose to lead by reminding people of the power of sticking to our values. I said that our recent success with our first-ever safari was only one data point, but it was an example of our value in innovation (thinking up the idea in the first place and figuring out how to make it work), execution (actually making it happen in a high quality way from start to finish), and teamwork, (not one of us could have pulled it off on our own). I admitted that I didn't know what we might invent in the future as far as fundraising innovation, but I felt certain that consciously exercising other values through continuous improvement, optimism, and all the rest, would—coupled with some luck—help make each safari, on average, more productive than the last. Most importantly, the action of putting our values to work in this way was 100 percent in our control, and it feels energizing to be in control of something! I was under no illusions that it was going to be easy and admitted that thinking about all the funds needing to be raised over the long term was intimidating for me, too, but I believed if we remembered to be guided by our values and stayed persistent and aggressive, we would find our way forward.

A second frequent reminder was to focus on the vision as often as possible. I believe that the more you stop and try to fully understand the comprehensive, highly detailed vision, the more powerful the image becomes as a force to pull the entire organization forward into the future. However, a tricky concept is that you can be inspired by a vision, even while many elements—as far as how you are going to make it happen—remain elusive. Visualizing ourselves having raised all the needed funds for the project and not knowing exactly how we would get it done is an example. Believing that we would create a result over the long term that provided ongoing mutual benefits to the vast majority of the region's stakeholders, and knowing early on some, but not all, of the details on how we would make that happen, is another.

The main detail that Curt and I included in the vision from the beginning was a wildlife spectacle in terms of population numbers and species diversity that exceeds most anything else in the majority of the Lower 48. But beyond that, we wanted visitors to have unforgettable wildlife encounters in place that felt impossibly big, quiet, and aesthetically beautiful. Bringing back large numbers of wild species primarily by providing millions of acres of habitat for them was one measure of success. But a conundrum remained: How could we help ensure that wildlife was spectacularly abundant in myriad places across the 250-mile-wide reserve—meaning it is frequently visible and, importantly, that their behavior, even when humans were present, matched what historians indicate was common for thousands of years before the arrival of European settlers?

Historical records from the earliest European travelers—late 1700s to the early 1800s—tell a story of vast numbers of wildlife but also that elk, wolves, bison, grizzlies, pronghorn, coyotes, and other animals were relatively unconcerned about human presence and did not flee at the first sight of people. Today we can only speculate at the combination of factors that may have contributed to these behaviors. For some species, like wolves, historians suggest they had minimal fear of humans because it was generally not common for Indigenous peoples to hunt or harass them; for countless generations of wolves, humans were not seen as a threat. For other regularly hunted species such as bison, for thousands of years they remained unconcerned until humans were quite near to them because the effective killing distance of the hunter's weapons—thrusting spears, atlatls, and small, non-mechanically assisted bows and arrows—was short, perhaps twenty-five yards or twelve meters at the most. Another factor that can still be observed today in a few places in the world is that the sheer numbers of wildlife far exceeded the numbers of hunters. This creates a situation that is not uncommon in nature where, for instance, you can watch an elk herd of perhaps 150 animals remain watchful but calm as a group of seven wolves walk the periphery of their group, searching for the one elk that they want to try to pull down. And once the hunt is over and that elk is down, it is common for the rest of the elk to go back to grazing versus fleeing at top speed for miles.

But now, when most hunters are using high-powered, ultra-long-range weapons that are capable of killing one or more of them from a distance of an eighth of a mile, the elk have become accustomed to seeing humans as a significant threat. The result is that often the entire herd starts to flee as soon as they detect humans at any distance and keep running until the entire herd is well out of sight. This is a very recent phenomenon.

Given this situation, one rather small contingent, i.e. hunters that make up roughly 6 percent of our total annual visitors to the American Prairie region, is having an outsized effect on the behavior of many of the wildlife species—pronghorn, black bears, elk, deer, bighorn sheep, coyotes etc.—that the vast majority of our visitors have come to see.

So how do we change that so hunters can still hunt in some places in the region while wildlife viewers, by far our largest contingent, enjoy a Serengeti- or Yellowstone Park-like wildlife viewing experience? We've carried this question with us for many years, knowing what we wanted in the end and weighing up possible solutions as we acquired more habitat and worked to restore wild populations. Today we are making some early, partial progress on achieving that end result, but it is a good example of leaders needing to first be very clear on what they want in the future, and why they want it, and maintaining confidence that, through much persistence and innovation, they will one day succeed in making it a reality.

Realizing the Value of Good Board Members

Elizabeth Ruml was a risk management executive who for many years held positions at Bankers Trust, Deutsche Bank, and Solomon Brothers. She was an avid supporter of WWF, and in the fall of 2001, many months before American Prairie was an official entity, she asked to talk with Curt Freese out in Montana to learn more. After just one phone conversation with Curt, she booked a flight to come see the proposed project area for herself. At a breakfast meeting the day after she arrived, Curt introduced Elizabeth to me as the soon-to-be leader of the soon-to-be American Prairie organization.

The next morning Curt, Elizabeth, and I embarked on a four-day tour of the prairie, sitting on our rented pickup's bench seat and talking nonstop as we clicked off the hundreds of miles toward the project area's center. One of Elizabeth's roles as a risk management specialist was to evaluate investment uncertainty at banks; she had deep experience and unusual acumen in finding holes in people's grand plans. Hour after hour, Curt and I tried to provide satisfactory answers to her inquiries. Elizabeth wanted to hear my definition of what financial soundness meant for American Prairie, as well as the estimated long-term management costs of the Reserve. She wanted to understand how much other entities, including WWF, the federal government, and the state government might possibly cost share along the way. She wanted to know what sort of financial horsepower I thought we needed on American Prairie's board of directors, once we were an official nonprofit business.

About four hours into the trip, the big mountains of western Montana were well behind us, and the rolling prairies punctuated by small, isolated mountain ranges loomed on the horizon. Elizabeth began paying closer attention to the unique landscape. Her questions changed from ones about business to ones about the final wildlife vision—specifically, on the assumption that we were successful, what it would be like to drive through this area in, say, twenty-five or thirty-five years. Curt talked about the return of species that once inhabited this area hundreds of years ago: The grassland birds thriving in vast stretches of protected habitat (Elizabeth is an avid birder), reptiles, pollinators, bats, predators, and so forth. I discussed our hoped-for changes in the experience of local Indigenous communities, who had for generations felt the painful and devastating loss of prairie wildlife.

On the second night, from 11 p.m. to 3 a.m., we helped US Fish and Wildlife Service Senior Biologist Randy Matchett search for black-footed ferrets. Then, from 3:30 a.m. to 7 a.m., we helped catch or "net gun" a flock of twenty-plus sage grouse using special lift rockets affixed to the corners of the thirty-by-thirty-foot net. The captured birds were banded and collared for radio tracking and then were released.

As the sun came up on that morning of the third day—very sleep-deprived but still talking about the big vision—Elizabeth, Curt, and I took a circuitous two-track route to another remote section of the project. We stopped on a high spot, left the pickup, and walked over to a barbed wire cattle fence with red metal posts. From there we could see many miles to the south, across sweeping grassland valleys that turned into forested breaks above the Missouri River. Curt once more described a scene in which the prairie was black with bison along with myriad other ungulates, all grazing together, all being trailed by big predators. Elizabeth listened, and, for the first time in three days, asked no questions. We stood silently for a few moments watching far-off raptors riding thermals above a ridgeline to the east.

Elizabeth stood with her arms folded, her eyes still trained on the stunning vista. "I think I'm in."

Two months later she provided American Prairie with a $25,000 general support grant and then gave another $100,000 the following April. She remained a very generous financial supporter over the following twelve years. By June 2002, she had joined American Prairie's board of trustees and agreed to serve as finance committee chairwoman. As important, she became an endlessly valuable mentor to me. Elizabeth's choice to become a part of our effort was a turning point for my confidence. To have someone so accomplished and so discerning about the quality and resilience of organizations approve of us, and what we were attempting, meant everything in the world.

The First Cornerstone of a Big Dream

At long last it was time to start physically creating the Prairie Reserve. Our staff and board team were growing slowly but steadily, and for once we had some money coming in. It was finally time to start looking at land purchases.

The 20,000-acre Weiderrick ranch, located fifty miles of

gravel road south of the small town of Malta, had been for sale for several years. Curt and I had toured it at least four times in 2003, and we'd realized from our very first visit that it was ideally suited to be our first land purchase. It would also provide us with one built in friendly neighbor: the 1.1-million-acre, US Fish and Wildlife Service-run Charles M. Russell National Wildlife Refuge. The ranch contained sagebrush uplands, high ridges and bluffs, and ephemeral creeks. It also carried a two-million-dollar initial asking price. Our general fundraising was improving in fits and starts, but success still meant covering our monthly operations; we'd not yet made much of a dent in building our land acquisition fund.

We knew we had to obtain a loan to buy our first piece of land, but no Bozeman bank would take a risk on us. We were too young, had no collateral, no credit history, and too few donors to assure lenders we could meet loan payment obligations. Curt suggested The Conservation Fund (TCF) in Washington, DC, might be a long shot, but worth considering.

TCF provides a bank-like function to nonprofits that conserve open space for the public's benefit. Their loans were usually short-term—about a year or so—and at a relatively high interest rate. They were the last crucial puzzle piece for fledgling organizations like American Prairie that couldn't yet swing a land deal through donations and traditional financing alone. In part due to our association with WWF, Elizabeth and I were able to secure a meeting with one of TCF's founders and several of their staff.

The Washington, DC-based TCF group was immediately impressed with Elizabeth's knowledge of complex banking. They also seemed quite intrigued with my vision for the reserve and for the organization's long-term success. After ninety minutes, we'd roughed out an agreement on a one-million-dollar loan to be paid back in full exactly one year later. As the meeting was wrapping up, two parallel and distinct feelings roiled through my body: The first was a kind of disbelief that someone was *actually* going to loan us a million bucks to help acquire the property. The second was abject fear and anxiety. How in the world could we pay back the loan in eleven months, twenty-nine days, and twenty-three hours?

The following week I called the Weiderricks' realtor to make an offer on their property. After a month of back-and-forth, the Weiderricks,' all of whom had been amenable, fair, and more than patient throughout our negotiations, agreed to a deal that would work well for both parties. They also agreed, as part of a five-year lease back arrangement, to incrementally reduce their total number of cows each year so the native prairie could transition toward supporting the most abundance and diversity of wildlife. And they also promised not to kill coyotes or prairie dogs or otherwise disturb in general any native plant or wildlife species.

My two-hour drive home from Billings—after our final three-hour negotiation meeting in the basement of a bank—was transformative. It had been nearly three years since American Prairie opened its doors. Something vitally important was at last moving from theories and plans to tangible reality: We had just reached an agreement on the terms for acquiring our first property.

On the afternoon of January 17, I watched the outskirts of Malta, Montana, growing smaller in my rearview mirror as I headed south toward home on US Route 191. I'd just left Phillips County Title Company where, after a five-hour drive up from Bozeman that morning, I finally signed the thirty-page closing documents on the Weiderrick property. As the sky darkened, the local radio station paused its regular programming every ten minutes to announce that all roads in and out of Malta might soon close due to an imminent winter storm packing heavy snow and fifty-miles-per-hour winds.

Forty-five minutes later I crossed the Fred Robinson Bridge that spans the Missouri River where, 195 years earlier, Lewis and Clark pulled their boats upriver during their two-thousand

-mile journey from St. Louis to the Pacific coast. My mind imagined all the things we could do with this new property. We could figure out which sections of barbed wire cattle fence to remove to make easier passage for pronghorn, elk, bighorn sheep, and deer. We could begin stream restoration efforts on Telegraph Creek that flowed south through the property, in anticipation of later restoring beavers there. Our donor visits would change in tone and impact now that we'd be hosting groups on our own land. I even thought about the possibility of soon bringing in a small group of bison, which had all been hunted to extinction in this region over a century earlier. I still didn't know where I would find the money to pay off the TCF loan, but this afternoon, it didn't matter. We now had 20,000 acres of private and leased public lands to work with.

As I continued south of the Missouri, the radio reported that all roads behind me leading in and out of Malta were now closed due to high winds and heavy snow. Elated from the day's events, I enjoyed cruising slowly and carefully south through the darkness, completely alone in this beautiful stretch of northeastern Montana. Home was still four hours away, but I didn't need the radio or any other diversions. Boredom was not an issue. The myriad future implications of what we had just done unfolded in my head as one of the most fascinating and invigorating movies I could ever recall. The initial steps to rewilding a protected area larger than Yellowstone could now begin.

The next ten months were both exciting and nerve-racking. On one hand, actually owning land significantly improved potential donors' confidence that we could get things done, and we brought in $700,000 in new commitments that year. Yet, when our loan was due, we were still $300,000 short. Elizabeth and I explained our situation to TCF's president, who graciously agreed to a six-month extension. Over the next half year, we scrambled, doubled our fundraising efforts and— thanks to some of our board members stepping up with their largest-ever gifts—we cobbled together the needed funds. In late fall 2004 we settled our debt. We now owned our first property, free and clear.

Over the next two years, we purchased three smaller, less expensive properties that connected to the Weiderrick ranch to create one contiguous twenty-eight-thousand-acre block. We named the land unit Sun Prairie after a post office that once sat at the crossing of two local dirt roads. Like so many small rural schools, the post office building had long ago been razed as a casualty of continuing human depopulation, but the name of the crossing was embedded in the local culture. Over the years, due to incrementally reducing cattle numbers and leaving water in the streams rather than tapping them for irrigating hayfields, Sun Prairie's valleys, ridges, undulating prairie, and winding creek bottoms slowly began transforming into richer and more varied wildlife habitats.

As the plant diversity slowly improved, one noticeable change was the increasing variety and numbers of grassland birds: Kestrels, loggerhead shrikes, Lark buntings, pelicans, and ferruginous hawks became more abundant as the years went by. Due to our ban on hunting prairie dogs, their small towns began expanding as well. From the plant biologists we worked with, I learned to pay attention to the subtle changes occurring in the mosses, forbs, grasses, sage, and other flora. With fewer cows grazing in the Telegraph Creek bottoms each year, more and more cottonwood seedlings flourished. These conditions would set the stage for one day reintroducing beavers. These early changes were subtle, but also visible, measurable, and satisfying to observe.

—

During these first four years, countless issues emerged and frustratingly slowed our progress. For instance, many scientists long ago corroborated the fact that certain wildlife species need a minimum population to be genetically viable and to make their ecological impact on an ecosystem. But, maddeningly, Montana Fish Wildlife and Parks (FWP) regularly gave out hunting permits for species that were already far below these population floors. Some cattle ranchers felt that species like elk and deer cost them money by damaging fences and consuming grazing forage on their leased public lands, so they wanted their natural populations permanently reduced. With cougars—which drew little to no complaints from most ranchers—FWP was reluctant to restrict hunting permits on their below-genetically-viable populations because they did not want to limit "hunter opportunity" for people who liked to kill lions for sport. They also endeavored to keep cougar populations artificially low because of other hunters' complaints that the cougar's preferred prey is mule deer. Many hunters also want to kill mule deer for sport and don't like having to compete with cougars. At the time, FWP tended to rely less on hard science data regarding the prairie landscape's capacity to provide space and food for these wild species. Instead, they made many wildlife management decisions based on hunters' desires.

We were successful in growing and improving the quality of the habitat over which we had control, and we succeeded in raising some species numbers like nongame birds and prairie dogs. But our requests to FWP to significantly raise the population ranges of many other prairie species went unheeded.

Another example: The Federal Farm Bill was providing over eight billion dollars per year for the Conservation Reserve Program (CRP). The effect in our project area was that agricultural producers were incentivized to plow up the native prairie, plant a non-native monoculture cover crop such as crested wheatgrass—marginally useful as wildlife cover for a few species but not so much for forage—and receive nontaxable annual payments for leaving the land out of production, meaning not creating any commercial food products. Many large-scale, successful ranchers in our project area, whose personal net worths are in the millions of dollars, were—and still are—receiving as much as fifty thousand dollars in federal assistance every year to leave portions of their land fallow (idle and unused for growing food) in the CRP program. Not only does the plowing up of these tracts of native prairie adversely affect wildlife, but the tens of thousands of idle acres reduce the need for local labor as well as fuel, equipment, and supplies from local businesses. These and other frustrating economic forces were hard to live with, but we always found ways to keep our challenges in perspective, to keep taking the long view, and to continually refocus our energies on what we knew we had the power to change.

CHAPTER SIX

The Art of Momentum

I knew going in back in 2001 that large, ecosystem-scale restoration was a tough road throughout the world where many others were also attempting it. And in our own situation, I was more than challenged to find the right approach to fundraising, keeping our organization's finances stable and predictable, and determining when the right time was to focus on increasing populations of which species, etc. But there was one aspect of the project that we needed to get absolutely right from the get-go and each year afterward. My confidence was high that even in a situation where progress often felt like two steps forward and one step back—or worse on some days—I at least knew how to focus myself and our organization on things that we could control and put the right systems and processes in place that would help move us steadily toward our vision.

As step one in this effort, I told every team member repeated stories about how, while working with Catalyst, I'd seen in a surprising number of client organizations exhibiting a tendency to spend a great deal of time not just acknowledging factors out in the macro world that were distressing or concerning, but an inordinate amount time worrying and talking incessantly about a myriad of things over which they had little or no control. In contrast, the most effective clients we encountered were those that spent some time acknowledging concerns about things over which they had no control. However, they then consciously chose to spend the vast majority of their creativity, energy, and problem-solving skills laser focused on their much smaller area of influence; the area in which they potentially, or definitely, had direct or indirect control. The first thing I worked to establish at American Prairie was the strong expectation—as part of the culture we were creating—that no matter how large we became, we would maintain the discipline of spending most of our collective time focused on that area of influence, instead of our much wider area of concerns.

Regarding getting the right systems and processes in place, I wanted to create an environment where each team member could feel as powerful and influential as possible in contributing to the progress toward our unwavering long-term vision. As I noted earlier, while working at Catalyst in Santa Cruz, we developed a tool we called The Catalyst Vision and Strategy Process.

Forty years later, it continues to be used extensively in many organizations, industries, and cultures around the world to help individuals and organizations stay focused on the items in their circle of influence as they pursue their goals. The process is intended to help groups formulate their own highly compelling story about where they are today, and where they would like to be at a defined point in the future. If done well, it has the effect of keeping an organization not only energized, but also continuously learning and improving while pursuing their distant vision. (Think John F. Kennedy's audacious— some said outright crazy—challenge, laid down in 1962, to put a person on the moon by the end of the decade. The large team of people working on that effort stayed highly focused on trying to do the impossible for seven straight years. The final touch down on the lunar surface came six months ahead of schedule in July, 1969.)

In the context of American Prairie, I believed that no matter what resistance we encountered, within our influence was the opportunity to keep building our land base, to improve habitat for wildlife, to manage our lands for wildlife abundance, to bring more financial supporters into the project, to invite the public to enjoy our private lands and provide unimpeded access to our leased public lands, to invest time in developing good relationships with Indigenous communities and other local neighbors, and to try to positively impact the local economy. No one could tell us we could not work incessantly on those things. No one had the power to diminish our penchant for innovation and quality execution. I knew from past experience that we possessed all the agency we needed to create an organization made up of energetic, innovative, trustworthy, and determined people who were obsessed with delivering on

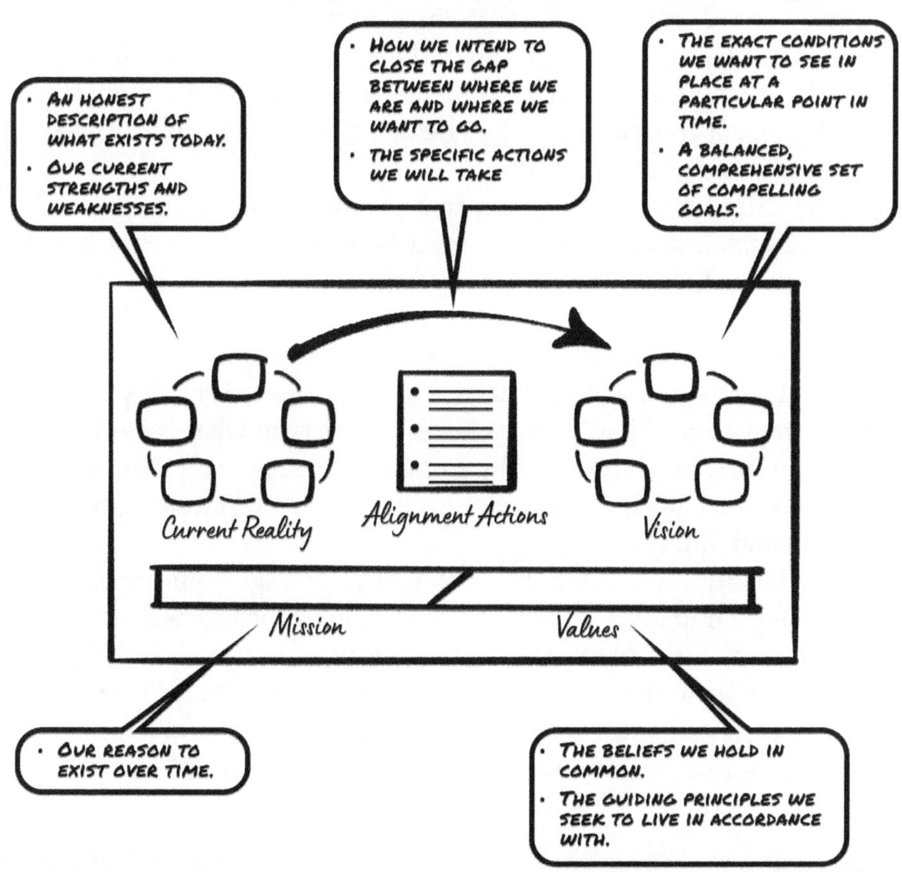

the promise of our mission.

The Catalyst Vision and Strategy Process includes five simple components that are essential for crafting a coherent story that helps sustain positive forward momentum: Purpose, Values, Current Reality, Vision, and Alignment Actions.

It is always helpful to start with your mission or purpose. This clarifies both *what* your organization is here to do and *why* you want to do it. Attracting people to work at your organization or inspiring them to support you—no matter *what* your organization does—will go better if you can clearly explain your overall purpose for existing. As the author and speaker Simon Sinek says, "People don't buy *what* you do; they buy *why* you do it." A clear, inspiring purpose or mission is a key part of your foundation.

Second, it is critical to produce a set of carefully chosen values. Values are an indicator of the boundaries within which you or your group intend to operate. A well-articulated, interdependent collection of values defines the intended culture of your group or organization.

Third, you need a vision that precisely defines—in clear and sufficient detail—all the results you want and when you want them. The vision acts as a magnetic force that helps you create a path of least resistance, like a winding river seeking the most efficient route toward its final destination.

Fourth, you need to make an honest assessment of your current reality that includes honest answers to what is working well, what your strengths are, and where opportunities lie. Conversely, it also makes clear your current weaknesses and vulnerabilities.

Finally, you create a short list of high-leverage/high-impact strategic initiatives, or actions steps, that you believe will help you move forward toward your visionary goals.

For these five things to be described, well-arranged, and agreed to can and should take time. Once finished and widely understood, conversations become more urgent, targeted, and powerful. It can also help create that unfortunately all too rare, highly satisfying feeling of being in close alignment with others.

We originally pegged American Prairie's long-term vision (somewhat naively) at around twenty to twenty-five years. Maintaining momentum over such a long stretch is challenging, so we broke it down into much shorter incremental markers containing specific conditions we wanted to have achieved by specific time periods along the way. For our purposes, breaking our incremental milestones into eighteen to twenty-four month segements worked well. We used those short time frames to push ourselves to achieve challenging goals in all aspects of our vision, including rewilding, our financial situation, the quality and effectiveness of our organization, our partnerships, local area relationships, and our national and international reputation.

The outcome was that everyone was intensely motivated by the audacious, holistic set of goals placed twenty-five years out, but on a month-to-month basis, we were—and remain—primarily motivated and driven by the one and a half to two-year increments whose goals were equally challenging.

We have never wavered in our end goals. We wanted to create a wildlife reserve consisting of a minimum of 3 million-plus acres where—unlike anywhere else in the remaining 180 million acres of the Northern Great Plains—nature and wildlife come first. We wanted it to contain all the flora and fauna that existed there for the past three to four thousand years. We wanted a reserve that would stand the test of time in its legal status and its protections against those who might seek to compromise its quality for commercial gain. And we wanted to deliver a result that would be cherished by local people and communities. Making small but consistent, measurable progress toward these goals became our organization's passion.

There's another key component to maintaining momentum in such a complex, long-term project. The first two, noted above, include focusing on those things you can control and becoming highly aligned as an organization. The third element is designing and engaging in multiple processes to help keep the first two components humming along at a high level. For example, one helpful process involves carving out three-day retreats—at least three times per year—to shut the outside world off and thoroughly reviewing the details and understanding of your organization's purpose, values, vision, current reality, and strategies. During my time at American Prairie, that meant bringing together twenty-five to thirty people, in person, to focus all day, each day, on that topic. The rolling dialogues, where everyone has a chance to be heard, helped tune-up the weak or confusing areas in the five-part Catalyst Vision and Strategy story, to adjust current strategies to make them more effective, or retire ones that were proving to be not worth the effort or resources. It allowed time for people to understand again how the current short-term goals were driving progress toward the far-off ultimate vision. It freshened up relationships across functional groups and between individuals. It allowed time for reflection on accomplishments and to once again make us feel like we were all in it together.

Another process was making sure each individual—from the person who oversees the safety and health of American Prairie bison population to the CEO—has individual quarterly objectives that tie directly to the organization's eighteen- to twenty-four-month goals. Progress toward those objectives was discussed periodically throughout the quarter, and adjustments were made if needed between the individual and their managers.

Yet another process was an annual or twice-per-year written performance review process, where each individual received feedback from colleagues about how they were perceived in terms of their value to the enterprise. The intended purpose for these reviews was to make people feel noticed as individuals, and to help them take advantage of the opportunity to keep growing professionally during their time with the organization. These are just three of many different aspects of this third component: Ensuring that the quality of organization alignment remains high, and people stay focused on things they can control and make measurable progress on.

These aspects of the American Prairie organization remind me of the current discussions on Artificial Intelligence (AI). There are many opinions about whether we should see AI as useful for humanity, be afraid of it, or both. Some fear AI becoming too self-sufficient, too good at learning how to constantly improve itself, without needing the direction of human programmers to help it, and then one day getting out of our control.

This potential downside of an AI algorithm—continuous self-initiated growth in self-sufficiency, effectiveness and capability—oddly, describes the best aspects of a high functioning organization. The leaders at American Prairie today know that if they carefully nurture these elements and metaphorically write into the code of our culture the right values, sideboards, and controls, the enterprise will in fact keep learning and in someways take on a life of its own.

Similar to quantum physics, in American Prairie there are super small elements that so far no one can actually see but you know they are there by the obvious, observable effects they have on clearly visible components. Some examples of the things you can see that are affected by the Vision and Strategy process and our supporting practices are the continued attraction of high-quality people who are hoping to one day secure a job at American Prairie. You can measure the attraction of new financial supporters who are increasing in numbers and in the size of their contributions. You can see the confidence in team members' decisiveness in execution that comes from being drawn toward a vison that—year after year—has maintained is sharpness and power to motivate. You can hear it in the comments from a variety of people who have watched our trajectory for a very long time and who still frequently ask, "How do you all do it? How do you seem to just keep building strength upon strength, and advancing so confidently toward your end vision?"

A partial answer to that is it takes a special kind of leadership team to keep this sort of algorithm working well. It requires their knowledge of what it is, the benefits it can produce, and the knowledge of how to keep tuning and improving the algorithm itself. But I believe the most important thing is the discipline of that leadership team to not get overly distracted with myriad other things and, like so many leaders do, slip into cutting corners or neglecting any aspect of it. If done well, the algorithm—the Vision and Strategy process supported by well-thought-out systems and processes—will do a lot of the work for an organization, so the team members remain aligned, relying less and less on sheer muscle to push forward, and instead using more finesse.

Early on as we began to assemble our organization, I knew that there were many unknowable factors that we would have to discover and to which we would have to adapt. But I was also convinced that it was within my influence—and later, that of our leadership team, after I was gone—to create an organization that would steadily become more resilient, capable, and smarter over time. I felt confident that we absolutely could maintain our momentum and eventually parlay that into an unstoppable movement.

Expanding Capabilities and Capacity

Our first few safaris bolstered our conviction that having people visit the project area was the most effective way to build a strong network of supporters. We soon realized that folks who had the capacity to provide capital gifts—which at the time we defined as over $50,000—were worth the time to build customized safaris. The trick was to coax them to travel to such a remote place and stay for at least two nights and three days, and slowly we were getting better at it.

Jeff Miller's first prairie visit is a good example. I first met Jeff and his wife, Karen, at a mid-January American Prairie event for twenty guests at Susan and Gib Myers' Bay Area home. At the end of my thirty-minute slide presentation and Q&A session, Jeff approached me and said that, because he was so impressed with our vision, he and his wife wanted to learn more about the project. "What would be the best time to visit?" he asked.

"Late spring, summer, or fall," I responded.

Jeff then asked, "How about early February?"

Despite my reticence, Jeff was undeterred by the possibility of temperatures as low as thirty below zero accompanied by howling winds and substantial snow. So, about three weeks later, Curt and I were touring the Millers around the project area. It was indeed cold, but the winds were light, the skies were blue, and there was less than a foot of snow.

The three-day, two-night trip was an eye opener for them. Despite the freezing temperatures, golden eagles, coyotes, and other hardy wildlife added to the wonder of the rolling ocean of white snow and spectacular blue sky. While traversing a frozen gravel road north of our Sun Prairie unit on our last day, a herd of about sixty elk burst into our periphery. I stopped our vehicle in the middle of the road and cut the motor. Something had spooked the elk to the east. Ignoring our presence completely, all of them—calves, cows, and thousand-pound bulls—jumped and flowed effortlessly over the four-foot-deep ditch running parallel to the road. Each of them crossed the road in three or four bounds, and once again flowed river-like over the ditch on the other side. They continued west at high speed, gliding over the prairie more like a murmuration of starlings than the huge ungulates they were.

Curt and I remained silent. There seemed nothing to add to such an experience. We watched the now far-off herd morph from sixty individuals into a receding blur of tawny color. "A few months ago, Karen and I spent two weeks in Tanzania and Kenya," Jeff said. "That right there was every bit an African safari-like experience."

Later, as I drove Jeff and Karen to the airport, after three days of getting to know him, I realized that Jeff was another example of the kind of board member I wanted. He clearly loved the project and, as a venture capitalist, he had served on many boards of fast-growing early-stage companies and had coached many young CEOs. I could tell he would have no qualms about pushing me to consider alternate strategies. When I visited him a month later at his firm, Redpoint Ventures in Palo Alto, Jeff not only accepted my invitation to join the board but also committed a six-figure gift.

From the beginning, the notion of having a board of directors was disquieting. I was worried too much about unsolicited advice. My nervousness stemmed from never having had a board with Catalyst, a privately held for-profit company, but my concerns would eventually prove mostly unfounded.

One of our first board members, Ann DeBusk, a longtime friend and ex-CEO of American Leadership Forum Silicon Valley (ALF), had agreed to join back in 2001, before American Prairie officially existed. She and I had previously worked together over eight years as she hired me to teach courses to her carefully curated groups of Bay Area leaders. Her decision to join first, when things were still a bit sketchy, was an enormous confidence booster.

Gib and Susan Myers joined six months later. Elizabeth came in mid-2002, followed by Jeff Miller in 2004. Mostly due to my own lack of experience interacting with and staying accountable to a board, our group process took a while to smooth out. But I realized I was gaining a collection of accomplished, engaged people who appreciated my total commitment to the effort and who were equally obsessed with the project's vision.

Early on, Jeff Miller advised me to develop our first property into as complete as possible a representation of the eventual larger reserve. It was a wise idea, and once we had purchased Sun Prairie, we began thinking about how to do just that. We wanted as many miles of fence removed as possible. We wanted to begin the rewilding process for species like reptiles, grassland birds, and prairie dogs. We wanted to have growing populations of the big grazing ungulates like elk, pronghorn, deer, and—at the top of my list—bison.

I began talking to Curt and Steve about how to make the bison reintroduction happen. Their first reaction was that, while bringing bison to the prairie was vitally important, it was a few years too early. Too much could go wrong, including the bison possibly escaping while we were still figuring out the best type of fences, and we needed more time to calculate how large the initial receiving pastures needed to be. Steve was particularly concerned about how to prevent injuries to the bison during transport, and, on top of all that, we needed a public relations strategy in case a few of the animals temporarily mixed in with local ranchers' cows.

Steve, who had been contracted by Curt to work with WWF NGP, was a lawyer and a meticulous planner and researcher. His approach was to determine all possible downsides by talking with people who had experience in this area. He thought we could get bison to the prairie in three to four years, but I pressed him to consider cutting that timeline in half or more. I wanted this to happen as early as possible as it would give our current and future donors something exciting to look forward to; after all, we would be returning bison to this landscape for the first time in more than one hundred years. I also predicted that local Indigenous communities would appreciate that, as a new neighbor, we were bringing back a wild species whose loss they had been lamenting for generations. This single accomplishment would help us sustain a sense of momentum and might accelerate our progress on numerous important fronts for many years.

It took some convincing, but Curt and Steve eventually agreed. After much research on where to select the highest quality wild stock—which meant no disease issues such as brucellosis and, given the best science available at that the time, no detectable cattle genes from crossbreeding with cattle experiments that had occurred in the late 1800s—Curt and Steve selected Wind Cave National Park in South Dakota for our initial eight bison. We calculated that our acclimation pasture size would require four hundred acres. Curt and Steve researched, designed, and directed the building of a bison containment fence. And, as described at the beginning of this book, in May 2005, we released what turned out to be sixteen bison in the middle of a rainy, muddy night on Sun Prairie. It had all happened roughly three years ahead of the original schedule.

High Stakes Wayfinding

Convincing Curt and Steve to bring the bison ahead of schedule turned out to be the easiest part of my plan. I'd anticipated there would be serious pushbacks from at least a few local ranchers, which there were, but I was surprised to receive some from supporters as well, including one key donor.

Each year the WWF annual board meeting was held in one of their ecoregions around the world so board members could get firsthand experience with various projects in which they were collaborators. In 2004 they'd chosen the five-state, two-province Northern Great Plains region. During this period, Curt Freese, Steve Forrest, and other NGP staff continued to contribute in-kind services, primarily in the form of their team's time, to our rewilding efforts. Curt was still devoting time to traveling with me now and again to help with American Prairie's fundraising efforts. The WWF board had requested the use of American Prairie's semipermanent-tented safari camp to host their two-day, in-person meeting. I was asked to stop in and provide the WWF board with a status update on our project.

As I wandered around outside of the large yurt waiting to be summoned for my presentation, I strolled down to a large pond to watch the Wilson's phalaropes, swallows, and the resident muskrat. I saw a lone man standing at the edge of the pond. Looking to be in his late sixties or early seventies, he was wearing khakis, a short-sleeved madras shirt, and canvas boat shoes. He stood silently, with his back to me, his hands in his pockets, engrossed in watching the bird and insect life around the pond.

I approached him and introduced myself. He said his name was John and explained that his wife, Adrienne, was on the WWF board and he had tagged along on her field trip. We stood in silence for a few moments until he began asking about my role in the project and my strategies for dealing with everything from political issues to local resistance and rewilding. After each of my answers, he stared at the surface of the pond, making no eye contact. He drew a breath and asked, "How are you going to get all the land you need?" This was clearly his main interest. We discussed that topic for twenty minutes until the door of the big yurt opened and someone invited me inside. They, too, invited John into the yurt to hear my presentation and listen to the Q&A session afterward.

Later that evening, I joined the board's barbeque dinner, where I sought out John to continue our conversation. I didn't know his background, but I appreciated his unusually sophisticated line of questioning. He was speaking a language I understood: It was the kind of strategic thinking I'd been around during my fifteen years at Catalyst.

After talking with his wife, Adrienne, I learned their last name was Mars, and later, from Curt, learned that they were one of the wealthiest couples in the US. John, along with his brother, Forrest, and sister, Jacquie, had taken over the Mars petfood and candy corporation from their father when it was grossing two billion dollars per year. Over the next twenty years, the siblings grew it into a $40-plus-billion enterprise with 130,000 employees worldwide. John had been CEO and Chairman of the Board during much of that growth period. The guy knew how to build and sustain large things.

As I left that evening, John asked me to visit him and Adrienne at their home in Jackson, Wyoming, in a few months. He wanted to learn more about the project and indicated he might consider giving a modest initial donation. My first two-hour meeting with him in Jackson went well, as did our subsequent phone calls in which we discussed American Prairie's business strategy. He and Adrienne eventually made a five-figure donation. Over the next few years, they made regular gifts, each slightly larger than the last. John later joined our National Council, which had no trustee responsibilities and existed to provide our staff and board members—mostly me in this case—with one-on-one advice on a wide range of topics. Elizabeth, Jeff, and Gib were important and valued mentors to me. But as time went on, I became increasingly grateful and appreciative for having John, an experienced and highly successful operational executive, as an ongoing advisor, coach and collaborator.

By the time the bison reintroduction idea was a go, John and I had, through many conversations, established a good working relationship. During one of our calls in which I was explaining my current priorities, I told him that I wanted to accelerate our bison timeline. We had overcome reticence from Curt and Steve, I explained, and the idea was picking up steam.

"I think that's a dumb idea," John said. "You're going to have all kinds of problems with those things." John was intimately familiar with bison: Bulls from Grand Teton National Park periodically jumped his and Adrienne's four-foot-high jack-legged fence and hung around harmlessly on their lawn, not fifty feet from their kitchen window.

"All you'll be doing is dealing with the problems they'll cause," John continued. "The ranchers will complain—even if there is nothing really to complain about—and you'll have to spend all your time calming them down. You'll have fencing problems. A few will escape, and you'll have to spend time and resources bringing them back. Bottom line, they'll create an ongoing distraction when you should be focused on acquiring land."

I tried to explain how we were systematically working through all these reintroduction issues and how well it was going. John wasn't buying it.

"As I've been saying from the beginning," he said, "you need to focus on land. Good executives have to resist being distracted by shiny objects, and that is what these bison are. Bison reintroduction can wait ten years. Focus on the land!"

John was late for an appointment, so the call ended abruptly. Once again, I was in unknown territory, not certain how to interact with donors whose strategic views did not completely align with mine. By the time we had a well-established customer base at Catalyst, it was relatively easy to walk away from a lucrative contract when we knew we weren't going to be a good fit. That was not the case with American Prairie. For these first seven years, we were hanging by our fingernails financially. I was still often feeling out of my element with the fundraising and often wasn't sure if we should stick to our guns or alter some of our noncritical plans to appease a key donor.

A similar interaction had occurred only a few months before. I had met a technology executive from California who had recently sold his company and purchased a large ranch in southern Montana. We'd spent a good bit of time together discussing the prairie, and it was my impression that he would become a donor. One day, while the two of us were parting after a half-day conference with some other conservationists, he explained that we should change our financial model from income derived from philanthropy into a portfolio of revenue-generating businesses. For instance, he suggested we could charge high fees for hunting, charge high prices to stay in our accommodations, and explore other profit-making enterprises to fund the Reserve's annual operations.

He had mentioned these ideas before and was frustrated that I'd showed little interest in pursuing them, but I had thought we'd settled into an agree-to-disagree situation. My reluctance to move to this strategy centered on my belief that, while these businesses might bring in some revenue, they would also require constant attention, skillful adaptation to changing conditions, and the need to retain a sizable group of experienced, business-savvy, and costly employees to keep them operating profitably. I reminded him that instead we'd decided to amass a large, university-type endowment. When the Reserve was complete, the interest from the endowment would cover our projected annual operating expenses of roughly five million dollars. It would take significant profit from numerous businesses to ensure that kind of steady net annual income.

Suddenly he snapped. "Endowments are communist! People living off them get sloppy and lazy when they know they have guaranteed revenue coming in!" We exchanged only a few more words before he stormed off. Over the next few months, I tried to mollify him, but our calls became shorter and less frequent. We remained amicable, but he no longer wanted to be a part of our efforts. Gib later reassured me that these kinds of situations would happen, but a strong leader stood by carefully chosen strategic decisions and defended them graciously but vigorously.

With Gib's words in mind, I called John Mars and told him that I understood his concerns, but I would be moving forward with my bison plan. I reiterated that I was betting that successfully reintroducing bison would build new excitement and momentum, generate positive press, and demonstrate that we could solve challenging problems and deliver on our promises. That, in turn, would bring in more donations, which we could use to acquire more land. To my surprise, John's demeanor had softened considerably since our last call. With a sigh or two, he acquiesced to the plan but admonished me to stay focused on the land. Without it, he said, there would be no opportunity to work on wildlife. "At least try to keep your herd size down to the bare minimum required to make people feel happy and excited," he advised.

Running an organization while pleasing all current and potential donors was not always possible. I wasn't accustomed to walking a fine line between what I thought was right and what others wanted me to do. Sometimes that meant picking and choosing donors. It meant turning down money with untenable strings attached.

Scott McNealy, the former CEO of Sun Microsystems, coined the phrase "disagree and commit" when he encouraged his managers to debate fiercely with each other but keep it short, and when a decision was made, get behind it and move forward. No foot-dragging or subtle sabotage of the idea allowed. To my great fortune, John and Adrienne Mars, and many other highly valued American Prairie supporters, operate like this. Their advice is invaluable, but sometimes it roams too far from our chosen strategies. Generally, when I moved in a different direction from their advice, they nevertheless continued their strong enthusiasm for both me as a leader and for the project overall.

—

A key leadership philosophy that was always operating in the background with me while leading the staff organization was, as I mentioned earlier, that maintaining momentum was a high priority. I believed that, with such a long project, the energy and spirit needed to keep people excited about a far-off vision and energized about pursuing it demanded that we regularly accomplished and celebrated things along the way. I saw it as important that our staff, our board of trustees, and our supporters all experienced and appreciated this aspect of us.

I sometimes got feedback about never being satisfied with our pace of progress and at times pushing too hard, but I wanted us to have an ongoing reputation for getting things done, and sometimes getting things done far sooner than many would have expected. Getting bison on the ground years ahead of plan is an example. As a young, small, nonprofit business establishing solid long-term relationships with partners like National Geographic and Smithsonian Conservation Biology Institute is another. And given our lack of experience in fundraising, getting our first seven figure financial gifts, and later even larger ones, much earlier in our existence than some observers might have expected, is yet another. Continuously and tangibly executing well against a big vision is one of the hardest things to do, but I believe if you can maintain exciting momentum, it tends to make other hard things about your efforts much easier.

Step by Step Toward the Dream

Those first five years continued to be exciting, rewarding, and nerve-racking. We demonstrated forward progress by growing our tiny bison herd, curtailing hunting on Sun Prairie, and improving relationships with our direct neighbors. And there were the never-ending adventures. On one otherwise excellent safari, the evening temperature dropped from a balmy seventy degrees Fahrenheit to well below forty in a matter of a few hours. As darkness fell the wind increased to the point that we had to use vehicles between the canvas wall tents as anchors to tie the tents down. Even so, by daybreak, which dawned sunny and calm, many of the tents had completely collapsed with guests still snoring on their cots inside them, their bodies artfully outlined in draped white canvases.

In another instance, Curt was presenting to a group of supporters in our one of our thirty-foot-wide yurts. Unbeknownst to anyone a surprising, isolated storm—locally called a microburst—was racing toward the camp. Cortland Barnes happened to look out the door, saw the purplish black clouds approaching at extraordinary speed, and noticed the walls of the yurt—which were rated to withstand seventy-mile-per-hour winds—flexing strangely. He alerted Curt who told the group to run to the vehicles parked outside and get inside. A few minutes later, screaming winds hit the camp and the yurt exploded into pieces, throwing all manner of metal cables and splintered two-by-four boards into the air. One eight-foot board drove through the windshield of one of the Suburbans and narrowly missed impaling the people in the front seats. We later learned that the mere twenty-minute weather event packed gusts of over one hundred miles per hour and had blown 250,000-pound railroad box cars sitting on a siding near Malta right off the track, onto their sides in an adjacent ditch. Wild prairie weather indeed.

Still, our fundraising improved—albeit unevenly and sporadically—and we increased our revenue each year. By 2005, we finally had a small but dedicated fundraising staff of two people, yet we were still far from being where I wanted us to be financially.

For the first few years we'd managed to get by without a major fundraising operation, thanks to our generous board of directors. They always came through when we were down to our final month or two of cash. I'd call Gib, Jeff, or Elizabeth, and they'd convince the rest of the board to pitch in another twenty thousand dollars here, and another ten thousand dollars there. They all knew we were an entrepreneurial effort and that we'd worked hard to minimize expenditures.

We'd kept our payroll low. We'd found the cheapest office space in Bozeman and outfitted it with used desks and chairs.

We often drove our own vehicles to and from the Reserve. Kayla and I often used our own tools to fix up the existing reserve visitor infrastructure. We housed volunteer student workers, board members, potential donors, and employees in our own house, and generally worked well beyond forty hours per week. After dirty and wet safaris, our eleven large canvas guest tents and other event gear would be set up in our front yard where Kayla, Dakota, and I washed, dried, and later stored them on racks in our garage, ready for the next donor outing. Every last cent we could spare was going to one singular purpose: buying land.

Holding the Line

Frustratingly, our financial difficulties increased. The dot-com crash and subsequent recession were fresh in the minds of wealthy donors, many of whom were hesitant to risk donating to a fledgling organization. I'd been making the rounds to wealthy enclaves in New York and California armed with a polished PowerPoint presentation extolling the virtues of conservation and why it was so critical to saving big, intact spaces before they were gone. I felt it made perfect sense—why wouldn't someone want to donate money to a cause like ours?

Every time my presentation was well received. Every time we received verbal commitments for thousands of dollars. And yet, when I followed up three weeks later, the enthusiasm from some attendees would have cooled. Eventually I learned that this was a normal part of raising money, and I came to appreciate why consistently successful professional fundraisers command high salaries. The job is much harder than I'd originally assumed.

By this time, each board member in turn had gently reminded me that there comes a time in every start-up's evolution when a decision must be made: Will it ever become self-sustaining? The subtle message: My board was done—for now at least—giving gifts to cover operations.

We had cultivated many potential new donors, but they needed more time to monitor our progress and decide if we were for real. We also had some current donors who were almost ready, almost, for a second or third donation. These gifts could be substantially larger than their first, but given what I'd been learning about fundraising, I knew I had to allow at least nine more months to prepare the ground for those larger asks. Still, in early 2005, we no longer had that kind of time—we were down to a little less than two months of cash, and we had no line of credit from which to draw operational funds. As a result, I was facing the possibility of laying off staff, perhaps as much as half or more of our seven people. One by one, I reached out to the board, becoming increasingly concerned with every polite "Not this time, Sean." Finally, I called Gib. Surely, he would come to the rescue like he had many times before. "Gib," I said, "I just need seven thousand dollars to help meet payroll for the next few months."

He sighed. "Sean," he said, "I've been in the venture business for decades. I've funded hundreds of businesses and staked hundreds of millions of dollars. My general rule is that I give them what they need for the first three years. But when they get to year three or so, they have to prove their solvency. You're my friend, and I believe enormously in what you're doing. But you're now at the end of year three."

I did not tell Gib, but this felt devastating. If Gib wouldn't contribute now, no other board member would. But he was right. I couldn't keep coming back to the well time and again. For the next week I considered my options. I caught myself briefly thinking there would be no shame in calling it quits: It happens to thousands of early-stage nonprofits and for-profit businesses every year. We had an audacious idea, we'd managed to buy a few parcels of land, and we gave it everything we had. Perhaps, I mused, it was time to hang it up and return to the consulting business. It was what I knew how to do, and after all, Kayla and I had a young family to provide for.

Except American Prairie wasn't a normal start-up.

Since first becoming involved in 2001, I'd come to love our vision and believed our business model—other than our inadequate fundraising productivity—was fundamentally sound. Our goals were clear, and with additional funding, we could adhere to our land acquisition timeline. We were restoring an intact and fully functioning prairie ecosystem, the largest of its kind in North America. Our success would be measured over a time frame of decades and centuries, not fiscal quarters. Unlike other nonprofits that are assessed by how many children are inoculated against polio, how many refugees are provided with food and shelter, or how many rescue dogs are saved from the streets of Puerto Rico (all good and worthy causes), our efficacy was measured by what might last for centuries.

I kept going back to the countless times I'd been on the prairie, often for many days and nights. The effect on me when I was alone out there, and on many others when we were together on that land, was a magical thing. The thought of what it could be, the uplifting experiences so many people in the future might enjoy, far beyond my lifetime, solidified my conviction that we had to keep looking for a way forward. I thought, "Why should the dream of an American Serengeti evaporate because I was an inexperienced, struggling fundraiser?" We were just going through a rough patch. I was not ready to quit.

One January night in 2005, Kayla and I again sketched out the math on a pad of paper. If we could make it to the end of the second fiscal quarter in June, the Packard Foundation might come through with a major infusion along with possible additional gifts from individuals in the pipeline. This would allow me to hire additional professional fundraisers who might be able to bring in a more predictable and sufficient flow of income. It would also get me to the point where I could finally make more five- and six-figure asks from our current donors. But no matter how we worked the numbers, the money wasn't there. Even after some layoffs, and with a skeleton crew manning the office, we'd still need a minimum of $100,000 to get us through until June.

But how? Kayla and I still had some time left on our mortgage, but a home equity loan was a possibility. However, we'd had enough experience to know banks wouldn't be keen on the idea of propping up what looked to be a foundering nonprofit with no clear path to solvency. As Kayla and I crunched the numbers, we avoided discussing the elephant in the room: We did have access to a stock account with $110,000 in cash—our kids' college fund. We'd been steadily growing that account for fourteen years by buying used cars instead of new ones, deferring other purchases, and diligently transferring four or five hundred dollars each month into the account as we also worked on paying down our mortgage and raising our young kids.

I drew a breath, "Well, Dylan is only sixteen. He's not going to college for a while. We'd have time to build some of it back up again. Worst-case scenario: What if…?"

I didn't finish the sentence. I looked at Kayla and found her nodding. "We could set it up as a loan," she added. "American Prairie would pay us back when the Packard Foundation comes through in the spring."

"*If* they come through."

Kayla and I had weathered some anxiety-ridden times in our twenty-three years together, but nothing quite like this. That she would even consider raiding our children's college fund spoke not just to her faith in me, but her belief in the importance of the reserve project. We spent hours talking openly and honestly about how American Prairie was the most meaningful project either of us had ever taken on. We decided to go for it.

The next day I took Dakota aside and told her my plan.

"Let me get this straight. You want to take all $110,000 from your children's college fund and lend it to American Prairie, with no guarantee you'll get it back?" she asked incredulously.

"Correct."

"The board will never go for it. Not in a million years."

"I'm not planning to tell the board." Then, after seeing the look of horror on her face, I added, "…Right away."

It took me half an hour to convince Dakota to initiate the transfer, but she reluctantly agreed. Once it was done, I felt queasy. There was no going back.

Yet even with this loan, we needed to lower our overhead. Our staff team was made up of terrific people. I did not want to lay them off only to start hiring again a few months later if the Packard Foundation came through. I assembled them and announced the good news: Going forward, everyone would get a three-day weekend. The bad news: We could only afford to pay them for a four-day week. But I promised we'd do everything we could to raise more money and return to a normal five-day schedule as fast as possible, although I couldn't promise when. I added that I would completely understand if they wanted to leave. Like me, they had kids, rent, mortgages, or student loan debt. Yet, after they had all thought about it, by the end of the week, no one had quit. On the contrary, in the months that followed I sensed the kind of resolve in my team that CEOs normally only dream of.

The next step was to inform the board. This wasn't going to be easy, and I invented excuses all week to avoid it. Finally, Dakota confronted me. "Sean, you have to tell the board."

"Maybe next week?"

She gave me one of her looks, chin down, head cocked to the side. Nothing said.

"Fine." I walked into my office and sent an email to the board executive committee—Elizabeth, Gib, and Jeff—requesting a short impromptu meeting. The next afternoon we gathered on a conference line.

Gib said, "Sean, what's the emergency? Are you out of

money again?"

"Actually, I have good news. We've got enough to last us until May."

"How the hell is that possible?" Jeff Miller, the no-nonsense venture capitalist, exclaimed. "You were begging us for $10,000 less than three weeks ago!"

"Well, Kayla and I loaned the organization $110,000."

"What are you talking about?" Gib asked, his voice rising. "You don't have $110,000 lying around."

I cleared my throat. "We cashed out our kids' college fund."

Stunned silence. Then Elizabeth Ruml, our treasurer, cut in: "You did *what?!*" As a retired risk management specialist, Elizabeth had heard her share of what she considered truly bad financial ideas. "Sean, this is exactly why you have a board of directors, so you can inform and consult with them. Emphasis on consult."

"Elizabeth, if I had consulted you guys ahead of time, you wouldn't have allowed me to do it."

"You're darn right!" she said. "This is the worst idea I've ever heard."

Meanwhile, Jeff started laughing. "You can't blame him, you guys," he said. "I have to say, if I was in his position, I probably would've done the same thing."

"I might have too," Gib said uneasily. "But Sean, you can never do something like this again. Ever!"

The conversation continued, but when Elizabeth realized that the executive committee wasn't going to stop me, she sighed and agreed to work with Dakota to smooth out any possible legal issues with the loan. But she still didn't like it. "What will potential donors think when they hear you had to cash out your kids' college fund to meet payroll? That's not the kind of operation you donate hundreds of thousands of dollars to. I sure as heck wouldn't."

In the end, to structure the arrangement as officially as possible, she insisted the organization write and file an agreement to pay Kayla and me back in a minimum of eighteen months at 4 percent interest—provided the business lasted that long.

The first months following our loan were filled with angst. But it was also a time of intense focus on fundraising. We dialed back our attention on habitat restoration and postponed public relations meetings in Malta and Lewistown to make more time to travel around the country in search of money. We broke the normal rules of fundraising and asked some of our current donors if they would contribute again sooner than they had been expecting.

By springtime, some of the people who had attended our safaris saw fit to send in $5,000 and $10,000 gifts. And, at long last, we received another donation from the David and Lucile Packard Foundation—this time for $200,000, their first gift since the original $80,000 nearly three years earlier. More astounding to me were the slew of $5,000 gifts from folks who had only attended our evening informational events outside of Montana and had not yet traveled to the Reserve. It was changing my thinking about what was possible in fundraising, and it inspired us to increase the time and effort it took to do presentations in people's living rooms around the country.

Six months after the time we made that fateful loan, we moved all employees back to full-time and full pay. American Prairie began making monthly payments to Kayla and me. And a little over a year later we'd been paid back in full—with interest. Still, the board voted on and adopted a new guideline that anytime the organization had less than a three-month operating cushion, a special meeting would be called to determine what to do, including taking out bank loans or even closing down the enterprise.

There were many more trying financial times over the next six or seven years, but none were quite as existential as that six-month period. It had been a wakeup call for me to step up our efforts even further to build a more productive fundraising organization. It remained hard for me to fully grasp how amazingly hard it is to do that. Based on advice from others, we began to segment our efforts into three categories: annual donors who gave $5 to $1,000 per year; mid-range donors who could be counted on, at least periodically, for gifts between $1,000 and $15,000; and capital gifts of $15,000 or more in a single donation.

We began to hire staff who would be focused solely on building our fundraising operation. Unfortunately, I made some early mistakes in hiring, primarily because I had never built a fundraising entity before, but eventually we began to attract and retain people who had the skills to match our specific challenges. There were plenty of times when it felt like three steps forward and two steps back, but consciously acting on our value of continuous improvement helped us get better bit by bit. The improvements were aided along the way by careful planning, the addition of very talented fundraising staff, and an engaging and helpful board. We also owe continued progress to some happy accidents at various junctures along the way.

Stopping to Notice Good Fortune as it Floats by

One morning I was headed out the door at home when Kayla mentioned that Alison "Ali" Fox was in town for a few days. I had to stop for a moment to remember the last time I'd seen her and in what context. Kayla reminded me that she was the girlfriend of an intern who had worked with us for a short while. Ali had made quite an impression on Kayla when the two of them met briefly. Kayla now said I should consider hiring her.

"Hire her for what?" I asked. Ali was in her mid-twenties with minimal work experience—her only professional gig being a short stint in high-tech communications, and, regardless, I had no position openings or wiggle room in the budget. Nevertheless, Kayla felt Ali was a very smart, quick-thinking, eminently likeable self-starter, and she had just graduated with a master's in nonprofit management with an emphasis on marketing. "Just meet her for coffee," Kayla suggested.

Reluctantly, I agreed. I ended up being quite impressed and, some months later, we figured out a way to hire her. Due to my for-profit business background, I was trained to believe that sales and marketing go hand in hand. American Prairie didn't yet have a marketing department, so I put Ali in charge of its creation and asked her to help the fundraising group. Importantly, Ali eventually began carrying a limited portfolio of entry-level donors I'd assigned to her. It wasn't long before she was growing the portfolio on her own, both in numbers of donors and in size of their gifts. She had a knack for it I hadn't thought to look for in the beginning, but to our organization's benefit she slowly expanded and honed her skills, steadily improved her ability to maintain quality donor relationships, and brought in increasing amounts of badly needed revenue. Ali's joining us and getting on a productive and valuable track so quickly was not the result of me being astute and awake to opportunities that were right in front of me. I was head down at the time. I likely would have missed it. It speaks to the importance of having others around—in this case Kayla—who are in fact paying attention, who care about you and the enterprise, and who will persist in putting the opportunity in front of your face—repeatedly—until you finally take notice.

Innovation as a Core Value

One of the reasons I had felt some confidence taking on this job was my mindset for innovation, much of which came from working in Silicon Valley, where people are continuously figuring out extraordinarily creative solutions to difficult problems in the world of medicine, biotechnology, computing power and capability, and many other disciplines. But innovation has always been part of my methodology at some level.

From the very beginnings of American Prairie, I realized the answers we'd need to keep the project moving would be found not only in the US, or just in the world of conservation, but, in a world of eight billion souls, other places that would be far ahead of us. I also assumed it couldn't be all that hard to find those people and places if we put our minds to it.

Of the many books I recommended to our employees over the years, *Steal Like an Artist* by Austin Kleon became one of the most popular. By the word *steal*, Kleon means that we don't waste time trying to be completely original; instead, he encourages you to build on already existing ideas that could be converted into solutions for your most vexing problems. At American Prairie, we seldom had time to come up with answers to all our problems, so I wanted the staff to look everywhere outside of themselves for ideas on how we could move more efficiently toward our goals.

For instance, as we continued to add acres to what would one day be our core wildlife reserve, a common conundrum no other reserve seemed to have adequately solved was nagging at me. The issue: Whenever you try to create a really large protected area, you will most likely be surrounded by an established industry where people are making money from the land or the water, creating potentially serious conflicts. Big marine reserves are often surrounded by the commercial fishing and shipping industries. Land-based reserves are often surrounded by logging, farming, or cattle and sheep ranching. Wildlife versus livestock industry conflicts still plague Yellowstone National Park more than 120 years since its inception. Grizzly bears, bison, and wolves are seen by many neighboring cattle ranchers as, at a minimum, an inconvenience, or more often, an outright threat to their operations.

As an example of some typical mitigation practices to lessen this issue, in Montana each big game hunter with a wolf permit is now allowed to kill thirty wolves each year for sport, but also to ostensibly aid the ranching industry in reducing livestock losses. The profit-producing livestock industry wins; the wolves lose. These species change, but this story is replicated wherever in the world big nature reserves and money-making industry collide.

I wanted to find a different solution and searched around the world for answers. Finally, in 2008, while on a three-week trip to Namibia and Botswana to learn best practices from well-established reserves, we visited the Cheetah Conservation Fund. There we learned from Executive Director Laurie Marker how her team helped local ranchers learn creative tools and techniques to help them live in harmony with wild cheetahs and leopards. Laurie had also come up with a concept of helping ranchers market their beef as certified "Predator Friendly." In theory, this would make them more money if they refrained from killing big cats.

Borrowing from that general idea, a few years later American Prairie launched a similarly successful program called Wild Sky that pays ranchers for being more wildlife friendly. It worked well with our first early adaptor cattle rancher participants, so we started on a path of continuous improvement to make it better every year.

Thanks to the continuous seeking of new ideas from Laura Huggins, one of our American Prairie team members, we learned that the Northern Jaguar Reserve in Mexico placed camera traps around a participating rancher's land and paid them hundreds of dollars every time they obtained a photo of a live jaguar. We borrowed that idea, added it to the Wild Sky program, and we now pay livestock producers cash for photos of a variety of wild species. Participating ranchers are now making more money by keeping those species alive than by killing them themselves or allowing hunters to do it. The Wild Sky program is growing each year. As of 2024, sixteen participating ranches with approximately seventy-two thousand acres (one hundred twenty square miles) of private land had enrolled, more than five times the size of Manhattan

Island in New York City.

In keeping with our value of continuous improvement, we were perpetually looking for ways to enhance our potential donors' experience on the American Prairie. Our goal was to get them highly engaged with the project by visiting the reserve more often and staying longer while they were there. We were, however, really struggling to figure out how to entice more people to carve out the time required to come spend sufficient time on our project area. The combined flying and driving time in and out of remote northeastern Montana was daunting to many potential visitors. We needed a better hook.

While in Namibia and Botswana, we were impressed by how different the reserves approached the visitor experience when hosting guests in very remote areas. The emphasis on the quality of the guides was far beyond anything I'd ever experienced. They were friendly and outgoing, which was not surprising. However, new to me was how they expertly described their environment holistically. Each guide could identify nearly every plant and explain the behavior and unusual characteristics of most mammals, insects, reptiles, and birds that we encountered. Moreover, they eloquently described the intricate interdependencies between species and how the local ecosystem worked as a whole. I'd never experienced that with any guide, horse packer, or outdoor trip leader anywhere in the US.

Replicating on American Prairie what we had experienced would not be cheap. It took me more than a year to convince the American Prairie board of directors that having a Namibian- or Botswanan-style camp would entice far more potential high-level supporters to visit us than had thus far.

As we got started, Kayla was tasked with choosing the camp's location, designing it, managing the year-long construction process, and outfitting the accommodations to resemble the surprising comforts, excellent food, and protection from the elements found in the camps we'd experienced on the African continent. The resulting facility, now called

Kestrel Camp, dramatically increased our potential supporter visitation. Many supporters who we'd concluded would never come eventually did come and have returned numerous times with friends and colleagues, many of whom have also turned into contributors. These adventures have been a catalyst for many millions of dollars of increased financial support over the past twelve years.

When people compliment us on our innovative approaches to things, I always reply that in most cases the original idea for the innovation came from somewhere or someone else. We are just good at looking far and wide for such things, bringing them home, and applying them in ways that help us accelerate toward our vision.

CHAPTER SEVEN

Making Change

As the years progressed, I became clearer on my favorite aspects of this job. The best, maybe, was being out on the reserve area with a small group of my colleagues, camping for multiple nights and spending time during the day and evenings talking over the future vision and brainstorming ways to achieve it effectively and, if at all possible, faster.

But another favorite aspect was hosting and touring people who had never experienced the grasslands, knew little about the history of wildlife there, and had little knowledge of how an intact grassland ecosystem functioned. These included journalists, authors, film makers, potential donors, and politicians. I liked it because I got to be out on the ground—away from emails and phone calls—in beautiful and interesting country, with people who were enormously curious about how the project came to be, why we thought it was important, and what made us think we could make it happen. But as interesting to me was their curiosity about the history of the place, as well as about the individual plants and animals and how the whole ecosystem worked. I loved how, as we drove around in or walked across the landscape, their questions tumbled out not unlike a seven-year-old child who is obsessed with understanding how things work and how things came to be. And I liked it because the days were filled with unscripted conversations that followed the visitors' interests and whatever we happened to stumble upon as we moved about the land.

One early summer day, we'd been touring around four visitors who at first were adamant about wanting to see two of the three all-important ecosystem engineers: bison and prairie dogs. We had a successful morning first locating both with our vehicles, and then by walking a bit to get better vantage points. Midmorning we returned to the old ranch house that was the precursor to the Enrico Science Center.

The visitors went inside to use the facilities and to fetch cold drinks from the fridge. I waited outside in the driveway, marveling at the early-summer bird activity around me. I looked to the horizons and above me to check for large raptors but saw only a vast, empty, and gorgeous ultramarine sky. I lifted my powerful binoculars to see if there might be anything out of my normal vision range flying high in the ocean-like void above. Almost immediately I found roughly twenty huge American white pelicans straight above me, lazily wheeling slowly in two irregular and interlocking circles. I lowered my binoculars and looked at the same spot. They vanished into the blue. Looking again through the binoculars, I saw the graceful avian ballet reappeared.

I leaned back and laid comfortably across the hood of my tour vehicle and was discovered in that position as the guests returned from their break. They looked up and asked what I was seeing. Without saying what it was, I told them to fetch the binoculars that we'd supplied them with and check it out. Soon the ooohs and aahhhs began, followed by a myriad of questions: What are they? How big are they? Aren't pelicans water birds? What the heck are they doing way up there in the middle of nowhere on the Montana grasslands?

We had a lively discussion about American white pelicans as natural prairie inhabitants during the breeding season: Adult wingspans can be eight to nine and a half feet, they can weigh between eleven and twenty pounds, generally feed on small fish and amphibians, and seek out shallow lakes and ponds, wetlands, and rivers, which are more abundant on the prairies than most people realize. While hard to say for sure, it is possible this bunch was passing through, maybe moving north from wintering grounds to the prairie pothole region of Montana, or possibly further up to Saskatchewan or Alberta. But often when they are that high and are using thermals to stay aloft with essentially no effort, they are scoping out their next potential resting—and possibly summer breeding—spot that has water of some kind. They may also be trying to suss out the area's relative density of their predators like racoons, coyotes, gulls, crows, and eagles, all of which like to eat the eggs out of the pelican's easy-to-access, ground-based nests.

We delayed our planned departure to view the Missouri River and instead stood for a long while just a few hundred yards from the Enrico Science Center, enjoying the horned larks, crossbills, lark buntings, and loggerhead shrikes flitting all around us. I told about the shrike's strategy of catching everything from grasshoppers to small rodents and then—as a storage tactic for future consumption—impaling them (some would say gruesomely) on whatever kind of spike they could find, including the barbs on a barbed wire fence or the hyper-sharp, three-inch thorns of mature greasewood bushes.

While touring in the vehicles, we talked about grassland birds the rest of the afternoon and again that evening. I would have never taken this particular group as birding enthusiasts, but that is where their attention, enthusiasm, and curiosity went as the day wore on, and they couldn't stop talking about what they were learning about bird migrations, species inter-actions, and threats to their habitats. An unanticipated part of the prairie had come alive for them and made their day far more interesting.

A big part of the fun of being on the prairie is that not all is what it seems. Glassing a seemingly empty sloping hillside a half a mile away can reveal a coyote leisurely hunting voles in the warm sun. Getting up early on a wet morning and walking across a sparsely vegetated area to see if elk are about might instead reveal hundreds of wolf spider webs, all glistening with dew and sparkling crazily in the raking light. And pointing your binoculars straight up into an empty sky can illuminate a species that sends the rest of the day's conversations in an entirely unexpected and delightful direction.

Experiencing Loss as a Constant

One day in 2010, Curt entered my office with some news. His wife, Heather, had secured an attractive position at a university in Westport, Massachusetts, as head of the art department, a position she'd always dreamed of. After all the support she had given him as he'd changed careers, Curt explained, it was time to reciprocate. He would be retiring from WWF, leaving Montana, and moving back to the East.

Curt and I first met in 2000 when the project was still a dream. We had become fast friends and accumulated thousands of work hours together. I likely wouldn't have joined the project if not for the opportunity to work with him: He brought vitally important credibility to the project not only through his background but also his presence, whether it was at yet another fundraising event, a joint interview, or a late-night campfire on the prairie as we drank whiskey with potential supporters. I greatly appreciated that he always pressured us to keep our goals as large as possible, to not let caution creep into our attitudes and mindsets; he was a highly valued partner in championing unwavering boldness in regard to our big vision. He made it clear that stopping the plow-up of the Great Plains was not enough. Regarding habitat and species loss, we needed to try swing the balance back to having plenty of room for all lifeforms—including humans—to thrive in the ecosystem with no species being forced to the margins or eradicated altogether.

It was more than strange to think of him no longer in the fray. I supported his decision and realized how much it mirrored the situation with Bill Underwood and me ten years earlier. Like Bill, I knew I would be missing Curt as a friend and colleague a great deal for quite some time.

Going forward, American Prairie would still have a relationship with WWF NGP, although a significantly reduced one largely because the WWF corporate strategy developed back in Washington, DC, had evolved for the ecoregions. Their new focus would have the efforts of WWF NGP's Bozeman staff of six or so spread more evenly across five states and two provinces in their huge ecoregion, with much less emphasis toward on-the-ground projects like American Prairie. It was simply another transition and the end of an eventful and successful start-up era.

—

During my fifteen years with Catalyst, I never experienced any acrimony over our business operations. Nobody wrote letters to local newspapers demanding we should be stopped. No one in the California State Assembly tried to pass laws to put us out of business. Our customers liked what we did and that was that.

Not so with the American Prairie. I'd been warned before taking the job that we would encounter animosity. For the first few years, I didn't worry too much about it. I spent a good deal of time in surrounding towns getting to know people at government agencies, local businesses, and neighboring ranches. I introduced myself around and made myself available by giving talks in VFW halls, high school gyms, gatherings of the National Audubon Society, and local community halls; presenting to the board of a local dinosaur museum; and attending the Charles M. Russell National Wildlife Refuge bimonthly working group meetings. In general, I was largely consumed with trying to acquire habitat and trying to get our organization to at least minimal financial viability. But by year four or so, local radio and newspapers were starting to cover us. Some reporters, rather than focusing on our long-term goals and our many ideas for benefiting the area as our project grew, increasingly asked questions to heighten their reporting's aura of conflict and drama; local resistance to our plans became the anchor of some reporters' print and radio stories. With reluctance, I decided it was time to bring the issue to the forefront for me, our staff, and the board.

One morning in 2006, I was visiting a woman named Ann Boothe in Malta (population 2,500), situated an hour north of our project area. We were having coffee at the Great Northern Hotel and Restaurant with the warm aroma of eggs, hash browns, and pancakes permeating the large dining room, surrounded by tables where clusters of ranchers sat discussing the weather and cattle markets. Ann, in her early forties, was stylishly dressed compared to the ubiquitous rancher's garb of jeans, canvas jackets, and mud boots. We'd never met before, but I imagined she'd heard many opinions about American Prairie. She had been recommended to me by Ron Scott, a native of Malta and the president of the local bank we used for various business accounts, as someone who might provide thoughtful feedback about how American Prairie was regarded in the area. Perhaps she might have some good advice on how to improve our standing.

Due to the challenge of making a living on small- to medium-sized ranches—meaning fewer than about two hundred cows—one spouse or the other often took a job in town to supplement the couple's ranch income. In Ann's case, besides ranching with her husband in a small place fifteen miles north, she earned additional income as the head of the Phillips County Economic Development Council.

I asked Ann if she thought American Prairie might one day be seen by ranchers as an asset to the local economy. She studied her spoon carefully as she slowly stirred her coffee. "You guys talk about the potential economic boost from your efforts, but a lot of people aren't buying it," she said.

"For instance," she continued, "through the Economic Development Council, I'm currently trying to win a contract for a small regional prison. I can tell people around here exactly how many jobs that contract will provide: nine. Maybe nine new jobs don't sound like a lot, but at least it's something. The problem with American Prairie is that no one here has seen anything like it. They don't understand how many jobs it could bring or when that might happen. They suspect you don't know either."

She went on to say that our comparing of American Prairie to, say, Yellowstone National Park, wasn't as positive as I'd imagined. Many locals felt that Yellowstone must be grossly mismanaged simply because it was run by the federal government. Others thought it was a waste of good land that could be used for livestock and hunting.

While Ann was talking, I noticed several ranchers around the room glancing at us. I hoped my presence would not get her in trouble.

Ann continued, "Many folks here are also afraid of your plans to bring back bison. They don't know much about these animals, but what they think they know is not all positive. They worry about livestock diseases and damage to their property."

She also explained that the locals considered me an outsider. Growing up in Great Falls and attending Montana State University didn't count for much, especially since I'd lived in California for a while. I talked differently, I dressed differently, and my ideas were different. I radiated a lot of positivity about our plans, but all that potential change scared people. "Here," she said, "change is not seen as a good thing."

Later that afternoon, I drove south on Sun Prairie Road with Otter, my black English-setter-mix rescue dog. Otter's head stretched out the window as he squinted into the wind and sunlight, watching gangs of lark buntings, meadowlarks, brewer's blackbirds, eastern kingbirds, and raptors. He whined excitedly at coveys of sharp-tail grouse rocketing across the road in front of us. Deep, sunbaked wheel ruts left over from rains earlier in the week turned the usual one-hour journey south into nearly two. This slower pace gave me more time to ponder things.

To influence local views, we would need to point to actual jobs created, demonstrate how the economy was improving, and prove that bison and other wildlife would not be an inconvenience to ranching operations. And, as Ann had reminded me, change was generally not a welcome idea in this region, so, even if we did everything right, it could take a very long time for some of the more reticent folks to conclude that our vision had some merit.

The belief that American Prairie simply did not belong in the region was reflected in opinion pieces in local publications asserting that if we were allowed to continue, it would threaten the very existence of the western livestock industry. One of the most cited quotes came from one rancher who repeatedly claimed that "For American Prairie to succeed, we ranchers have to fail." State legislators, in their attempt to stop our progress, tried to pass laws stipulating that no Montana nonprofits could own as much land as American Prairie now has or plans to have in the future. Others, like those initiated and promoted by the Montana Attorney General and even Montana's Governor, focused on challenging decisions by the federal Bureau of Land Management that allowed American Prairie to graze bison on public lands, which previously had been the exclusive domain of beef cattle. One newspaper editorial explained that bison, like the dinosaurs, had had their day and it was time to move on: "There was no longer any practical need for them in a region devoted to raising cattle."

The book *Seven Arrows*, by Hyemeyohsts Storm, helped me frame the issue. Storm was Metis, which refers to a mixed ancestry of roughly half Native American (in his case Northern Cheyenne) and half Western European, often linking back to the French fur trappers working for the Hudson's Bay Company in the 1700s. *Seven Arrows* is a collection of Indigenous stories focused on understanding Indigenous origin stories, beliefs, assumptions, and the importance of hearing and trying to understand the viewpoints of others.

I'd always appreciated one story in particular. It begins with a group of elders sitting with some youngsters in an open field seated around a big circle of stones representing a medicine wheel. At the wheel's center was a sculpture. About three feet high, its elements were multifaceted and nonuniform: It sported a unique combination of wooden shapes, varied pieces of animal pelts, some splashes of paint derived from local soils, some strings of shimmering beads draped at different lengths, and some raptor feathers. No one side of the sculpture was the same as another. The elders instructed each participant, after sitting and gazing at it for a while, to create a convincing story about what the sculpture represented. After the youngsters studied the sculpture, the elders invited them to share their stories, which were entertaining and told with conviction. When all stories had been heard, the head elder spoke.

He commended them for all telling such artful stories, for their enthusiasm and their interpretation of the sculpture. The elder then explained the life lesson for that day: When you are crafting a story about what something means, it is helpful to rise from your seat and walk all the way around the subject. Observe it thoughtfully from different vantage points. If you take the time to view something in this way—before you begin shaping your own story—there is hope for us to be more open to others' interpretations of what something is or what it means, even when we are all looking at the same thing. He encouraged the youngsters to be more curious and more respectful of others' points of view, which have been informed by what they have seen and experienced.

While at Catalyst, I'd used many models and theories promoting this same idea. Part of our job was to help clients uncover their own confirmation bias that could contribute to errors in thinking. But despite my best efforts, after five or so years into running American Prairie, I was at times making some classic mistakes. In my haste and intense focus on keeping us in business and moving forward, I was sometimes forming opinions based on minimal data and settling too quickly on simple explanations for complex problems. I had thus far, by invitation, attended many gatherings of local people in community halls, high school gyms, and city council meetings. There I did my best to calmly answer questions about who we were, what our plans and goals were, and why we wanted to pursue them. Some of those interactions went well, and most people appreciated the opportunity to exchange views and learn more firsthand about American Prairie. At other times things were a bit more contentious.

Given my many decades in Montana, I'd thought I understood the local culture well enough, but I was learning that there still hadn't been enough time to truly understand the complex, deeper nuances of what had been happening in the region for decades before we showed up that had led to some frustration, confusion, and sometimes resentment against outsiders. This history contributed to the way some ranchers were feeling about our vision and how it might affect them and their already changing communities. If I was going to lead this project effectively, I needed to somehow make more time to hear more viewpoints, like I'd done with Ann Boothe, and along with everything else I was responsible for, I needed to do it more consistently.

On my occasional monthly stays in the project area, I began adding a few days onto either end of my trip so I could visit folks I knew and get a general idea of what the locals were saying about us. In Zortman, I'd meet with Terry Brockie, a highly respected and admired Tribal member from the Fort Belknap

Indian Community and then superintendent of Blaine County schools. In Malta, I'd have coffee with Ron Scott, the president of the First State Bank. Sometimes I would stop into the local Bureau of Land Management (BLM) office to see Dennis Linghor, a thirty-year veteran of the agency who'd been assigned to oversee American Prairie's public lands leases. (After retiring from the BLM, he would become an American Prairie employee.) I knew these people well enough to ask directly how our project was viewed, and I trusted them to respond honestly. I learned that, unsurprisingly, the locals could not be lumped into one neat category.

I was reminded of a particularly useful model of change I'd learned while at Catalyst that helped me view this resistance topic in a more structured way: Michael Hammer's 20-60-20 model. A well-known writer, business consultant, and professor at Massachusetts Institute of Technology, Hammer's model focuses on how groups of people—in organizations or in society—tend to respond to an impending change that will affect them. Hammer's research shows that, whatever change is afoot, people nearly always fall into one of three categories and in somewhat predictable ratios.

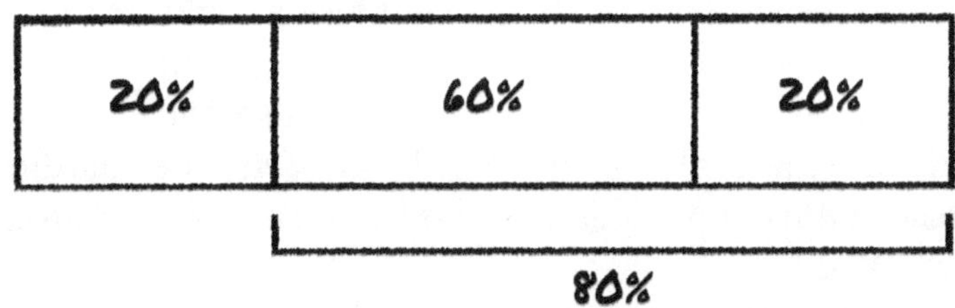

On the far right side, roughly 20 percent of people become supporters of a proposed change upon hearing about it. They like it and need no further persuading. On the opposite side, 20 percent of people will adamantly oppose an idea, often for a variety of reasons. These folks are not likely to embrace the idea in the near-term, if ever. The middle 60 percent of people will be the ones who ponder pros and cons. Many would say they are reserving the final judgement until they see how the early stage of the change goes. Given my experiences with Ann Boothe, she seemed like someone in Hammer's middle 60 percent: generally calm, open-minded but somewhat skeptical, willing to wait-and-see.

Hammer offers three pieces of advice to increase your chances of success when leading complex change efforts: Don't become overly focused on the people on the far right. They can give you false confidence and cause you to miss important steps you should be taking to execute your change more effectively.

Avoid spending too much time trying to directly address the issues of those on the far left. Sociological research indicates that usually no amount of data will change their minds immediately. If you are lucky, some might come around later if some of their peers have, too.

Focus most of your creative energy on the 60 percent in the middle. If you can incrementally earn their trust, you can often add enough of them to that 20 percent on the right to one day achieve your goal.

As I worked to understand why we were struggling to win over some locals, Hammer's 20-60-20 model kept coming to mind. Many local people thought our vision could create more access to public and private lands, and they liked that it focused on bringing back native wildlife. They also felt the project could help the local economy, which had been in decline due to a steady human population exodus from the area since around World War I.

Still, I wanted to better understand the resistance from the 20 percent who were most adamantly against our plans. Channeling Hammer, I didn't think we should attempt to change their views for now, but they had a right to feel heard and understood. I also wanted to be able to talk with our board and staff about the complex nature of their resistance from a well-informed place. And I wanted us to respond effectively when we sensed the negativity was reaching lawmakers who had the power to influence our progress.

To work on gaining the trust of the middle 60 percent, we made sure that the fences keeping bison off of our neighbor's property were state of the art and impeccably maintained. We health-tested our bison frequently and made our herd health records available publicly. We tried to be clear that we did not want to see anyone going out of business as a result of our efforts—on the contrary, we recognized that agriculture would likely remain, by far, the dominant for-profit industry in roughtly one hundred and eight million acres of the Northern Great Plains. Our efforts would result in conserving for wildlife just 10 percent of the twenty-two million acres of land that makes up northeastern Montana.

And, in the end, we also tried to be understanding that much of the animosity directed toward us stemmed from people being frustrated and saddened by the unwelcome changes that had been underway for the past eight decades. Those changes included locals steadily moving away due to ever-increasing mechanization and streamlining of processes and techniques associated with large-scale cattle ranching. That situation has led to today's record high yields in cattle production while steadily reducing the need for human labor. The result was a decade-by-decade closing of rural schools and business and, ultimately, the diminishment of a way of life. The trend continues to this day. Sadly, there was nothing we could do or say that would change those stark realities.

Michael Hammer's 20-60-20 model helped me to keep perspective while growing American Prairie in the first ten to fifteen years. As a leader I made sure that, as an organization, we talked about the model and discussed what we were learning and how it should affect our actions. I tried to make sure that, as a team, we made it clear that we appreciated and preserved the sentiment of our champions on the far right of the continuum, respectfully disagreed with the folks on the far left, and directed most of our efforts toward those in the middle 60 percent, some of whom might one day recognize value in our mission and vision.

As we continued taking the long view on our project, I kept in mind a story about the transformation of one particular person who began solidly in the 20 percent on the left on Hammer's model but later ended up in the enthusiastic twenty percent on the right. Clifford Peter Hansen was a Wyoming cattle rancher as well as the state's governor from 1963 to 1967, and a US senator from 1967 to 1978. Throughout his earlier years, he was a vocal opponent of the expansion of Grand Teton National Park. He feared it would negatively impact local ranchers and even the entire cattle industry in general. But over time his perspective evolved. One day while governor he was the keynote speaker at a luncheon in New York City for a group of oil company executives. A quote from his speech helps illuminate his transition: "I fought against the establishment of the Grand Teton National Park as hard as I could, and I lost, and I want you all to know that I am glad I lost, because I was wrong. Grand Teton National Park is one of the greatest natural heritages of Wyoming and the nation and one of our greatest assets."

All of us have experienced ourselves changing our perspective on one thing or another given enough time, new information and accumulated observation. I know its speculation, but I remained convinced that many similar personal transformations are underway at this very moment in regard to the future value of American Prairie.

—

One sunny but cold January afternoon in 2014, I drove north on the fifty miles of gravel called Regina Road that led to Malta. I arrived and drove slowly through the quiet, tree-lined streets to the Kirkwood Memorial Chapel where I was attending the funeral of a friend and neighbor named Gene Barnard, who'd died at the age of ninety-five. Afterward, in the large reception at the Lutheran Church a few blocks away, I joined about 150 people sitting at round-top tables, chatting quietly and eating church-social fare: Ham sandwiches on sliced white bread, macaroni and potato salads, Jell-O, cookies, and coffee.

As I walked through the tables looking for a place to sit with my plate of food, I received some smiles and hellos, but also some cold stares and whispers. I paused at one table with an empty chair. As I approached, I noticed a purse sitting on it. I smiled at the woman sitting next to the chair, presumably the purse's owner. The woman looked up at me passively, glanced down at the purse, and slowly turned away, toward the person sitting next to her, and resumed her conversation. Understanding her message, I walked away.

Just then a kind and jovial Malta resident I'd known for a while, Vance Spencer, strode across the room to greet me, reaching out to shake my hand with both of his, and said with exuberance, "Mr. Gerrity! Good to see you here. Glad you could make it. I know you were a friend of Gene."

People at nearby tables looked up to watch Vance treating me so graciously. He grabbed my elbow, led me back to the table I'd just left, and stood me behind the chair with the purse. Still holding my elbow, he addressed the table, a bit boisterously but cheerfully.

"Hi all, do you know Sean Gerrity here? He runs that American Prairie outfit."

I looked around the table and said, "Hi." A few people said "hello" back.

"You know, folks," Vance continued, "I'm a religious man. And lately, as I have been hearing some of the negative things about American Prairie, I have been studying my Bible. And you know what? I've looked through it backward and forward, and I can't find anywhere in it saying what American Prairie is doing is wrong." He paused for effect. "And the way I figure it, if what those folks are doing is okay as far as what's in the

Bible, then it's okay with me too. Who am I to judge them?"

I stood still, next to Vance, holding my plate with a stupid smile on my face, not knowing what else to do for the moment. Vance smiled and slowly looked at each person around the table.

He said, "How about Sean here joins you, and you can get to know him a bit?" With a flourish, he pulled out the empty chair with the purse on it and signaled for me to sit. The woman whose bag was on the chair, still not looking at me, lifted it, put it under her own chair, and again turned to face her friend.

When the eating and visiting was over, I'd come to think my table was a microcosm of Hammer's idea. Of my seven tablemates, I detected one or two who might already appreciate our vision. Maybe three or so who seemed unsure but were also curious, asked questions and seemed open-minded. And the other two or three? Well, maybe someday.

CHAPTER EIGHT

Semi-Relaxing into Level Flight

From 2001, as we were getting prepared to officially launch American Prairie, through around 2008, our three main criteria for success were: To stay in business; to keep forward momentum; and to establish and constantly strengthen a reputation for being exceptionally good at getting things done.

All this happened, but it was still not yet clear whether the ultimate success was ours. Yes, we added more land year by year. Once we had some bison, we carefully grew their numbers and expanded their habitat. We slowly and carefully tried to demonstrate to our neighbors that we did what we said we were going to do, such as welcome people onto our private lands, keep access to public lands open, and make the lands we controlled progressively better for wildlife, and hiring local businesses and individuals.

Our relationship with local Indigenous leaders continued to develop as we spent more time with each other, attended events at each other's locations, and continued to talk about mutual interests. And our fundraising productively—on average—improved year after year. It all felt like substantial and satisfying progress toward our vision.

But as expected, with such a long-term and complex project, as long sought after interim goals are finally achieved, the next set of problems soon loomed on the horizon.

By 2012 or so, I finally became convinced that even with the inevitable controversy of such an effort still trailing us, our project was indeed succeeding and getting stronger all the time, and—while a great deal of work remained—was likely to achieve its full vision. This belief grew out of a combination of events that happened over a roughly seven-year period between 2008 and 2015.

In 2008, my longtime friend Clyde Aspevig invited me to a lunch with Roger Enrico, who was then the CEO and Chairman of PepsiCo. Clyde and his artist wife, Carolina Guzman, lived outside the tiny rural town of Clyde Park, Montana. They became friends with Roger and his wife, Rosemary, who had a summer home a few miles away in the Bangtail Mountains.

Clyde knew Roger was curious about virtually everything. Moreover, he was a lover of the outdoors, so Clyde figured he might like to meet me and hear about American Prairie. By this time, we had acquired seven large-scale properties and were on track to close on two more in the next ten months. Over sandwiches at Clyde and Carolina's house, Roger quickly became fascinated with our vision and what he viewed as our surprising progress after just seven years of existence. He asked if I'd ever met anyone from National Geographic. I hadn't. He said he was Chairman of the Board of the National Geographic Society (NGS), and he would introduce me around.

Six weeks later, I was at National Geographic Society's headquarters in Washington, DC, meeting with Terry Garcia, the organization's Vice President of Explorer Programs. He, too, was quite taken with our vision and asked if I would return the following month and tell our story again, this time to a larger group of people.

Four weeks later, I was back in the same conference room, talking to Terry and to the heads of Geographic's many departments, a meeting that launched a long-term relationship with the nonprofit National Geographic Society (NGS) and the for-profit National Geographic Partners (NGP) orga-

life and their habitats and was passionate about saving nature for future generations. As we talked, I was sitting on the bank of ten-acre lake at American Prairie's White Rock unit trying to talk over the din of waterfowl landing and taking off from the water's surface. On the brightly reflective surface of the water were greater yellowlegs, gadwalls, coots, Canada geese, a raft of pelicans, and even a few white swans. I appreciated that John kept interrupting the flow of our conversation to ask for a description of what I was seeing and what specific birds were creating such a cacophony.

John complimented me on our progress and asked many detailed questions about our most urgent needs in the next two to three years. At the end of the call, he said that he'd like to learn more at a later time but, without my asking, he'd be sending in an initial donation. Two weeks later we received a wire into our bank account for $500,000. I was stunned. I had never met the man in person or otherwise, and he had never visited the Reserve. After being told about the wire, I sat thinking about our situation and marveling at what a very different place we were now than a decade earlier.

Six months later, I wrote to John and asked if I could come visit him at his Newport Beach house while I was on a trip to Los Angeles. He agreed. We stood in his native-plant-covered front yard talking for more than an hour while watching California brown pelicans gliding single file along the tops of curling waves far below us. Thoughtfully and graciously, he asked me question after question about our philosophy on public access (which he appreciated for its inclusivity), how we would join all the public and private lands together, and how we would bring wildlife populations back. I didn't ask him for more money.

Instead, I saw the dialogue as a means to get to know each other and to continue responding to his curiosity about us. A few weeks later, we received another wire for $500,000 followed by a short note—created on a typewriter—saying that

John had many philanthropic interests and didn't know when he would donate to us again, but that he admired and valued our project very much.

By this time, I'd successfully asked for and received larger donations, but I will always remember the interaction with and contributions from this fellow as a particularly special marker in time. I never got to see him again in person as he passed away a few years later, and at that time he held the distinction of being the largest single donor to conservation to date in California. His decision to contact us on his own after only reading one letter from me was powerful. It confirmed, once again, that our compelling story, supported by solid data and sound rationale, could and did capture the imagination and enthusiasm of some of the world's most discerning and accomplished people. The funds we needed were indeed out there. If we continued to somehow first find and later get it in front of these individuals, we would be fine over the long term.

Not all our donors were at John's level of wealth.

One day in 2009, a young intern who processed our mail stopped by my desk and handed me an envelope. It contained a handwritten letter from an elderly couple in a rural farming region of South Dakota. They explained that they had admired American Prairie since they had first read about it the local newspaper and were pleased to be annual donors. Wanting to do more for us, they decided to sell the silverware set that they had received as a wedding gift fifty-five years ago. Enclosed in the envelope was a check for $650—the proceeds from that sale—with instructions to spend it on whatever we deemed most important.

I found the couple's phone number in our donor database and rang them up. The husband answered, and after I identified myself, he put me on speaker phone so his wife could join us. We talked for half an hour. They explained that, given their age, they might not ever visit the Reserve, but they so enjoyed knowing our project was on its way to success. This conversation didn't provide a great deal of money but did offer me an enormous amount of satisfaction and inspiration. It's one I'll never forget.

As donations started coming in, so did requests to speak at well-known organizations. In 2013, I was asked to speak about American Prairie on the main stage at the Aspen Ideas Festival, where dignitaries, well-known media personalities, academics, and other professionals gather annually for a week to discuss cutting-edge projects and ideas from around the world. Not long afterward, I spoke at *Talks at Google*, the Smithsonian Earth Optimism Conference, and *The Goldman Sachs Talks* in New York; I even delivered a keynote talk to six hundred people at the Global Big Cat Conference in Baku, Azerbaijan.

At the same time, articles and film stories were finally tipping to the positive instead of the previous overly dramatized American-Prairie-verses-the-agricultural-industry stories. Sometimes the reports started out with that old saw but changed once the reporters began to dig deeper into the details as they constructed their stories.

For example, in 2014, I was interviewed by the veteran CBS newsperson and journalist Dan Rather. He was planning to make a one-hour documentary on the status of bison in the American West with a focus on the myriad controversies surrounding them. After arriving at a house in a quiet Bozeman neighborhood that Dan and his five-person film crew had rented for the interview, I found Dan and his team already in their professional mobile studio full of bright light boards, boom-mounted microphones, and numerous TV cameras. The two of us sat on high stools facing each other, *60 Minutes*-style. Just a few minutes into the interview, a large, very hot light board crashed to the floor near us, lit on fire, and began kicking up copious amounts of smoke. The film crew shooed Dan and me outside and instructed us to hang out on the front steps until they were ready for us to return.

During our unexpected and unscripted half-hour chat,

Dan asked me how I was feeling about the film's focus. I told him that, frankly, I doubted it would end up telling a meaningful, comprehensive story. Taken aback, he asked me to elaborate. I explained that for the past thirteen years, journalists had been framing this same story as a fight between wildlife conservationists and cattle ranchers. (I'd learned that the working title of Rather's documentary was *Range Wars*.) In my experience, filmmakers and print journalists rarely sought opinions from the majority of locals who were either indifferent about or in favor of reintroducing bison—that middle 60 percent, and the enthusiastic 20 percent on Hammer's model—and instead always focused on interviewing the most colorful people from the proportionally small, but highly upset and vocal contingent: the 20 percent on the far left. My second problem was that, to date, no journalist had included views from any of the thousands of Indigenous people who lived in the region, many of whom were enthused about seeing bison and other once-eradicated wildlife return. The stories were always reduced to white ranchers versus bison conservationists.

Dan listened calmly and thoughtfully, asked many more questions, and said that he would think about our discussion as the crew built out the story over the coming week. A month later, I learned they had altered their goals and returned to Montana with a larger film crew with the intent on expanding the show to two full hours. The final documentary spent a great deal of time on Indigenous people's relationships with bison and their opinions on the animals' return to the prairie in large numbers. Surprisingly—though it remained titled "Range Wars"—the program ended up being favorable toward American Prairie.

For quite a long time, I saw each of these financial gifts, these opportunities to speak on a stage, these interviews with a publication, and these films as anomalies. But now I began cautiously accepting them as a pattern. The size and frequency of donations was steadily increasing as American Prairie was being spotlighted by news outlets with large followings and with more sophisticated stories. All this was such a welcome change from those difficult first ten years. Yet it was only about half of what I needed to feel confident that we were on our way to achieving our long-term vision of a genuine American Serengeti. As important to me as consistent donor enthusiasm, press interest, and opportunities to speak around the world, was our progress in the project area itself.

—

We'd worked hard there for years on many fronts, including habitat and wildlife restoration and opening our lands to the public. And finding common ground with our immediate neighbors was an ongoing priority.

When I first saw the remnants of Prairie Union School, fifty miles south of Malta, it was a twelve-foot by twelve-foot delapidated shack in the middle of a cow pasture. One wall had collapsed some time ago. Twenty or so cows stood around the structure while three or four stood inside on a floor piled high with logs, dirt, and dried manure.

This artifact came along with a property we'd purchased from the Shores family. I recalled a warning from one of our earliest National Council members, the historian and author Robert "Bob" Righter of Moose, Wyoming. Bob advised me to be thoughtful about what we removed from the landscape as we acquired properties. "One hundred years from now," he said, "we might be surprised what visitors would find fascinating regarding the complex history of the area."

Bob's advice got me to thinking about a restoration project and, after asking the Shores for a detailed history of the school, we decided to restore it to its old glory. Two years later it was ready, thanks to some historical-preservation-minded donors and Montana-based architects and builders who contributed much in-kind time, as well as descriptions gleaned from students, now in their sixties and seventies, who'd attended the school from kindergarten through the eighth grade.

Once done, we decided to have a celebration although we weren't sure how many residents would want to be seen associating with us. Still, we recorded a short public service message announcing the date and time on a radio station that reached numerous small towns in a sixty-mile radius.

We soon learned that more people than we'd originally expected wanted to attend, so we rented two school busses, each of which ended up fully occupied, to help those who weren't comfortable driving uneven, rutted roads deep into the remote southern section of Phillips County. The only surviving teacher, now in her eighties and living at a retirement home a hundred miles away, presided over the school's dedication. She was just twenty-one years old when she taught at the school where she also lived by herself, in the middle of nowhere. But her memory was excellent, and she told wonderful stories about her students, most of whom were in attendance, some of whom had not seen each other for years. I talked with many of the guests, some of whom I gauged to be in Hammer's middle 60 percent regarding their views on American Prairie—as well as a few from the 20 percent who didn't care for it at all. Despite our differing views, I have found that when it comes to historical preservation, we can often come to not only tolerate one another but enjoy each other's company.

Once we made it a priority to be more consistent, we never ceased in our efforts to improve local relationships, and this was especially true with the Aaniiih and Nakoda Tribes. For a number of years, before natural birth rates were sufficient to keep our bison population growing, we imported animals from Elk Island National Park in Alberta, Canada, and in May 2012, we released seventy Elk Island calves onto 14,000 acres of American Prairie land. To help us celebrate, we invited our friends from the Fort Belknap Indian Community. We were guessing that a dozen Tribal members might make the mostly-gravel, seventy-mile journey to our Sun Prairie Unit. To our surprise and delight, two large school busses lumbered into the driveway carrying more than fifty grandparents, high school kids, parents, and leaders from both the Aaniiih and Nakoda Tribes. They exited the busses carrying folding chairs and food to contribute to the "feed" we were putting on just before the release. They joined American Prairie, WWF NGP staff, and members of the Confederated Salish and Kootenai Tribes for a celebration of youth: seventy rather bewildered and nervous two-hundred-pound calves. Meanwhile, our resident bison welcoming party of 125 adult females, yearlings, and two-thousand-pound bulls stood knee deep in the silvery sagebrush a quarter of a mile to the east—downwind from the human crowd and the calves—quietly watching, listening, and sniffing the air for news of what might be happening.

These Elk Island calves were descendants of animals moved from Montana to Elk Island in 1907, when the US was not ready to create a national bison sanctuary. Marcia Pablo, a member of the Confederated Salish and Kootenai Tribes, attended our event with her family. Her great grandfather, Michel Pablo, had owned and helped arrange the transport of those bison—some of the last left on the Great Plains—back in 1907. Marcia explained that in her Tribe (and many others) there's a tradition of considering the impact any decision made would have seven human generations into the future.

Standing next to her as she addressed the group were two of her grandchildren—descendants exactly seven generations removed from Michel Pablo. She said in her written remarks:

"We are honored to be part of this celebration, to see descendants from the Pablo herd coming back to Montana, coming home...In Native American beliefs, the circle is a sacred symbol. Today we see the circle being completed, as the descendants from the Pablo herd are back in the United States once more, thanks to American Prairie."

George Horse Capture Jr. of the White Clay (Gros Ventre)

Tribe stood next to the temporary holding corral and also addressed the crowd, saying that he was very pleased to see the changes that had occurred on American Prairie over the past decade. He explained that there were fewer buildings and barbwire fences, and that the land was slowly looking more like the past. Tears clouded his eyes when he commented that the sight of these young bison on the landscape was a sign that slowly things were being set right again.

After the speeches and lunch, the crowd moved out to the corral where the uneasy calves awaited their freedom. When Marcia Pablo and her grandchildren ceremoniously swung open the steel gates, an initial stream of fifty or so calves exploded out of the enclosure like Fourth of July bottle rockets, careening toward the waiting herd that opened like a half circle of musk oxen to accept them. But twenty or so hesitant and edgy youngsters remained pressed against the back rails of the corral. The crowd of humans waited ten minutes or so.

Robe Walker, also from the White Clay Tribe, asked, "Shall we sing them out?" The rest of us remained quiet as he gave voice to a loud and beautiful song in the White Clay language, translated as "It is Good to Be Young." Another burst of calves soon charged out of the gate and made the crossing from the human crowd to the waiting bison herd. The bison spent the rest of the afternoon quietly integrating the newcomers into the matriarchal culture, eventually wandering off to the east with their new charges, until they all disappeared over a high ridge and then down slope into the safety and quiet of Box Elder Gulch.

Had we not invited people to join the release, or had no guests shown up, it would have been just another day of rewilding logistics for our Reserve team. Instead, it became a cherished memory for everyone there as we celebrated incremental, multifaceted progress in this very long-haul project.

Our interactions with the Aaniiih and Nakoda Tribal members have stayed steady. We travel to Fort Belknap reservation periodically to provide updates on our project at the Tribal Council, high school assemblies, and other gatherings. We invite them as guests at American Prairie's Antelope Creek campground at Mars Vista for outdoor group lunches, celebrations, and discussions. Tribal members use the large Clyde Aspevig Community Room for their own meeting purposes at the American Prairie National Discovery Center on Main Street in Lewistown. And when journalists and film makers contact us to come to learn about American Prairie, we always make sure they consider including multiple tribal perspectives in their written and film-based story telling about the region. After twenty-two years of relationship building, not everything that could be done has yet been done, but it feels like we are on a sustainable, long-term track of continuous improvement based on sincere intentions and growing trust in each other.

Despite all these successes, we still had a few worries. As compared to other easier-to-access places, I fretted that few would want to spend time in what some people viewed as a desolate landscape. But slowly events began to accumulate that convinced me otherwise.

As our relationship with National Geographic continued to expand, Roger Enrico eventually convinced Tim Kelly, President of National Geographic Television, and Terry Garcia, Senior Vice President of Explorer Programs, to make a short visit to the prairie. It took many months to coordinate their busy schedules, and when the date arrived, it was in August, which is sometimes blazing hot and largely devoid of wild animals and birds, at least during the heat of the day. I was hoping to get lucky and show them at least something that would prove inspiring.

Flying north from Billings, Montana on a small Cessna 210 with no air-conditioning, we sweated profusely throughout the ninety-minute flight into Malta, our backs sticking to the vinyl seats and furnace-like hot air blowing in our faces through the open windows. Terry, who had arrived in

Montana directly from Johannesburg, South Africa, was horribly jet lagged and kept nodding off during my commentary as we flew over the Missouri River. In a rented Suburban, we drove south on Regina Road toward Sun Prairie. The outside temperature indicator on the Suburban's dashboard read 105 degrees Fahrenheit.

Mile after hot mile there seemed to be nothing but dry grass, dust, and heat mirages rising up off the dirt road ahead of us. My mood turned grim. I was losing faith in finding anything that might rouse their interest. I was wondering if I could possibly salvage a reasonable evening tour when it would hopefully be cooler—maybe spot some prairie dogs or burrowing owls—when Tim Kelly from the back seat asked about those animals in the distance off to the left. I stopped the vehicle and didn't need my binoculars to tell what they were. Thirteen bull elk, each of them sporting tremendous antlered racks, stood milling about in the scorching sun on a gently sloping hillside. Seemingly unable to agree on what escape route they should take, they finally chose to stand stock still and stare back at us.

So many mature bulls hanging out with each other is a rare site. On a whim, a few days earlier I had rented a 300mm lens to use during the trip on my Olympus camera body. Once we'd started driving, I figured I would never even take it out of its case given the unfavorable conditions, but now I carefully unpacked it, attached it to my camera body, and began snapping images.

We sat there a long time, windows down, the sultry afternoon air wafting through the Suburban, talking about how elk were originally a plains animal and how what we were now seeing was what we hoped would be a common occurrence for future visitors. Tim and Terry were indeed impressed by this vision. I believe it helped inspire many years of productive collaboration between American Prairie and National Geographic Society and National Geographic Partners.

—

After Curt Freese retired from the project in 2009 and WWF's role steadily tapered off given their change of corporate strategy, the role it was originally intended to play—a lead science project partner—went unfulfilled. But a new partner soon appeared. In 2014, I was invited to Baku, Azerbaijan to give a keynote talk on saving big natural areas and their endemic species to a global conference for saving big cats around the world. Azerbaijan, and its neighbors—including Armenia, Iran, and Georgia—are the last places on earth that are home to the heavily persecuted and overly hunted Persian leopard, of which fewer than one thousand are left in the wild. While touring the country in the days after the conference, I met a scientist from the Smithsonian Conservation Biology Institute in Washington, DC, who had also presented at the conference. We stayed in touch months afterward, and I was eventually introduced to his boss, Steven Monfort, the head of the Institute then.

Steve and his staff, intrigued with our big vision, came to visit and spent three days touring with us. Not long afterward, the Smithsonian decided to make American Prairie their flagship big-landscape science and rewilding project in the US, which meant—as with their other projects around the world—they would remain as a constant partner to American Prairie for many decades at a minimum. I was astounded that they would choose us and formally commit to such a long effort, but they explained that they seek to become deeply embedded with conservation projects around the globe that are well run, have grand ambitions, and demonstrate a high likelihood of ultimate success. Ours qualified, and as of this writing, there are more than twenty-five graduate students, post-doctoral scientists, and others working seasonally under the Smithsonian banner, living and working on site at American Prairie.

From approximately 2014 and beyond, it became common

for those I was touring around the prairie to ask how, after all the years I had been with the effort, optimistic and confident I was that the trends in this region were in fact in our favor and that we would eventually achieve the original vision. I would respond that there were many local trends and global trends that I believed would help us overcome much of the lingering doubts about, and some remaining resistance to, our long-term goals.

At the local level, more and more people in that middle sixty percent—those open-minded, yet wait-and-see types, of that societal change model—were increasingly telling us they were witnessing the many benefits of the project and that they appreciated us slowly becoming a part of the social fabric of this region. The annual number of visitors from near and far who came to view wildlife, hike, bird-watch, float the Missouri River, and stay in our huts and campgrounds is still growing, and they often report that they wanted to return and visit different parts of the Reserve. Our predictions about incrementally adding to our habitat base year after year continued to be accurate. The federal government's steady movement toward allowing public lands to be used for more than just making money for private industries like logging, mining, and agriculture continued. For instance, the newest evolution to the BLM's approach to managing public lands includes the recently ratified Conservation and Landscape Health Rule. The rule recognizes—for the first time ever—conservation as an essential component of public lands management, on equal footing with other multiple uses of these lands. That means managing the land for biodiversity, nature, and conservation, are as important as mining, logging and livestock production. Like many new rules and programs in this political era, this rule may be blocked by our current congress and executive branch but due to its broad public support, I believe it will one day move forward. New rules like this help to validate our model of joining private lands with public lands with the express goal of benefiting both nature and people.

On a more global level, effective techniques for co-prospering with wildlife, including large predators, are being developed, shared and adopted with increasing frequency. The practice of permanently replacing physical livestock fencing with invisible virtual fences is gaining acceptance. The use of virtual fencing helps to defragment landscapes while reducing livestock producer's operating costs. Reducing impediments to wildlife movement between protected nature areas is becoming much more common, including the installation of roadway underpasses and overpasses to enhance the effectiveness of critical wildlife corridors.

Most heartening to me is the fact that many people are beginning to view large landscapes differently as a result of new models of ecology being shared more broadly. As one local example, a recent change is underway in Montana in the way people are viewing the state and its wildlife.

For the past 100 years or so, government officials and the public viewed Montana's wildlife situation largely according to the late 1800s and early 1900s baseline, which noted that the state's remaining wildlife species were present mostly in the mountainous, western forty percent of the state. Efforts to rebuild wildlife populations in those areas—including between the Greater Yellowstone Ecosystem and the Continental Divide Ecosystem—have been encouraging and reasonably successful in recent decades. But the eastern grasslands that make up sixty percent of Montana—and where historically most of the wildlife was once known to exist in spectacular abundance— were passed over for both protections and restoration efforts. For the past twenty-five plus years, however, the Northern Montana grasslands have attracted increasing attention.

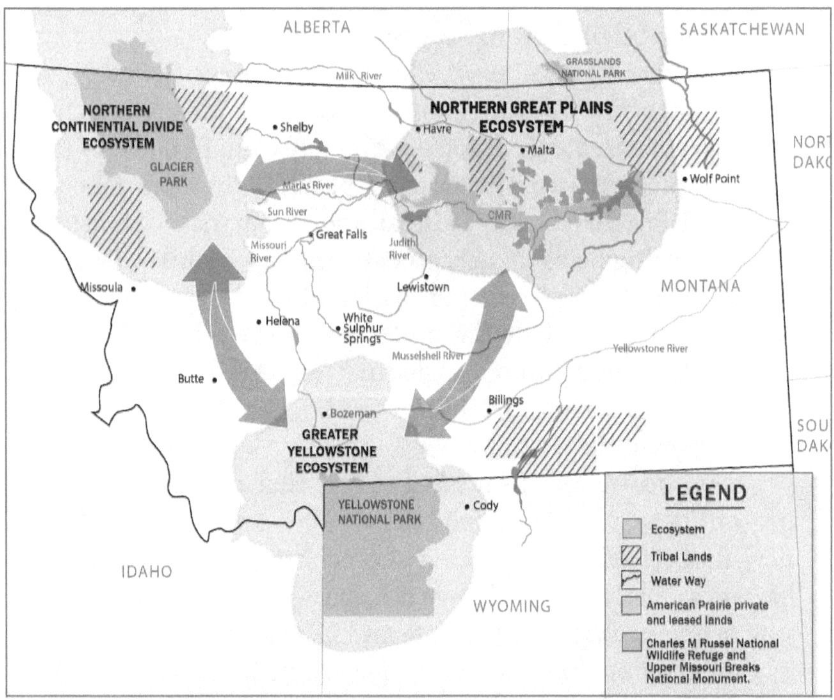

This graphic represents a future concept that would highlight a third large scale ecosystem in Montana, thereby creating the Montana Triangle.

Today, more Montanans are beginning to recognize the value of a more holistic, core areas connected by corridors approach that ensures robust and genetically diverse species populations into the future. The Northern Continental Divide, the Greater Yellowstone and the multi-million acre prairie-based ecosystem surrounding American Prairie, are all home to recovering species like grizzly bears, wolves, cougars, and others. As one example, grizzly bears who were eradicated completely in Northeastern Montana approximately 120 years ago, have now travelled roughly 250 miles back to that prairie region from both the Greater Yellowstone and the Northern Continental Divide Ecosystems. Sightings of both males and a female with cubs have been repeatedly verified in various areas in the region.

Due to increased appreciation for the interconnectedness of these places, I predict that in the decades ahead various people and organizations will choose to more actively support improvements to this important system—which could be referred to as The Montana Triangle—and in turn help increase the abundance and resilience of all of Montana's nature and wildlife. In particular, I envision organizations, including the existing Yellowstone to Yukon (Y2Y) and others that have not yet formed, will play a vitally important role in better connecting these large protected areas with safe-passage corridors for all manner of wild species.

I predict as this Montana triangle concept continues to take shape and becomes normalized, it will increasingly be thought of as one of the most innovative and effective models worldwide in successfully returning wildlife abundance at an enormous scale, and as it had existed for thousands of years.

—

Looking back now, it seems like often the smallest indicators of progress were for me the most gratifying. They didn't involve formal celebrations, lots of high fives, or positive stories about us in the press.

Early one summer morning, I was driving north up Sun Prairie Road on my way to an appointment in Malta. I slowed down as I was passing our recently opened campground, Buffalo Camp, to see what might be going on there. As the years unfolded, I'd become better at resisting being in such a constant rush while on the Reserve. I was more frequently stopping now and then, being more present, and noticing and absorbing what was happening in the world around me. I pulled over to the side of the gravel road and shut the motor off. There was only one occupied campsite in the thirteen-site campground. From my vantage point a few hundred yards away, I saw the vehicle was an early 1990s vintage Road Trek camper van.

Looking through my binoculars, I could make out a local Phillips County license plate. Next to the van was a large tent. The picnic table sported camping staples: Coleman stove, coolers, and lanterns. In the shade of some large cottonwood trees sat an elderly man wearing a floppy canvas fishing hat, reading in a camp chair. A woman of a similar age, wearing a one piece, peach-colored velour leisure suit, stood on the edge of their campsite holding what looked like an older model Instamatic film camera. A short distance below her, on a sunny, grassy slope lay nine very large bull bison. They were contentedly lounging ten or so feet apart from one another, some of them dozing and some placidly gazing here and there while meadowlarks and Brewer's sparrows flitted around in the sagebrush just in front of them.

The woman was taking photos but mostly held her camera with both hands to her chest as she carefully studied the bison. Every minute or so, while pointing at the bulls, she would turn to her husband to say something I could not hear but presumed was a description of what the bison were doing. Each time she spoke, the man looked up from his book, said something back to her, and returned to his reading. After each exchange, the woman took another picture or two and then studied the animals some more.

I found much that pleased me here. I thought about the items we most often celebrated that indicated our momentum, as when we closed on another piece of property, when we'd secured significant funding, or reached the end of an often Kayla-led construction project. But more recently, I was experiencing the most satisfying feelings of momentum when I was on my own like this—in quiet moments—and while taking stock of where we were with the project in general.

I sat in my truck watching this scene which I'd witnessed many times in Yellowstone, Glacier, and other national parks; scenes that involved someone having an enjoyable and mind-expanding wildlife experience. It could be watching a beaver cutting and ferrying willow branches along a riverbank or seeing a single coyote sitting in a field, patiently cocking its head to one side then the other, listening intently for ground squirrels under the dirt below. It might be a moose standing knee-deep in a pond, repeatedly dipping its head below the water's surface and coming back up with a mouthful of dripping, mushy plants. And here was a local woman whom I imagined had perhaps never seen a bison up close, having the chance to stand quietly for as long as she liked watching them. Ands she was doing so from a remote, peaceful campground, made comfortable with a water supply, power, and shade pavilion for under twenty dollars per night. And she could enjoy the fact that the bison were acting naturally. They were on that slope because that is where they wanted to be then. If later the animals decided to move, they could get up and wander around in a space of forty-five square miles of prime wildlife habitat. This felt wonderful. It was absolutely a Yellowstone-like experience, happening right in front of me, which is what we had been shooting for since the beginning. I thought, "This is going to work."

I can't say I ever truly relaxed, and perhaps I never will about this project, but through the combination of all of these pieces, I finally allowed myself to believe that ultimate success—even though years of hard work and much problem solving remained—was becoming ever more likely.

CHAPTER NINE

New Endings, New Beginnings

In 2016, fifteen years into the project, I was in my mid-fifties, and it was slowly dawning on me that I did not want to continue leading the organization into my sixties. This thought triggered a complex mix of emotions that I mulled over for the better part of a year. Following our start-up years, when we were struggling merely to keep the lights on, the work remained challenging, but most days I experienced a highly satisfying sense of being a part of something important. But my long-held vision for what I wanted to be doing in my sixties conflicted with the demanding role of full-time president.

Kayla and I had always designated this period of our life for traveling to far-flung places, doing more volunteer work, and possibly—if we got lucky—one day enjoying time with grandchildren. I loved my job with American Prairie, but I'd run into far too many people who'd left their demanding positions quite late in life, had neglected to effectively pass on their role to younger people, and wondered why they hadn't transitioned sooner. As heavily invested as I was in the success of American Prairie, I didn't want to be one of those folks.

I was aware of many stories about founders and their attempts at succession planning. Many, if not most, were cautionary tales (to say the least) about how often they do not go well. I wanted to leave American Prairie set up for long term success, so I wanted to do my best to make this transition a good one. My hope was that the next leader would be, or soon become, a more appropriate and effective CEO than I might be during future phases of the project.

I began talking with a few board members, seeking their help in figuring out a smooth as possible transition in the years ahead. Each of our board executive committee members was supportive yet uncharacteristically subdued at my news. The same reaction occurred when I informed the entire board a month or so later. As Dakota later explained, "They're quiet because it scares the bejesus out of them to think of you not being the leader after fifteen years. Just give them some time."

I'd started thinking about bringing in a CEO in from outside American Prairie and had loosely identified several candidates, but all were employed, would need to take substantial compensation cuts, and would have to relocate thousands of miles to Montana. Moreover, I felt queasy about the effect an outsider might have on our culture. Our operating style, aligned by our Vision and Strategy process, was uncommon, and our carefully selected values were important to our continued success. Because I hoped that those values and that process would continue well beyond my tenure, an internal candidate made more sense.

Alison Fox was the first person who came to mind. Since I hired her back in 2007, I'd always appreciated her near obsession with the project. She sincerely believed that it was important, not just for nature and wildlife, but for humanity. As the years unfolded and her responsibilities increased, she and I spent hundreds of hours together in meetings, on airplanes, at donor events, and on the Reserve. All the while she became increasingly admired, well-liked, and respected in the organization. Her reputation grew stronger even as she became a member of the senior executive team in our then-thirty-five-person organization.

Before talking to her, I conveyed my thoughts to the board.

There was some initial hesitancy as Ali was young and had no prior experience leading an organization. Some board members pondered: Could she command the respect of the staff? I was convinced she could. I started bringing her to board meetings, and to help them get to know her, I asked her to conduct presentations that I would have normally done.

When I told her we were considering her as the next CEO, she was pleased but also surprised. We checked in frequently over the next six months. Through continued exposure to her, the board warmed up to the idea. After Ali had completed a multi-city tour to share our latest marketing and fundraising strategies with board members around the country, our board chairman, George Matelich, called me to check in.

"How was your meeting with Ali last week?" I asked him.

He replied, "I really like her—she's full contact!" What he meant was that, although pleasant and gracious, Ali did not shy away from revealing her honest thoughts.

Many months later, at one all-hands staff meeting, I arranged to have Ali sit with me during a regular segment called the President's Fireside Chat, which was a ninety-minute, free-form dialogue where I talked and answered questions with the whole staff. We placed two bar stools at the front of the room. I parked myself on one. Ali took the other.

I began by saying that there were some changes afoot with my role. Many on the team already knew that someday I wanted a less intense role with American Prairie. I continued, saying that the board and I had decided on a way forward. "Beginning soon," I said, "Ali will report to me, and everyone else in the organization will report to Ali." I took a deep breath and continued. "Then, at some point, she will take my job." Uttering those words evoked many emotions for me—some relief, a bit of confusion, and much more anxiety than I'd expected—but it also felt like the right thing at the right time.

At our February 2018 board meeting, three years after I'd started considering this transition, Ali officially became CEO.

Now, by design, I reported to her.

My new schedule consisted of four days per week overseeing only the Reserve operations and wildlife restoration, a much more relaxing role than being responsible for the entire enterprise. I liked having three-day weekends. In time, I began thinking that four-day weekends might be even better. Five months later, I dropped to three days a week and got off the senior management team after seventeen years of leading it. A year later I retired from the staff entirely, and my primary function became serving on the Board of Directors.

—

Reflecting back on my years leading American Prairie, I wish I could have raised more money and faster, acquired more land, and helped to rewild the prairie more quickly. I'd like to have done this for all the generous supporters who've believed so much in this vision and wanted to see it largely realized in their lifetimes. But they witnessed the launch, many years of substantial and exciting progress, and the formation of the talented, fired up, and vision-obsessed people who constitute the staff, Board of Trustees, and Emeritus Board members today. I feel confident that today's and tomorrow's leaders at American Prairie will not be deterred in the least by temporary political conditions, by downturns in the economy, or periodic bouts of fatigue during particularly challenging times. For a quarter century American Prairie has weathered all of that and more. The vision is the thing; and the enthusiasm and commitment of those who get up each day and keep working the plan.

Today, our supporters enjoy a continuously growing wildlife-centric landscape: An increasing population of bison roaming the prairie and swift fox have been reintroduced after a ninety-year absence. Female and male grizzly bears—not seen in this region since the 1890s—are now making their presence known and thus far appear to be settling in the area.

If I get to be around on the planet for a while longer, I look forward to seeing examples of all the major pieces of the Reserve in place. I would cherish the experience of standing on a high point looking down on a curve in the Missouri River, watching a mother grizzly and her young cubs ambling along the bank, snacking on rose hips, and turning over rocks or listening to resident wolves howling on a winter's night. And, as Meriwether Lewis reported long ago as his expedition passed through this area, I would like—while standing on the top of a high cut bluff—to turn away from the river and look out over the vast, fence-free plains to see wildlife in every direction, all moving about in one common pasture.

Most of all, from the start I have hoped that if this endeavor became a complete success, it would result in multi-million-acre, wildlife-rich region of the North American grasslands. And like Yellowstone National Park and other sanctuaries for nature, it would draw people to want to experience it time and time again.

I have also hoped our success would provide a tangible example that, with the right group of people all aligned toward a big idea, it is still possible these days to achieve high-impact conservation results, even when starting from scratch in many cases. I believe the world today is abundant with nature conservation opportunities like American Prairie on the land and in the oceans. Each diamond in the rough is there waiting for a regular group of people to notice and then act.

I think it's time we seriously consider these questions: Is it reasonable to imagine that we now have the opportunity to go far beyond just trying to save what nature we have left and instead work to bring back a great deal of what we have lost? Is it possible that the best period of exciting nature restoration and preservation is actually in front of us? Might we actually be on the front end of a long-awaited renaissance in rewilding nature for the benefit of all life on earth?

Interlude

During the time I was leading American Prairie and, in the years, since, I have spoken to audiences about our work on stages, on radio and TV shows, and on podcasts. For the longest time, I was surprised that I was sometimes asked nearly as many questions about my own career journey as questions about American Prairie itself. Two issues kept coming up: First, they wanted to know how I was able to align my own interests and passions so well with the two very different phases of my career at Catalyst Consulting and later American Prairie. Second, they wanted to know how—given my relatable, seemingly-unremarkable background—I became adept at simply getting things done. Was I born hardwired to achieve results? Or had I figured out some specific secrets along the way?

My honest answer is that I mostly learned by observing many other people whom I admired and—over a long period—trying to incorporate some of their ways of operating into my own. I'm the first to admit that I failed at a lot of those efforts; there are many things I wish I could claim are now a part of who I am, but for various reasons—lack of talent, laziness, and other factors—haven't happened. What *does* now come naturally to me is being consciously intentional about finding work that matches my interests, my penchant for getting things done, and my ability to often disregard conventional wisdom in favor of even bigger possibilities.

The story of American Prairie has always been bigger than one singular organization. It's also a story about how change happens, and about how people get good at *making* that change happen. Over the years, I've come to realize that there's a hunger for both parts of the story—and, in writing this book, I believe it's as helpful to explore "the how" as it is to share the tale of American Prairie itself.

What follows are some of the more essential practical concepts, tools, and ways of thinking that I've picked up along the way. Each one has benefited me a great deal and, with much time and experimentation, I found the right combination that made me more effective and more fulfilled in what I set out to do. That mix will look different for each of us, as it should.

Some of these concepts may be passingly familiar, and others may be things at which you already excel. I tried to provide here a general overview of each topic; some contain an exercise or two to help you understand what it is like to work with them. For those subjects you find particularly interesting, you'll find ways to learn far more about it in the "Further Resources" section later in the book.

But I hope that the practical ideas I've included here will be interesting and useful to anyone who, like me, occasionally wonders how to make the most of our time and talents on a planet in desperate need of our collective attention and care.

While these ideas that follow can be helpful no matter what significant change or transition you might be considering, I think they can be particularly helpful if you are considering a transition into the complex yet highly rewarding world of enhancing our natural environment. Indeed, I'd be pleased to think you may be headed in that direction, because nature needs all the help it can get. It needs you.

CHAPTER TEN

Wayfinding

When American Prairie's Wildlife Restoration Manager, Daniel "Danny" Kinka, was in college in Florida, having always been fascinated with people and cognition, he majored in psychology thinking that one day he'd become a child psychiatrist. But after a few years of study, Danny discovered he wasn't attracted to that field, and so he tried a new track: abnormal psychology, which seemed to suit his fascination with the complex human behaviors associated with mental disorders.

After obtaining his bachelor's degree, Danny entered a graduate program in Virginia to pursue a master's degree in psychology, where he loved the rigorous neurological research that matched his interest in hard science. But something gnawed at him: Outside of teaching, he couldn't see any practical application for his neuroscience research. Furthermore, he was repelled by a career lifestyle that, because of the need to control all environmental variables, required working in dim, windowless and sterile laboratory environments. Still, he persevered in the subject matter he assumed would be his career.

One day, Danny felt like he was suffocating in his lab, which reminded him of a sensory deprivation tank. Seeking fresh air, he decided to test the building's second floor hallway exit door, where a sign read "Do Not Open. Fire Alarm Will Sound." Curious, he opened it a crack. No alarm went off.

Instead, like Alice going through the looking glass, he stepped out onto the roof where he was overwhelmed by the campus's expansive vista of beautiful plants, trees, and other foliage, all under a clear blue sky. While breathing in fresh air that carried the scent of flowers, grass, and musty oaks, he felt alive again. Flooding back into his mind were the best memories of his youth, when he spent countless hours outdoors with his family exploring inland waterways by canoe and searching for wildlife. Danny found an old wooden classroom desk and chair and lugged them onto the flat roof, which now became his makeshift office where he would write his thesis.

He also underwent an internal transformation. The fragmented interests that had been swirling in his consciousness for the past few years—his fascination with human beings, penchant for hard science, and the love of outdoors and wildlife—began to coalesce in his brain. He was becoming clearer on the distinction between what was important to him and what wasn't. Still, psychology was his intended career in some form or other.

That summer, Danny's parents invited him to join them for a few days in Shenandoah National Park; he gladly accepted. While hiking, Danny met a young woman who'd just landed a job as a park ranger. He was struck by the utter pleasure she took in her work—being outdoors all day, leading interpretive walks with visitors, getting them excited about the natural world—even though she was likely making a meager income. He realized he wanted to one day have a job that he relished as much.

After getting his master's degree, Danny headed out west and ended up near Jackson Hole, Wyoming, where he applied for a job at Grand Teton National Park as an assistant in a study about wolves, a role for which he was completely unqualified. Danny knew nothing about wolves; furthermore, the role required backcountry skiing ten to fifteen miles a day, five days per week, to cover the large study area looking for wolf tracks.

Having grown up in Florida, Danny had never been on skis before, nor had he ever done any backcountry field research.

Still, after much lobbying, Danny convinced the hiring supervisor to give him a chance, and eventually he became skillful at all of the requirements. He lived in Park Service-provided housing with a group of others his age, also making very little money, but having a ball skiing all day to gather data on wildlife and relaxing together in the local bars come evening.

After three field seasons of work, realizing how much he liked working outdoors, Danny learned of a Ph.D. program at Utah State University focused on wildlife and the emerging field of Human Dimensions of Ecology. Danny enrolled and began a study on how livestock producers could use specially bred dogs as a nonlethal way to help prevent predator conflicts with their livestock. Although his goal of becoming a university professor was slowly losing its appeal, Danny felt the first inkling of a possible match between his interests in people, hard science, wildlife, and nature. As months and years went by, while he had no idea what career might miraculously include all of these things, he could feel the rich combination of interests starting to morph into an outright passion.

As he was completing his PhD in 2017, out of the blue, a friend told him about a position in Montana with the American Prairie. Danny had no idea what American Prairie was, but the job sounded like an excellent match for his interests, so he applied. We liked him, and we hired Danny shortly before his thirty-second birthday. At thirty-seven, he became our Senior Wildlife Restoration Manager, which also included working with a team that preserves wild species by helping ranchers coexist with them through our Wild Sky program. Now he is Director of Rewilding. He works with our science partner, the Smithsonian's National Zoo and Conservation Biology Institute, using both hard research and socio-ecological theory to help inform strategies to build what will one day be the largest wildlife reserve in the Lower 48.

Danny is grateful that he gave himself the time to identify his true interests through years of trial and error, rejecting what he assumed was his future as a neuroscientist professor in academia. "It took a lot of time, work, and reflection to identify my true interests," he says, "but once I did, an opportunity presented itself that I might have missed had I not embarked on that long discovery process. Now I get to live out my passion most every day!"

—

This chapter is not about how to land a job. It's about creating a situation where you are truly engaged in your work because it matches your current interests and values and, through your work, you have a chance to create lasting change that makes the world a better place. You can increase your chances of doing both at the same time, no matter how old you are and no matter where you are in your career.

It is also—and this is not insignificant—about taking the risk to test societal-expectations; to open doors that have signs on them warning, "Do Not Open. Alarm Will Sound."

A few years ago, I was asked by my friend Chris Johns, the former editor-in-chief of *National Geographic* magazine, to be a guest virtual speaker for his environmental journalism class at the University of Montana in Missoula. Chris was hoping I could tell his graduate students about my varied experiences with journalists throughout my seventeen years as president at American Prairie.

I explained to the group that I generally interacted with journalists maybe eight or ten times per year, perhaps over time totaling over one hundred interactions with national and international newspapers, television, magazines, podcasts, and other mediums. Midway through our allotted time, I was surprised by a question that shifted the conversation to something completely different. A young man asked, "As we get closer to graduation, we're all being told that we should find and then pursue our passion in life now. It's an intimidating challenge! But you seem to have pulled it off over two very different and long-term careers. What can you tell us about discovering your passion and finding a job that matches it?"

The ensuing discussion was quite lively, and after the class wrapped up, the same young man mentioned that he and several of his classmates were hoping I might meet with them again to keep talking about the topic. I agreed to do so. I then started polling other young people, including my daughter Siri, who was twenty-seven at the time. She agreed that many of her friends were determined to find a meaningful career they were passionate about, but many were struggling with how to go about it. Talking with still more people about this topic, I noticed it's clear that this challenge is common for people at any age.

Here's what I now tell people when I'm asked about finding meaningful work: First, you have to devote sufficient time to truly understand your interests. This is most likely to happen through years of deliberately widening and diversifying your experiences, which can include being exposed to different people and cultures, reading broadly across a range of topics, getting more formal education (if that is available to you), and, if possible, trying a wide variety of jobs and hobbies. While doing all this, you will zero in on your interests sooner and more accurately if you are consistently reflecting upon and keeping track of your thoughts and feelings.

You may think I am mostly talking about the classic stage of one's early to mid-twenties when some people are working hard to try to get to know more about who they really are and who they want to be. Sure, but I also did it for a second time—for nearly four years—in my late thirties and early forties. And I know others who have done it even later in life.

Over the last twenty years I have been asked countless times, "Have you always been a prairie fanatic?" No, I have not.

It began by accident when, having just turned forty, I happened to meet two people, Curt Freese and Steve Forrest, while they were working with the WWF trying to start a project to rewild a portion of the northeastern Montana grasslands. Initially, I was not at all captivated by the idea. Having been exposed to the area since the 1960s, in my mind the vast region was largely empty except for a lot of barbed wire fences and cows.

But Curt and Steve explained the deeper history of the area, which I'd never been taught about in Montana public schools—specifically, the fairly recent wholesale slaughter and eradication of the area's fauna, including tens of thousands of bison as well as all the grizzly bears, wolves, elk, bighorn sheep, and countless other critters.

Intrigued, I read every book and article Curt and Steve recommended about the lives and habits of pronghorn, cougars, grassland birds, prairie dogs, and the complex ecological system that had existed there for thousands of years.

As a result of looking at something I'd been familiar with all my life from a new angle, over time the idea of restoring that entire ecosystem evolved from a passing interest into deep-seated passion. It was an unexpected accident that resulted from me being curious, talking as often as possible with highly informed people, working hard to identify my current interests, and making the effort to look at things in a new way. And this was all happening generally around my fortieth birthday.

Over the next year and a half, I started imagining how it would feel to have a role in its restoration: I tried to visualize many generations of people coming to visit a transformed landscape, witnessing vast, unmolested populations of wild species that had returned in huge numbers for the first time in centuries. I discovered that, for me, meaningful and important meant helping to right a wrong that had been done by humans to wildlife and producing something of value regarding nature that could be enjoyed by people now and long after I was gone.

—

Like many people in their early to mid-twenties, I was adamant that when I got a "real job" I would be doing something that greatly interested me. I didn't want to be pushed into a career because it was well-paying, because it was expected of me, or because society deemed it worthwhile. I learned in my psychology classes that many young adults, as much as they might like to do otherwise, bow to societal norms when pursuing careers, particularly given the enormous pressure to not fall behind. Psychological research suggests that, for some people, ignoring or subordinating your true interests and passions to choose a more traditional vocation can over time result in malaise, drudgery, and depression. I tried to resist that natural tendency to want to fit in, at least while I was figuring out my interests.

In my early twenties, I studied the theories and practices of authors, therapists, philosophers, and poets who were resolute about getting to know themselves. Trying to emulate people who were well known at the time like Hermann Hesse, William Blake, T.S. Eliot, Dr. Wayne Dyer, Carlos Castaneda, Thich Nhat Hanh, and others, I journaled steadily, wrote letters about my thoughts to family and friends, and entered therapy for the first time. I also read extensively about how to minimize the distracting, sometimes negative voices in my head telling me I was lazy, inattentive, not particularly smart, and perhaps incapable of attaining my dreams.

Slowly—over some years—my interests became clearer. As I noticed where my mind went naturally in my free time, I found I was fascinated by the human brain, what motivates us to make good and bad decisions, and how we often get tripped up by our fears and anxieties. I became particularly interested in how—much as we would like to believe otherwise—we unconsciously draw heavily on our upbringing and local culture to form our lifelong beliefs and worldviews.

I slowly realized I was interested in learning more about and working with people—but how? I resisted the idea of becoming a therapist because I didn't have the discipline nor patience to sit still indoors all day. I wanted to focus on action—the parts of our psyche that inspire us to tackle sometimes intimidating yet meaningful challenges. With William Glasser, Carl Rogers, Abraham Maslow, and others as influences, this kernel of interest would later become a key aspect of Catalyst Consulting's mission, and years later, also of American Prairie's.

WHAT LIGHTS YOU UP?

Over the years I've learned that it's always helpful to mull over provocative questions in different environments, during different experiences, and while in different moods. Here are just a few questions that helped me during my twenties, thirties, and forties. The overlap and redundancy—the same question is repeatedly asked in slightly different ways—are intentional and can help you arrive at clearer answers.

- Setting aside what others expect of you, what sorts of things are you more than just casually interested in, as impractical as they might seem?

- If you set aside the assumption that making a career out of your interests requires getting an expensive and time-consuming advanced degree, what would you *really* love to do?

- What do you love doing so much that you'd do it for free?

- What skills have others noticed in you that might be important to remember and consider applying more consciously somehow?

- What things have you or others noticed in you that you are actually good at, at which you are naturally competent, or at least it seems to come easier to you than for many other people?

- What activities make you lose track of time?
- What topics or ideas do you love thinking about, and about which you can talk for hours?

Write down your answers. Talk about them with others. As you improve at answering these questions, over time a deeper understanding of your current interests and maybe even some passions will emerge and evolve. Keep them to review later—in a few days, or when you feel compelled to return to the questions years down the road.

It can be challenging to start and stick with this type of process, and there are different methods for this type of introspection. But I find putting thoughts in writing yields rewards. Journaling most days, which I'll touch on more later, is particularly useful for me. Tenzin Gyatso, the current Dalai Lama, recommends lists as a critical component to attaining happiness:

> *"It is quite simple. In addition to cultivating compassion and altruism, you need to train your mind for happiness. To begin, you make two lists. The first contains all the things that you feel lead to happiness for you. The second list is all the things that you believe contribute to your suffering. Then you commit to steadily reducing thoughts and activities that lead to your suffering while trying each day, week, and month to bring into your life those things that you know feed your happiness."*

He suggests that many people who claim they want happiness will not follow this advice. "In fact," he says, "most people won't even take the time to create the two lists!"

Figuring out your own interests and passions works the same way. It requires being organized in your approach and committing to long-term attention on the subject.

"Sean," you're probably asking, "'you're saying I need to become a nerd in this area and spend years cogitating about my experiences, feelings, and thoughts in order to discover some true interests and passions?"

Exactly.

—

MANY PEOPLE wrestle with finding a decent job that provides a comfortable living, much less finding the right time to ditch that job for one that they could become truly passionate about.

I first started thinking seriously about the "when" question in my mid-twenties, a year or so before graduating college. This was before I'd traveled extensively or began a string of eclectic jobs in restaurants, hotels, construction, and on farms. Still, I knew I wanted a career that matched my interests, but I also tried to be patient—and thus began a years-long investigative journey of getting to know myself better.

I took on a variety of odd jobs, both during college and afterward, partly for the money, but also to meet interesting people and to gain a broader perspective. For example, bartending at the Eagles Club in Bozeman until two in the morning on weeknights while in college didn't do much for my grade point average, but accumulating countless hours listening to and talking with its wide range of customers made me realize that Montana's culture was not nearly as homogenous as I'd assumed. Another job helped illuminate an interest I still hold today: I discovered helping others find purpose and satisfaction in life while doing summer work for Bozeman's Human Resource Development Council and learning about the extraordinarily difficult issues facing at-risk teenagers.

In my third year at Montana State University, my parents ended their financial support, as we had planned, so I took out a series of short-term loans each semester to pay for my tuition and books, working many evenings and weekends to pay them off before the next semester. But when school debt finally got ahead of me, I was barred from attending classes until I paid them off and had to forgo one spring semester to make some money—fast. One friend suggested heading to Alaska to work on salmon boats as some of our friends had done. Another suggested the oil rigs in the Bakken oil fields of western North Dakota. The latter being the closer option, I headed out in my 1971 Ford Falcon and spent the better part of a week driving hundreds of miles of gravel roads in the oil patch, stopping at rig after rig, asking for work.

Despite my lack of experience, I landed a roughnecking job with Westbourne Drilling, making what was to me the incomprehensible high wage of $100 per day (roughly $330 in today's dollars) and another $150 with overtime. We worked six days on, two days off, rotating each week from the day, evening, and graveyard shifts in western North Dakota's high desert, just north of Teddy Roosevelt National Park.

In the middle of one night, during a downpour, we took cover into a small, steel box high up on the rig platform where the driller stood monitoring the rig's hydraulics. After an hour or so of sporadic banter, on a whim I asked the group: "How much money would you have to save to finally get to do what you really want to do beside this? And what, exactly, *do* you really want to do?"

My coworkers sat in their damp, greasy coveralls, quietly staring at the opposite wall, sipping coffee, and munching donuts. Finally, each in turn said they hadn't thought about those questions but figured they would get to it once they had enough money to quit the rigs. A few decades later, during countless fundraising trips to New York City for American Prairie, I spoke with many twenty-something professionals working for Wall Street firms who had a similar philosophy. A typical response was "I'm only working in finance for a few years until I have enough money saved up to do what I really want. I just don't know what that is yet." Unsurprisingly, many of them were still there—in the oil patch and on Wall Street—years later, primarily defining success by continual pay increases.

My eclectic experiences, from rigging to fundraising to facilitating strategic planning sessions, have made me realize surprisingly few people take the time to think through what they truly want in life, what their true interests are, and in turn, what they might want to do as a vocation. As a result, they stay—for far longer than they'd intended—in jobs they once swore were only temporary.

My time in the oil patch netted me a lot of money, but more importantly it inspired me to step up my efforts to expand my experiences, so I took on other jobs, traveled extensively outside the US, and tried to learn more about myself and my interests. All this added breadth and dimension to my self-knowledge.

Not everyone agreed this was a wise course. My dad and other adults predicted I'd fall behind if I didn't get back on track with a "real" job. Other folks said the same thing when I left Catalyst in my late thirties and deliberately allowed myself a number of years to better understand my interests during that phase of my life. Yet I can honestly say I've never felt behind in my adult life and would not trade those accumulated, extended "interest and passion" discovery periods for anything.

Sometimes Life is Like Running the Hash

In the fall of 1983, while exploring Southeast Asia, Kayla and I were traveling through the hot, humid jungles of southern Java, where we met some expats from Australia, France, and the US. Each month they gathered in some fresh, unfamiliar area of the jungle to participate in a traditional running pastime known around the globe as the Hash House Harriers. One day they invited us to join in.

Hash runs (at least the Indonesian variety) vary in length

depending on the environment they're held in. First, the "hare"—usually someone in excellent shape who knows the territory—takes off about fifteen minutes before the crowd of forty to sixty runners is released. She carries with her a satchel of paper confetti and drops handfuls of it here and there to lightly mark the trail. She also diabolically lays false trails two or three hundred yards in length. When you haven't seen confetti for a while—and find yourself deep in the jungle surrounded by giggling local children jumping up and down and pointing in multiple directions to throw you off—you know you've been had, and you must stumble your way back to the main route. An hour or so after the start, the mud-splattered, sweaty, and wheezing runners arrive at the "end," which is an opening in the jungle marked by the presence of large beer trucks with kegs of cold Bintang beer on their tailgates. The exhausted runners grab mugs of beer as they laugh, sing drinking songs, and tell stories from the trail.

I have often thought back to this experience as an unusually apt metaphor for life. Unlike a more traditional footrace, both the nature of the trail and the finish line are unknown at the start. To the casual observer, it can appear inefficient and messy. Metaphorically, you can't get too bummed out when you have enthusiastically run down the trail of one of your interests only to later find it sputtering and diminishing in intensity. That's just how life goes. You must turn around and try to find your way back to the main trail. Yes, it can look unproductive to an outsider, but if you're paying close attention, you're learning important lessons about yourself.

During my late 1990s semi-sabbatical from Catalyst and a few years before I settled on my new path at American Prairie, I became involved in something call the Entrepreneurs Foundation (EF). Based in Silicon Valley, EF was started by Gib Myers, who thought up the idea following a highly successful thirty-year career in venture capital. Through EF, he hoped to entice early-stage companies to give back philanthropically both financially and through volunteering to their communities before they became successful. He knew many companies find it hard to adopt this altruistic ethic once they have gone public and then become hyper-busy maintaining their financial success.

Gib called me one day asking for my help in scaling up his idea. EF had already brought on thirty member companies, but Gib was shooting for hundreds more. I loved the concept as well as the chance to work with him. One thing led to another, and in addition to coaching Gib and some of EF's employees on scale-up strategies, I agreed to take on the writing and publishing of EF's newsletter to their member companies. I called it *The Venture Philanthropist.* In theory, it all seemed like a terrific fit for my interests. I liked the idea of inspiring businesspeople to do more for their communities, plus I could research, write, and assemble it at home. It felt like an amazing new opportunity—until it didn't.

The job became drudgery once I ventured beyond the initial writing and layout. I didn't like editing and assembling the newsletter or keeping an accurate database for distribution. I tried to nurture my interest in the undertaking, but even though every condition for a very cool assignment seemed to be in place, my energy fell flat. Slightly confused and a little embarrassed, I relinquished the role, turned around, and searched for the confetti that would take me back to the main trail. American Prairie happened not long afterward.

This may happen to you more than once. Maybe it already has. Budget for it psychologically. Become the kind of person who actually follows an interest long enough to see where it might lead. Nurture it carefully through reading, viewing it from different angles, talking to others, and simply trying it out. Get your hands (and the rest of your body) good and muddy. Try to have some fun in the process and don't beat yourself up for spending time on something that ends up being a dead end. Don't listen to others who say you are wasting time or being unproductive.

Engaging in a quest to home in on your interests takes time and persistence. If you devote the time to making this style of hunting a habit, you may well find one or more true passions.

Get Clear on Your Interests

It can be really challenging to carve out large chunks of time to explore your interests when engaged in a high-pressure job or buried in demanding school commitments. This can be particularly true for many folks who feel as if their worth is doubted if they're not being hyper-productive and chronically overscheduled. Often real courage and thoughtful planning is required to extract yourself from this mindset and to give yourself the time needed to discover unexpected, previously unknown aspects of yourself.

As one example, I came up with the conviction to start a new business not at a desk, but while sitting on a beach in Thailand. I'd financed my portion of the trip by first working six months as a carpenter and handyman in Washington, DC, and getting free rent and board by being a live-in nanny to a five-year-old boy.

In 1983, Kayla and I wandered throughout Southeast Asia for five months. Like other young travelers at the time, we easily managed to live—collectively—on ten dollars per day for food, ground transport, and lodging. (That equates to about $33 dollars in 2025 currency, though some relative costs have changed.)

This being 1983 (zero emails, texts, or social media), we had limited means to communicate with others back home. With the exception of sending a few handwritten letters to our families, we happily resigned ourselves to being completely out of touch with just about everyone for nearly half a year. The spaciousness these conditions allowed for in our minds was marvelous.

The idea for a new kind of organizational development

business coalesced in my brain toward the end of our trip, in what was then the tiny, sleepy enclave of Ko Samet. The idea—which eventually resulted in Catalyst Consulting—almost certainly would never have come together had we not spent those months traveling far outside the typical rhythm, fast pace, and often intense pressures of American society.

You may be thinking, "That's great, Sean, but many people don't have the luxury of embarking on months and months of international travel." Ok, but carving out significant time away from the rat race can take different forms. I had to keep working three days per week myself in my late thirties while simultaneously stepping back to consider what I wanted in my next phase of life. But consider this: The more time you take for yourself, the better quality your next career choice may be. At the very least it may simply mean taking—for a good long stretch of time—a lower paying, but far less stressful job that just covers the bills but affords you the time and headspace to thoughtfully contemplate your next move.

What if You Have No Applicable Degrees or Formal Experience?

You likely don't need an advanced degree to secure a wonderfully rewarding and valuable role. When I joined American Prairie, I only had a bachelor's in psychology from an inexpensive public college and a previous career in Silicon Valley where I learned about assembling small organizations and how to get people to coalesce around a shared vision. At the time of this writing, less than 20 percent of American Prairie's employees—including the CEO, CFO, and most senior managers—have previous academic or professional backgrounds in wildlife conservation. If you're passionate about the mission and can bring some relevant skills to the party, it's likely that soon after joining a nature preservation-type organization, you will be able to continue to learn and grow indefinitely from within the organization.

When it comes down to choosing something that aligns with your identified interests, how do you make that choice with confidence knowing it's the best one? There isn't only one perfect answer—for you, for me, for any of us. There isn't just one "right" organization or opportunity. In my case, Catalyst Consulting and American Prairie both felt like truly important work—and they were—and yet they were extremely different from each other. But even after realizing how important American Prairie felt, I continued to travel around the world, which introduced me to many other projects that could also have been my life's work.

Forty miles off the north coast of Honduras on a visit to the Bay Islands, I learned about an effort there to protect more than twenty-five miles of spectacular coral reef adjacent to the island of Roatán. As I returned there numerous times over the years, it occurred to me that under different circumstances, I could have just as easily lived there and become a crusader for marine biodiversity instead of wildlife on Montana's grasslands.

If you've done your homework, meaning you have become much clearer on your true interests, you'll likely know a good thing when you see it. It does not have to be the one perfect opportunity. Resist stressing out about making the "best" choice. Just make a choice from one of many terrific things that you might imagine yourself doing. The critical thing then becomes focusing on how you will pull out all the stops and do absolutely everything within your power to make it a good decision.

As the psychologist Abraham Maslow was nearing the end of his life, he summed up his seminal research, the hierarchy of needs theory, by remarking that the only happy people he knew were those highly engaged in something they considered important. That, Maslow felt, was the only universal truth for his self-actualizing subjects.

I have frequently sat alone on the prairie contemplating our organization's end vision; a five thousand-square-mile reserve where wild nature is the top priority. I see it being surrounded by tens of millions of acres of the Northern Great Plains largely devoted to for-profit industry, but where people are much more amenable to having fabulously abundant wildlife as compared to past decades. I might be watching a pronghorn buck frantically trying to keep his harem of females from being poached by an interloper buck, or I might be observing a gorgeous ferruginous hawk sitting quietly on a large glacial erratic while taking a break from her morning hunt. I think about how one day this muti-million-acre wildlife reserve will once again hold an astounding array of native wild species. And I imagine that scene containing people who, in various places on the reserve, are enchanted with the opportunity to observe wildlife that is fairly unconcerned with human presence because humans are not experienced as a threat, except at very close distances.

Looking further afield, I think about species like elk, moose, grizzlies, lions, and wolves plying the corridors between Montana's Rocky Mountain front range, the Greater Yellowstone Ecosystem, and American Prairie, ensuring the continued genetic diversity of all manner of terrestrial species for hundreds of years into the future.

Contemplating this scene always helped me stay positive through those trying early years and kept me energized and optimistic for the nearly two decades I was directly involved. I could have chosen a variety of careers back in 2001 at forty years old that might have been far easier to get off the ground. But wildlife conservation fit my interests perfectly, and my skills were a good fit for what was needed to move the project forward; it seemed achievable, and I believed that the mission was important and meaningful. Those conditions were enough for me to give it a shot.

Start with allowing yourself more time than you might have ever envisioned to discover your interests and how to apply them to a future you feel is truly important. Allow yourself some fun on this quest. Stay open to being surprised. Make it a long-term project and keep at it. It'll come, and down the road, you may find yourself in a more exciting and fulfilling situation than you ever thought possible.

CHAPTER ELEVEN

Purpose and Values

Most of us hope to find satisfaction and meaning in our careers—and rightfully so, given how much time and energy we spend at work and working.

Finding purpose, personally and professionally, is complicated. Not only does it look different for each of us, but it can be hard at times to truly escape the daily demands of juggling responsibilities, relationships, obligations, opportunities, and other stressors on our emotions, time, and brainpower. Getting clear with yourself about your purpose takes time—and it takes making time—but doing so can act as a powerful stabilizing force over years and even decades.

For those of us who aspire to help make the world a better place, our ability to do so successfully is helped a great deal by taking the time to determine two key concepts: your current purpose and your current values.

Think of your purpose as describing what this current or soon-to-be phase of your life is about—or what you want it to be about. Your values are a customized set of principles you hope to live by during that phase. If your purpose is your North Star, pointing the way to your desired future, your values are how you live your life on your way to that destination. But here's the reason it actually matters to stop and spend some time clearly defining this stuff: When you get it right, this list of values helps you live your life in a way that makes it more likely to get to that destination.

Over the past thirty-five years, when updating my own purpose and values—and periodically helping others figure out theirs—I begin with the following four questions that help get me in the right mindset:

What are the few things that truly interest me these days?

If I had the chance to change the world for the better, how would I most like to do it?

What are my top five priorities in this current phase of life?

What overarching principles are helping to guide my decisions and actions during this time in my life?

Try these yourself. Take some time to think about your answers. In combination, your answers can be a doorway into thinking more richly and clearly about how to pursue the life you want to lead.

Personally, I think knowing one's fundamental purpose that will last a lifetime is rare. For most of us, it's more common to have different ways to define our purpose during different phases in life. (I've experienced five distinct phases of my life so far. If I'm fortunate to live a while longer, I may undergo a few more.) But how do you determine what period of life you are in so you can articulate your purpose to match it?

We measure the phases of our lives in many ways: specific milestones—getting that big promotion, moving somewhere new; the passage of time itself—your early twenties, thirties, middle-fifties; and, sometimes, by things coming to an end—a major breakup, or your children moving out of the house to start lives of their own.

One of my longer phases lasted a dozen years, from about twenty-eight to forty. The previous phase lasted seven years when I was single, exploring my interests and expanding my options. That twenty-eight-to-forty phase was an eventful one: Kayla and I moved from Seattle to Santa Cruz. We got married. We had two kids. We cofounded an entrepreneurial business and spent fourteen-plus years helping to grow it. In my early thirties, I crafted a purpose description to try to capture the basic elements of this phase. Here's what I wrote:

My Purpose: From 1987 until…?
- To learn how to thrive, versus feeling overwhelmed, within all the big choices I've recently made.

- In my marriage, to learn how to best contribute to a healthy, constantly evolving, and mutually satisfying relationship and learn to be the kind of partner that helps Kayla feel like she made a good choice in deciding to be with me.

- To learn how to be a good dad. (I am curious about what exactly that means in these times and am currently nervous about learning it on the fly.)

- To help Catalyst Consulting become a highly valued, sought-after provider of the services we are offering now and those we'll offer in the future.

This list was far different than that of my twenties, and very different from the following two phases as well. Many years later, around 2001, another new phase began, partly centered on the start of American Prairie. I wrote this new purpose around my forty-first birthday:

Purpose: 2001 to 2010 onward
- To make time to enjoy family life in Montana, including getting our two children out into nature as often as possible.

- To help grow and improve my marriage during this unusually busy time through good communication and demonstrating improved, more consistent attentiveness, appreciation, and affection for her.

- To apply my background in building and fine-tuning organizations to successfully launch American Prairie.

- To learn as much as possible about northeastern Montana's past—from sixteen thousand years ago through today—regarding its wildlife and human history, to help me be a more thoughtful and effective leader of American Prairie.

DRAFT YOUR PURPOSE

Feel free to craft your own list in a set of bullet points or in a one- or two-paragraph narrative. What's important is that it serves as a brief, high-level summary of your life, or what you want your life to be during this particular phase. Here are some additional questions that you might find helpful as you are attempting to craft a purpose:

- What phase of life are you in right now? How would you summarize it for someone else?

- Are you on the cusp of a major ending or turning point of some kind?

- Are you in a state of uncertainty where something significant has ended but a distinct next phase of life has not materialized?

- Does it feel like you may be about to embark on—or are already engaged in—some kind of significant new beginning?

Based on your answers, what do you see as your fundamental purpose right now? Once you get your draft purpose on paper, review it often. Try to further shape and improve it each time you revisit it. As simple as it may feel, you will find comfort in having it explicitly articulated.

If you asked a number of people, "What phase of life do you see yourself being in right now?" many people will respond, "Good question. I haven't thought much about that."

So, think about it. Your current purpose, especially once it is coupled with your values, will help produce more clarity, calm, and steadiness in your life.

THE FIRST time I understood the importance of my personal values was by accident. My mother was raised Presbyterian, and my father Catholic. When they decided to marry in 1951, both sets of their parents refused to attend the wedding if was to be held in the other side's church, so my parents eloped and were married by a justice of the peace. Perturbed by this event, as well as what he viewed as other rigid and illogical doctrines, my dad later disavowed the Catholic Church. Rather than listening passively to a sermon, he began taking his spiritual inspiration from nature, which he found in abundance in the wilds of the early 1960s Montana.

My mother loved nature as well, but she felt my sisters and I should, at least from a cultural-awareness standpoint, have some basic familiarity with the Christian faith and the values it espoused. Though it would cut into our weekend camping time, dad reluctantly agreed to let me and my sisters attend the Presbyterian Church and Sunday school until we were suitably oriented, provided he didn't have to go with us.

During my short, organized religion experience, I learned that I was supposed to be God-fearing and accept unquestioningly the Ten Commandments as my own personal values. I had a hard time with that expectation since most of them started with the stern admonition "Thou shalt not..." followed by, I assumed, "...or you'll be in a heap of trouble."

Two years later, with my dad's patience wearing thin at the lack of family camping time, Mom figured we'd acquired a decent religious foundation, our churchgoing tapered off, and our family's weekend outings resumed. I was happy to be sprung from those ten draconian values that had been imposed upon me, and it was none too soon: I'd fallen for my lovely and intoxicating fragrance-wearing second-grade teacher, Mrs. Trask. While her husband was technically not my neighbor, I was indeed coveting his wife, putting me in clear violation of the Tenth Commandment.

My second experience with imposed institutional values came soon after the end of my churchgoing. I joined the Cub Scouts to learn outdoor skills, make new friends, and try to fill my official Cub shirt with sewn-on merit badges. Our first mandatory commitment was that a scout should always be "trustworthy, loyal, helpful, friendly, courteous, kind, obedient, cheerful, thrifty, brave, clean, and reverent." These felt more reasonable and potentially attainable than the Ten Commandments. My parents had already hammered into me the courteous and kind bits. Bravery often eluded me—but I was only eight. My mom's standard for my hygiene was "clean enough," so that was easy. I had no idea what *reverent* meant, no matter how many times it was explained to me, so I let it go.

But I eventually drifted away from scouting—along with unquestioning allegiance to all of those values. And in the following years, I neglected to replace those Cub values with anything better I could call my own.

When I was in my twenties, I finally realized that it was up to me to choose and assemble my own list of values—an insight that hit me while taking college courses in behavioral psychology and social and political philosophy. I learned that personal values are, at their most basic level, the ideas and principles that are most important *to you*. They can motivate you and help to inform your decisions. Without a clear understanding of, and close familiarity with, your own values, your decision-making and emotions are too easily influenced by outside forces.

Spending time on certain kinds of questions can help people to identify and articulate their values; I've included my initial answers as a twenty-year-old (as best I can recall) to one such set of questions below:

Q: If you had the power to do so, what few things would you most like to change about the world?

A: I would make it more normal and important in society to talk about what I'm learning in psych classes: What makes humans tick and why we are so attracted to a sense of belonging—to fit in—to being seen as valuable to our group or community.

Q: When you read or watch the news, what kinds of stories bother or irritate you the most?

A: When people criticize others who are taking the risk to make things better. I dislike news that are based on cynicism and overhyped negativity.

Q: What kind of current events or news stories make you hopeful or optimistic?

A: When I learn about individuals or small groups of modest backgrounds and means, devising and implementing solutions no one else saw as possible.

Q: What would you most like to change about yourself if you could?

A: I'd like to be thought of, by myself and others, as highly capable of making an important, positive difference in the world.

Q: What conditions are present when you are feeling good about yourself?

A: When I accomplish something that isn't easy for me to do and afterward, I feel better about my potential. And when I temporarily squelch the sometimes-negative voices in my head that undermine those good feelings and thoughts.

After thinking and journaling about my answers for a time, I was eventually able to articulate some, initial underlying list of values—and their accompanying definitions. At the time, this list fit me fairly well:

Innovation: Taking an intriguing, existing idea and successfully converting it from concept to reality.

Adventure: Shaking up my routine by spending time with new people, new readings, new places, and taking unusual jobs, all of which help to disrupt my sense of certainty about the world.

Optimism and Persistence: Staying enthused about the potential for an idea to work and sticking with the trial-and-error process long enough to give it a fair chance.

Finding Ways Forward: Taking the personal initiative to find a way forward to a better situation when I'm not content with my current circumstances.

First of all, I of course noticed that some of these values had not spontaneously appeared out of nowhere. They had the lingering aroma of much of what I'd been taught by both of my parents—separately and together—in unstructured ways. I also sensed at the time more potential values were floating just outside my peripheral vision, but this was a decent start. I was getting to know myself better. I began wondering: Why hadn't I done this earlier? Why hadn't somebody told me to do this sooner? Why isn't everyone taught to do this early in life?

Those college courses first inspired me to craft my own set of written values—and this slowly-growing list helped me begin to look at myself differently. I started thinking more about people who might help me to live in alignment with these values. I thought about what sorts of future jobs might do the same. By age thirty, my list was up to ten; in the years since, I've combined some, dropped others, and discovered more relevant ones.

But the most important thing—for me, and perhaps for

you—is the ongoing practice itself: simply know what your values are during different times in your life and keep them always on the front burner.

As a result, my values have—along with my purpose—been a steady force in every phase of my life. They serve the same function as the heavy keel on a sailing boat or ship. While the sometimes-raucous action is all happening topside, the keel lies invisible below the waterline, playing the critical role of keeping the boat relatively upright in choppy or some-times dangerous seas. Likewise, people are also often buffeted by unpredictable outside forces that contribute to stress, pres-sures, and debilitating strain. Based on my direct experiences over a decade and a half with Catalyst, I came to believe indi-viduals, and organizations, who commit to a well-designed set of values tend to suffer less emotionally, perform better, and often last longer at their chosen endeavors than people and organizations who don't.

Keep your list of values handy. When they are difficult to access, you're less likely to align them with your actions. One fellow I know keeps them on a three-by-five card in a front pocket of his pants. That's dedication! Another friend installed them as a screen saver on her laptop. Even though I have my current list well-memorized, I keep them in the Notes app on my iPhone so I can adjust them when needed.

When people ask how often to revisit their values, I suggest whatever works for you to make them a part of your thinking, emotions, and decision making. If you are just establishing a practice of having your values near, reviewing more often is better; maybe once or twice per week for fifteen minutes. Even-tually maybe twice per month. Then maybe once a month. You'll know.

—

In the early years at American Prairie, we had to make

many nerve-racking decisions. As mentioned, one was deciding to purchase our first property in 2004 when we had no money to do so. We devised a short-term loan arrangement with a willing lender, but we'd have to pay back one million dollars within twelve months. I had only the sketchiest of ideas of how we might accomplish that.

I'd already worked through plenty of business-school-type analyses of the situation. The conservative approach said this action wasn't worth the risk. The bold Silicon Valley approach said go for it. Needing to make a firm decision, I sat at home one morning contemplating the go- or no-go question. I pulled out the risk assessment tool, which I'd taught to clients and had used on myself many times over the previous fifteen years, and a blank sheet of paper, and started working through the tool's sequence of questions.

What is the best-case outcome I can imagine? If the best case occurred, what would I do next? These were easy enough to answer. What's the worst-case outcome I can imagine? That one felt so bleak that I almost pulled the plug right then. If the worst-case outcome occurred, how might I recover? At the moment I couldn't think of a way to recover if we defaulted on our first and only big loan short of closing our doors.

But my mood improved with the final questions: What do I honestly think might be the most likely outcome? My answers: Somewhere between the best case and worst case. We will probably find most of the money, but maybe not by the date it was technically due. The power of having the first property would increase confidence in our small list of potential donors which would then help us raise more money.

I then turned to my current list of ten values. Three jumped out immediately: optimism, innovation, and persistence. I felt an immediate change in the physical sensations of my body. There was some trepidation, sure, but there was more excitement. I realized that with enough determination and tenacity (persistence), creative thinking (innovation), and belief in myself to find a way forward (optimism), it was going to somehow turn out at least good enough. Though I couldn't yet see a clear path to getting this purchase done and paying the funds back on time, I felt confident we would somehow hack a path through the jungle and get where we needed to be. We went for it—and it worked.

Invoke Values Prior to Doing Something You'd Rather Not

I, or one of my colleagues, often used values to frame a conversation with an employee whose performance was sub-par and who needed to get back on track. We framed our conversations in these situations around their current struggles to uphold the values, such as teamwork, openness with respect, and execution. This often allowed the employee in question to identify new beneficial behaviors, but not always.

Some bosses might actually enjoy firing people. I'm not one of them. Unfortunately, having held various leadership positions over thirty-five-plus years, I had to do it many times, and I always felt uncomfortable. On one occasion, I was preparing to fire a top performer in terms of billable hours at Catalyst Consulting. I'd already helped verify the allegations of numerous female team members who reported him to be disrespectful, condescending, and dismissive toward them, and no amount of direct feedback had changed his behavior. Thirty minutes before our appointment, I sat down alone in a quiet conference room and reviewed our organization's values, one of which was "openness with respect," which he clearly had not followed. I also reviewed my own values, two of which at the time were courage and fairness. The session was difficult. He felt I was siding with what he called the "overly dramatic complainers" who were blowing things out of proportion. That dialogue only reinforced my belief we'd made the right decision.

As the adage goes, "Sometimes success in life can be measured by the number of uncomfortable conversations you're willing to have." Knowing your values well, and reviewing them before necessary but uncomfortable conversations, can help you perform better in these difficult moments.

Values, like interests, shift over time. We move, travel, switch jobs, learn new things. Relationships begin and change or come to an end. And occasionally, we encounter new people, books, ideas, places, or works of art that can shift—subtly or dramatically—how we look at the world.

Our values naturally evolve as we do. We rarely toss our values aside; rather, they are more likely to be gradually subsumed by newer ones. For example, while I was steadily reducing my hours at American Prairie toward the end of my time as a part of the staff, I noticed I was feeling less driven by my decades-long values of innovation and persistence. While these had been central to my success at Catalyst and American Prairie, once I was certain I was not going to start another enterprise, I felt less of a need to keep them in my core stable, even though I'm still an adherent to both.

Innovation and persistence were shifted to emeritus status, in favor of Essentialism. This happened as I began to think about my own mortality. Statistically, the average American male can expect to live around seventy-eight years. Mulling over the possibility of having just fifteen or so years left induced me to be more thoughtful about how I wanted to spend that time. I added Essentialism to my list and wrote a description of what the term meant to me.

Essentialism: This means asking myself, "Given the phase of life I am in, what really is essential today, this week, this month, and this year? What is not essential?" Essentialism means being aware of what I truly enjoy doing, and which people and experiences are most important to me now. It means choosing curiosity over certainty, engaging in some activities for the sheer pleasure of doing them, and attempting to eliminate or at least minimize most everything else.

The Struggle to Live in Accordance with Values Never Ends

In his book *Mastery,* George Leonard says we periodically experience distinct improvements or upward spikes in areas where we are trying to get better. This might include anything from painting with oils and swinging a golf club to learning to play bass guitar and trying to improve the quality of your close relationships. However, most of our time is spent between noticeable improvements, on long, flat plateaus where we continue practicing and trying, but don't immediately notice much advancement in skills or benefits. But Leonard says, we need to understand that while on those plateaus, really important micro-skills are accumulating beneath the surface. When they reach critical mass, we experience a noticeable bump up in competency, or returns on our efforts, and then we settle onto another, higher-level plateau for a while. So rather than feeling frustration, impatience, or malaise, we should believe that things are happening unseen beneath the surface and learn to love those plateaus while on them.

There have been times in my life when I struggled to live by a list of values, especially when I was in my mid-thirties with two preschool-aged children and in the early throes of an entrepreneurial start-up. I'd sometimes start my morning with coffee and a values review, but as the day's speed increased, I often neglected to think about them again or consider how they impacted my actions.

I don't recall a particular epiphany that caused me to shift my behavior but at some point, I recommitted to finding ten or fifteen minutes to meditate. No matter how crazy the day, I tried to devote the time to follow the well-known beginner's instructions: Just focus on in-and-out breaths and simply notice as much as possible about what was going on within me in that moment. Sure enough, those few minutes of stillness made a difference. I never achieved a blissful state of harmony in those intense years between 2001 and 2009 or so, but by mostly staying true to my new practice of daily meditation—an outcome of my mindfulness value at the time—I became conscious of my actions more frequently, and my relationships and decision-making improved.

The key here is to be awake enough to notice when you're off-centered, then to gently try to bring your attention and behaviors back in alignment with your purpose and your set of values. As George Leonard writes in *Mastery*, "Practice loving the plateau." The virtue and benefit are in the trying.

—

Remember, your current values should be the ones you decide are most important for this phase of your life. But values that have slipped off your core list are still important; they represent your evolution as a person. Honesty, fairness, innovation, optimism, humor, and tenacity are just a few examples of values that are no longer on my formal list. It doesn't mean I no longer care about or have moved on from honesty; just that it's no longer one of the most critical elements to guide me through this particular phase of my life.

And when you suspect you maybe need one of your older values to be back front and center for some reason, do it. Recently, as I worried frequently that too few people would be interested in this book, that maybe my views on life would be widely panned or publicly ridiculed, it occurred to me I needed to put courage back on my list of current values. I eventually settled on calm courage. It doesn't eliminate all my trepidation, but it helps a lot on some of my worst days.

CHAPTER TWELVE

Vision and Alignment

In such a complex world, it's only natural to wonder whether one person can affect any meaningful change. And, even if it's possible, thinking whether that person could possibly be me?

Over the course of my various careers, I have learned that one of the most effective ways to counter those doubts—personally and professionally—is through some structured planning and preparation. As I mentioned earlier, the Vision & Alignment (V&A) process we developed at Catalyst was the foundational framework for keeping our organization aligned at American Prairie.

I have found value in pursuing mastery of this process because many decades ago—after I'd first learned how to work with it—I noticed that when used at the personal level, it enhances one's sense of ability to influence outcomes. By this I mean the knowledge and belief that you can change and enhance your own life path, your thoughts, your behaviors—and the confidence that you can, in fact, handle a wide range of challenges.

As useful as this process has proven to be for teams and companies, the basic aspects of it were originally designed to benefit individuals; only later, with help from a number of colleagues, did we adapt it into an effective tool for helping organizations. At its most essential level, a Vision and Alignment plan works the same way in both scenarios: Once you get your personal Vision and Alignment process up and running, you'll feel a satisfying sense alignment between the sometimes-competing voices in your head.

As is often noted about the benefits of meditation, using this process helps you to feel far less fragmented and instead more integrated overall. You'll also learn to move beyond the tiresome oscillation you may experience when trying to decide whether to stay on your current course in life or pursue some significant changes. This oscillation usually involves back-and-forth movement between excitement about a potential new direction and feelings of hesitancy about not risking losing what you've worked hard to have already achieved. Those potential losses can include your current vocation, financial situation, relationships and certain aspects of your lifestyle. Using this V&A process will help reduce, or even eliminate, that oscillation.

So, I do think the process is vitally important, but I admit that learning to work it with for the first time can require considerable effort. It requires such effort not because it's hard to understand, but because it asks you some challenging questions that many people don't think about all that much. Answering those questions can take time, since the stakes are quite high; the focus is what you want the story of this phase--or the upcoming phase—of your life to be about.

You'll find it useful whether you are young and searching for a meaningful new job, or if you are decades into a career and looking to make a big change toward something like nature conservation, or anything else that feels compelling. And it will make the many choices you face on a daily basis feel like they are being made within a coherent context of your own design.

Over the past thirty-five years or so, I've honestly made this process a way of life of sorts, but you don't need to go quite that far in order to gain an enormous amount of clarity, direction, and confidence from your own V&A plan. This isn't just about strategy; it's about setting your own trajectory and taking control of your own unfolding story.

So, given all of that, this is probably the most important concept I can convey to you in this book.

As you begin, you first want to establish a stable foundation consisting of your current purpose and values. Next, you will define your first-draft set of compelling goals, the collection of which describes what you want in the future—your vision.

Your current reality is an honest assessment of where you are today, and your action plans will help you move toward the vision you have set for yourself.

The interplay of these five components—purpose, values, vision, current reality, and action plans—is what makes the process not just interesting, but actually effective and applicable to your everyday life.

As you begin assembling a V&A plan, keep this in mind: You also want your plans to be highly charged with energy. It's about feeling positive anticipation about moving toward your carefully constructed dreams associated with a particular phase of your life. In addition, once your journey is underway, it means feeling energized about incremental progress and the prospect of eventually fully realizing your vision.

The process of creating your V&A plan can become easier by using the visual template below. Most people find that keeping this visual in mind helps you to arrange your understanding of where you are now and where you hope to be in the future. When you complete the template, you will have an easy-to-grasp plan that will first create and then help maintain that feeling of energy described above.

If you are on the cusp of making a jump into conservation or another field that feels meaningful to you, aligning these five areas of your V&A plan is critical. Before you choose your new path, you'll need clarity on other aspects of your life, such as your relationships, your nonwork activities, your finances, and so on. Likewise, when you think about possible jobs such as conservation, you'll want to bounce those potential choices off your larger, comprehensive plan. This is exactly what I did just before finally choosing to go with American Prairie instead of one of the four other interesting vocations I was vetting at the time.

Lastly, if you are thinking of making some kind of move to another vocation, if you first get familiar with and become really good at working with these concepts at a personal level, you will be much better prepared in terms of skills and experience to deploy the same thinking at an organization level. This will be invaluable if your next role involves you being a leader in some capacity.

For now, getting started is all that matters.

YOUR VISION & ALIGNMENT PLAN

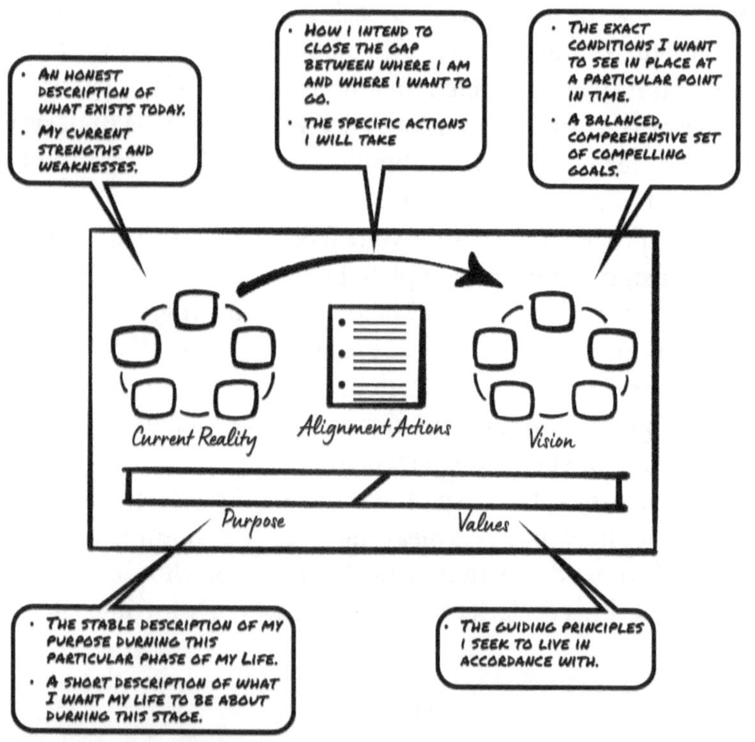

Step One: Begin by clearly articulating your current purpose and values.

Understanding your current purpose and current values provides stability and consistency—a preexisting foundation as you work though the rest of the V&A plan template. In contrast, your current reality, vision, and action plans in the template are the opposite of stability; together they tell a story about the movement from where you are now to where you hope to be.

Using some of the suggestions in the previous chapters, write down a reasonably good articulation of your purpose at this phase of life, as well as four to six core values or principles that you want to live by during this phase. Work them for a while until they feel fairly accurate, even if they could use some further editing later. "Pretty darn good" is fine for now.

Step Two: Current Reality and Vision

When working on both your current reality and your vision, it's helpful to arrange them in categories that apply equally well to both; it's simpler and more effective when you can draw apples-to-apples comparisons between these sections of your V&A plan—and between your own present and (potential) future.

Everyone comes up with their own custom categories. Select whatever feels right to you. Common ones include things like relationships, finances, career, mental/physical health, lifestyle, spirituality, and contribution to the world. Four to six categories are usually sufficient.

One benefit to this way of approaching this is that it forces you to develop and arrange your visionary goals in your desired proportions across all categories. It forces you to look at all the important areas of your life and think about what you really want in all those areas, rather than putting too much weight and emphasis on just your career, or another area.

—

Once you've chosen your categories, you can start articulating your current reality and the goals for your vision in each category. Working on them in either order is fine. Soon you'll be going back and forth between them as you try to fine tune the information and to begin building the tension between current reality and vision, so start on whichever side you like.

The objective in filling out the current reality side of the template is to accurately capture how things are presently going in each of your chosen categories. A collection of three to four statements about what is going well and what needs improvement or what is suboptimal in each of your categories will give you enough material to anchor this half of your plan.

The trick is to focus on what exists within your current reality, rather than why it exists. It can be tricky to separate the two, but here are some questions that can help.

What is going well in this phase of my life in each of these categories? What currently, in general, could be better or use improvement? What current conditions in my life—in each of these categories—feel less than optimal?

Write your answers out in full sentences, not just sentence fragments. It helps you to be clearer on what you feel is true.

For the vision side of the template, your aim is to specify what goalposts matter most for your future. The more precise you can be, the better: Specify clear conditions in each category that you really want to be true—but that are not true now—by a specified time in the future.

One last thing before you get started: Figure out the timeframe that you're picturing as you formulate your vision goals. Maybe you're thinking about this time next year, or maybe it feels more realistic to think about a four-year timeframe to move from one point to the other. The timeline can be short or long—as with everything else, this is your plan so it's up to you—but it's important that your goals, in all categories, should be scoped for that same future date.

I have probably done this process regarding my own life in excess of fifteen times in the past thirty years. I have found that about one and half years into the future is usually a good time-frame for me. Sometimes I go for two years into the future. Just allow yourself enough time that your goals are challenging to achieve and require some well-thought-out approaches, but you have sufficient time to achieve them. Pick a date close enough in the future that you feel slightly anxious about being able to achieve the goals you've set. Play with the date until it feels like it will keep your attention without feeling too unrealistic, scary, or debilitating.

As you draft goals in each category on the vision side of your template, remember:

- Write your goals as clearly as possible, in full sentences, and in the present tense, as if the condition already exists.

- Ensure each goal simply states what you want to achieve with no hint of how you intend to get there.

- Think carefully about the achievability of your goals within your chosen timeline. Is there too much pressure for this to be realistic? Too much time to keep the momentum? Adjust accordingly.

- The most important check: Ask yourself repeatedly, "Why do I want this goal?" Listen carefully to your answers and then use them to improve the goal to make it as on-target as possible.

Here is the reasoning for asking "Why Do I Want This Goal?" visionary goals are challenging to get right the first time around. For example, related to your work or vocation category, if you are hoping to move from a less-than-fulfilling career to something that feels more meaningful, you might first write the goal in your "work" category that you want to be true by two years from now like this:

"I've secured a job that pays just OK, but given it is in the world of nature conservation, at least it feels more aligned with my interests and most of my values as compared to my last job."

This first attempt is not bad; a complete sentence, in present tense that says what you want (sort of). But if you sit back and ask yourself, "Why do I want that?" then wait a moment or two, you'll discover helpful insights. Your answer in your head might be: "I want this because for too long I've done what others—including society at large—expect of me, or what I think I should do, not what I want to do. I want to wake up every morning excited about working on a mission I really care about, with people I feel lucky to be working with, and feeling that I may leave the world a better place."

With the answers to that "why" question still lingering in your mind, you review your first crack at that future goal and rewrite it something like this. (Again, this is stated as something you want to be true in two years.)

"I am very grateful for my career. It's a privilege to be a part of because I feel like I am indeed helping to make the world better through meaningful nature conservation. I feel certain that when I look back on it, this phase of my working life is likely to be the one in which I was most proud and found the most satisfying."

That's a little wordy, but it's better! So, you ask yourself again, "Why do I want that?" Once again, listen carefully to the voices in your head and see what you can learn to make your goal sharper and more inspiring. Your third attempt at the goal might be:

"Every day I feel grateful for my job, given I'm engaged with meaningful nature conservation, am helping to produce things that will last, and believe that one day I will look back on this period of my life with deep pride and satisfaction."

The goal may still need even more fine tuning, but with

each revision it is getting closer to describing what you really want. So, keep at this cycle until those voices in your head—and heart—answer the "Why do I want that?" question with, "Because that is absolutely, precisely what I want!"

If it feels really good to read it out loud to yourself, you are getting very close. That's how you craft high-quality visionary goals. It demands your attention. It can take a lot of time, but it's worth it.

Two or three well-crafted goals in each of your categories give you a collection of future conditions that comprise your whole vision. Importantly, you should have included goals in your categories that are not just about your vocation, because life is always about more than just our jobs.

Once you have a set of goals covering all categories, it is time to step back and take a look at how well the goals complement each other across your categories. Further tuning is usually required to make all your goals achievable in your chosen timeframe and to make sure that none compromise or hinder the achievement of any others. Achieving an elegant, complementary sense of integration and interdependency among all your goals will add power to your vision.

The more honest you are as you create a compelling vision and detailed description of your current reality, the more nerve-racking this is likely to feel. And I mean that literally. When you start to get it right, you're going to feel it in your body—and that's a very good sign indeed.

In many areas of our life, we often start with the easier stuff, and the same thing is true with any kind of intense introspection. We tend to begin by describing our current reality in a simple, straightforward way, and leave to the sides any elements of our lives that are messy, painful or seemingly unsolvable. This isn't some kind of willful self-deception, just the natural human tendency to keep ourselves safe and comfortable as long as we possibly can. When I talk about myself—in public, in therapy, or even with my closest friends—I'm am sometimes conscious of what I'm not saying (or in this case, not writing) at any given time; these tendencies don't just vanish because you're sitting down, writing out a V&A.

At various points in our lives, there are things we don't want to put down on paper, such as aspects of our current reality that we know we'll have to acknowledge (and, annoyingly, start to deal with) when we speak it out loud for the first time. Some dreams are so personal, so nascent and precious, that including them as part of your vision might feel genuinely terrifying. If we just leave it off, we're protecting ourselves from disappointment and heartbreak. But that very fear—that deep vulnerability and authentic passion—generates something else too, in all of us: a palpable sense of energy, our pent-up-for-too-long excitement. It's the best kind of ambition, mingled with anticipation and longing and hope.

It is well known that in art, music, films, books, and other forms of storytelling, skilled creators begin by envisioning how they want their finished product to look and feel. They focus on the reactions they hope their creation will provoke in their audience. Next, they contrast this final vision with where they are starting—an empty canvas, the first page of a screenplay, or a blank sheet of music. This continued, back-and-forth comparison between their current reality and their vision builds within them a feeling of tension, or stored energy. And the important part is this: as the tension builds, it spawns creativity which is directed at trying to relieve that tension. That's when the magic begins to happen.

As you may have learned if you've had a brief introduction to physics, all tension seeks resolution. Watch some YouTube videos of the standard twelve-bar blues. One reason this musical structure has persisted for over a hundred years is that it's among the simplest musical forms for building tension. It always resolves satisfyingly at the twelfth bar.

As human beings, we like it when everything from novels to films to musical riffs are resolved after a buildup of energy.

To get a sensual feel for this tension and resolution idea, think of what you experience during those long moments leading up to sexual orgasm. Tension can indeed be a desirable thing.

Unfortunately, many individuals' (and organizations') plans—even those packed with details—lack this kind of energy. It is often missing because people have never been taught about its power and value when trying to move oneself (or a group) forward toward a compelling vision. Like the artists mentioned above, as you get better doing the work—at repeatedly creating and then resolving that tension—you will far more often find yourself achieving your goals.

Step Three: Action Plans

Your action plan is about identifying the most effective ways to pursue your goals from where you are right now. On the V&A plan template, we are literally filling in the gap between current reality and vision with the list of actions that will help get us from here to there. Your job is to choose a very short list of the right things to focus on. Don't make things harder or more complicated than they need to be. And don't overload yourself with an unrealistically long list of actions. When in doubt, pare the list back.

Here is an important point: Don't think of the actions on your list as being solely about solving specific problems or challenges that lay ahead or stand in your way. Sure, you'll inevitably have to focus on problem-solving in order to reach your goals, but the primary aim of your action plan is to help you bring into focus what matters most day to day, and week to week—and to help you put into practice things that create momentum.

As you look at your entire collection of visionary goals, brainstorm a list of actions you might take to create movement toward all of your goals and to make them true in the timeline you've defined. You are looking for single initiatives (actions) that will—if executed well—have multiple positive impacts across the vision. This means your possible action will help you move in the direction of achieving more than just one of your goals.

Here is an overly simplified example: Say, a parent is trying to move in the direction of multiple goals she's identified for herself and is faced with seemingly not enough time the next day (Saturday) to make a little progress on all her goals. Among other things, her goals include:

1. Spending more time with her two grade-school-aged kids instead of using parts of her weekends to catch up on work emails.

2. Getting in better shape through consistent exercise because she is sitting too much throughout the work week and the sedentariness is catching up with her.

3. Getting her kids organized and excited for the ten-day winter trip they are about to take to the tropics next month.

4. Giving her spouse (who is always a helpful and attentive parent) some more frequent space and alone time on the weekends to catch up on house projects, exercise, meditation, or time with friends.

At first it seems like there is no way she could make progress with all four goals on one Saturday without running herself ragged going from one thing to the next. Then she thinks about the single action idea that will have multiple positive impacts. She decides to take the kids, with their new snorkels and masks they just got for the trip but have never practiced with, to the indoor public pool downtown. The kids end up loving the adventure with her, which included ice cream cones on the way home. They had a blast being with mom and messing around with and getting used to their new snorkels and masks. She got to swim laps most of the time while coming and checking in and playing with them periodically, and her spouse got some quiet, alone time at home.

She decided to go to the pool like this at least twice per week as the kids never get tired of playing in the water and she loves the swimming time for herself. One action, four goals impacted.

Your collection of goals will likely be much more challenging, and they may be set for two years out, but the thought process is the same. A list of four or five actions—maybe six—are more than enough if they are really high-leverage, high-impact actions. Push yourself to be innovative on this. If you find an action that hits only one or two goals, ask, "How can I add to or adjust the action so that it is likely to impact more goals if executed well?" You'll get better at this with practice. Soon you will be surprising yourself with how short a list you require for keeping momentum toward the vision rolling along; and momentum is the key thing.

Here are some prompts that may help when developing your initial list of potential actions:

- How might I best focus primarily on creating momentum, rather than strictly problem-solving solving, in the way I frame my potential actions?

- In what ways might I creatively reduce friction in the system—meaning finding ways to move forward more effortlessly—using less muscle and time, and more finesse and elegance?

- How might I enlist others, particularly those who care about me, in helping me both create and carry out one or more actions? How can asking for help from others aid me in my effectiveness as I try to move from current reality toward my vision?

- (It is astounding how many people—at least in American society—seem hardwired to not ask for help. Try to break out of that trait for this work; it will pay off.)

Day-to-day problem-solving can feel like a slog. Framing the underlying challenge for your action plan as "creating momentum" not only leads you to identify a smaller list of more powerful potential actions, it also helps you do so with as much innovation and creativity as possible. This approach is also more interesting, more energizing, and less taxing—which, in turn, makes it more sustainable and more likely that you will begin to use V&A plan repeatedly over the long term.

Stepping Back

I paint pictures with oil and watercolor paints. As I sit here writing in my studio, I am surrounded by lots of them that I have painted over the years and two or three in-progress ones that I rotate on and off of my easel. One of the first things I learned long ago from my friends and art mentors Clyde Aspevig and Carolina Guzman, is to take your time, enjoy the process, and importantly, remember to often walk away from your work in progress to view it or think about it from afar. Allow ideas for improvement to emerge while you're away from the easel, sometimes even just for five minutes. Return to your plan in a different mood, at a different time of day, and with a different attitude. Similarly, with this Vision and Alignment process, try to learn, step back frequently to contemplate the overall composition, look for balance, integration, and complementary ideas in your purpose, values, vision. Approaching your effort with a mindset of continuous improvement and belief that this phase of your life is indeed a work of art will enhance your results.

Remember also that a great way to increase your effectiveness working in this process is to repeatedly share your work and what you are up to with someone else. Just trying to explain your entire story to someone is a fascinating endeavor. And don't wait until it all feels perfect. Seek others' input while it is under development. Their reactions and feedback, for better or worse, will help you improve your plan.

It took me time back in my early to mid-thirties to get good at, and in a consistent rhythm with, this activity. Since then, it has taken me into some exciting and rewarding adventures and helped me to first imagine clearly many things I have dreamed of, and then later achieve them. The process, while it does require an investment of time each time you reset it, is straightforward, costs nothing but time to use, and has never let me down.

CHAPTER THIRTEEN

Embracing and Navigating Transitions

Heather Griner had achieved pretty much everything that makes a successful career in finance by her mid-thirties. A native of Alabama, she was enjoying life living in Atlanta while facilitating lucrative deals in commercial real estate, staying in upscale hotels while on business trips and pulling down a high salary. She owned a nice house and a new BMW convertible and indulged in wonderful vacations. But something was gnawing at her. She told her boss that she was losing interest in a job where her main purpose was to make wealthy people wealthier. She needed a change. Her boss suggested that she write down everything she required to initiate a transition. This soon boiled down to, "Sell my house, quit this job, and find a new lifestyle in a new place."

While she was in high school, Heather's parents had taken her on the classic American road trip out to the West to see the national parks. Since then, Yellowstone had stood out in her memory because, in addition taking in all its beautiful natural features, she'd encountered a bison standing in the Lake Hotel parking lot. The two creatures regarded each other for an unusual amount of time; Heather felt that the animal was somehow looking directly into her soul.

Heather's mother knew of her daughter's urge to move to

the West and mentioned this to a friend who, in turn, said she knew a man in Bozeman who was looking for a finance person and who, coincidentally would be visiting Atlanta soon. Heather met the man, liked him, and the following week she was offered, and accepted, a high-level finance job at Montana State University (MSU). However, the next day she got a call: Her new boss—back in Montana and pleased with having made such a great hire in the morning—had decided to take the afternoon off and went for a motorcycle ride along a winding two-lane highway. He never returned. He crashed his motorcycle and died at the scene. However, the caller explained, the job was still Heather's if she wanted it.

Stunned, Heather was on an emotional roller coaster: Elation one day, sorrow and confusion the next. But after careful consideration, she decided to take the position regardless. The job didn't turn out to be what she'd expected. But the silver lining was that the undemanding role allowed her to leave every day without any take-home work, allowing her ample time to contemplate other options.

During her few years at MSU, she'd told some of her work colleagues about her love of nature and conservation. One day, two different colleagues alerted her to a job opening as the finance team leader at American Prairie. Although she didn't know much about our project, she applied, was hired, and found herself squarely in her dream situation. She loved the idea of being involved in a project whose final product might last for centuries, eventually became American Prairie's highly respected Chief Financial Officer, and on top of that, she got to commune with the bison at American Prairie any time she wanted.

Six years have passed since when Heather first thought of leaving her job to working with us. But during her quest, she became very clear about her interests and what she wanted in her life, and, after landing at American Prairie, began enjoying essentially every condition she'd first dared to dream about.

Transitions can take time.

Perhaps you are someone who, like Heather, has already had a significant career and is considering a change, possibly to a role in conservation. Or maybe you're just starting out in life and thinking of altering what you previously thought might be your first career. In either case, you can benefit from an understanding of the generally predictable stages of human transitions. Being more aware of these stages won't eliminate all the uncertainty and anxiety as you progress, but you'll be less surprised along the way and more likely to stick with your effort until eventually arriving at a more desirable set of circumstances.

In his book *Transitions*, William Bridges offers a helpful way to think about the relationship between "time" and "importance" as key, interrelated aspects of a transition process.

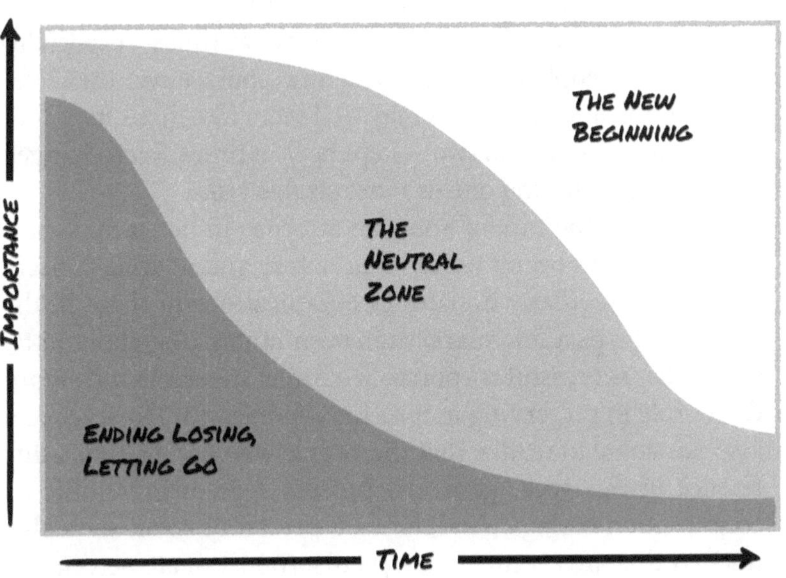

The beginning of the model is, paradoxically, about endings. As you begin to understand your feelings about your situation, you slowly become clearer on what is ending. It might be a long-term relationship. It might be your feelings about your current career or the geographic area where you live. More broadly, it might signify the end of conducting your life primarily based on what society expects of you and other people's definition of success, instead focusing on what you really want.

In my case, while at Catalyst, I realized that my interest in continuing to work in organization development consulting was slipping away—a confusing realization because I had worked very hard with my colleagues to build a successful business. However, once I understood there was no going back, I had to wrestle with the endings and my waning interest in something I used to be passionate about plus leaving friends, valued work colleagues, a well-paying job, and the beauty of Santa Cruz. On the other hand, no matter where I was headed, I knew I was not losing my family, my accumulated work skills, or a myriad of options for starting something new.

Navigating transitions can be messy at times—especially so for those people who like to feel total control over their life. Most significant transitions may well seem like three steps forward and one—or even two—steps back at times. Such changes also can mean taking one or more sizable risks.

Let's take the case of Sofia, an attorney in her early forties who has always been interested in nature and wildlife conservation. She regularly donates to organizations in these fields, but over the past few years, she's been fantasizing about jettisoning her successful corporate law career to seek a much more direct role in preserving nature and biodiversity. However, she also has come to realize that the people who are making a difference in this space generally possess degrees in wildlife or conservation biology. And, being a person of color, she's also noticed that area seems to have a disproportionate percentage of white people. On some days, she is excited about a possible career transition; on other days, she feels unsure as to how she would fit into this world.

When she reviews the latest draft of her written purpose

and values, it's clear that she would love to work in conservation to make a meaningful and long-lasting difference for future generations. To help figure out her next steps, she works through a guided set of questions to explore this potential transition in greater depth:

Q: Do you really understand the holistic nature of your vision? Is there anything that could make it stronger, clearer, or more compelling? Is there anything about it that is causing uncomfortable thoughts and feelings?

A: Nothing I can think of in the vision is making me uncomfortable. I like it a lot and am highly motivated to pursue it. I am concerned about how I actually get there, particularly as it relates to a job, and how I will be viewed and treated once I do.

Q: What are you imagining you might leave behind as you pursue your vision?

A: I worked long and hard to become good at my job. I am respected by my colleagues and clients. I earn a very good salary. I feel comfortably competent. At work, I am surrounded by other people of color. I feel confident that I can add value to any challenging client engagement. I am guessing that I'll be leaving behind at least some of these conditions if I jump into conservation with both feet.

Q: What fears and concerns are associated with starting this journey? Push yourself to think beyond your initial three or four responses.

A: What if I fail? What if I become financially insecure? What if I don't like my new choice of career? What if I discover I will have a very steep learning curve and will have created years of stress for myself? What if I don't end up feeling like I am really making a difference? What if…

Q: If those fears are strong enough to cause you to loop back and hold on to your current reality, what would that looping back behavior look like? What are the voices in your head saying? What feelings arise as you notice yourself looping back?

A: The clients I work with here as a lawyer are generally uninspiring and are mostly focused on maximizing profit versus trying to make the world a better place. Still, my role in helping them with their legal issues is familiar, and it pays well. Maybe I should be happy with what I have achieved and stop striving to get to the next rung of satisfaction, or a deeper sense of meaning and purpose. Maybe I should just wait ten years to make a move when my retirement account will be flush. The feelings associated with all of this are embarrassment and urgency. I'm embarrassed that I'm worrying so much, and I also feel a sense of urgency to get going on this transition.

Q: If you do let go of the old and move toward the vision, what might be the eventual sense of loss that you might experience?

A: Possibly the comfort of having paid off my school loans and becoming financially independent. Also, losing my everyday connection to my favorite work colleagues. Even if I'm successful in finding a satisfying position in conservation, I might never have as many great colleagues as I have now, or at least probably not in the beginning.

Sofia's thought process indicates she is somewhere between the ending phase and neutral zone of a transition. A "change loop" model, illustrated below, is a question-based thinking tool that can help illuminate the types of questions, doubts, and oscillation that she, or most anyone, experiences emotionally as the try to navigate high stakes change.

The Change Loop Experience

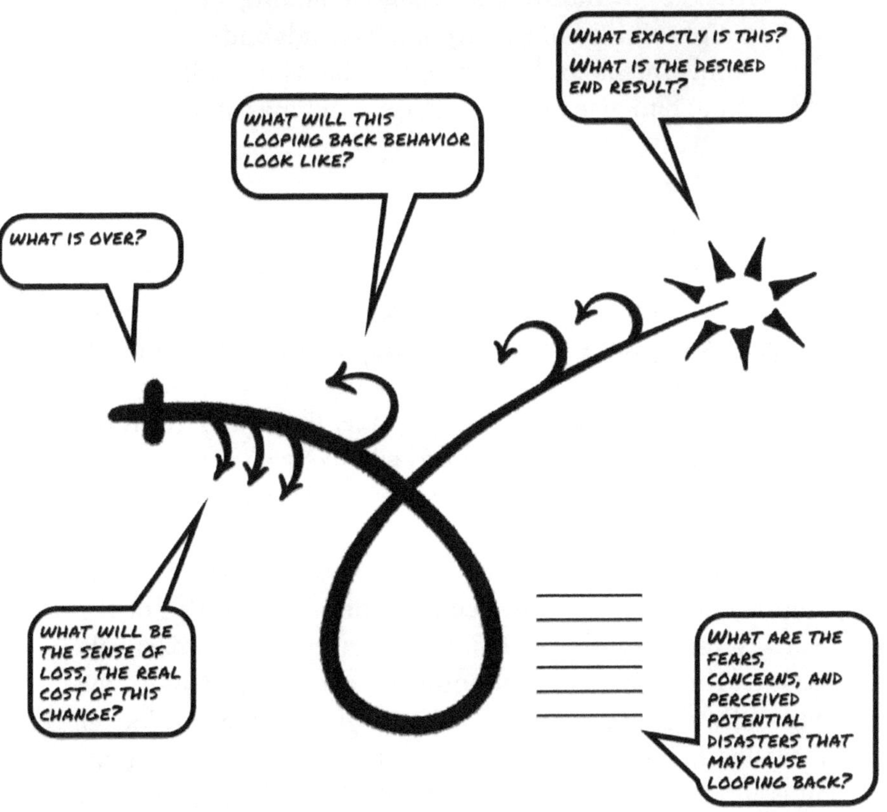

Reading back over her answers, she can see clearly her desire to pursue this vision, even in the midst of these doubts, and with the knowledge that with every change comes "costs. She then thinks about what could help her move past her concerns and make this transition a reality. Two initial ideas come to mind:

1. It would be helpful to have more examples of specific roles I could potentially play in nature conservation.

2. I'd feel better if I could broaden my understanding of the range of possibilities. I could use a friend or mentor who isn't bent on talking me out of this idea like many of my friends and family members, but who understands me well enough to give me solid advice about my future.

—

While contemplating—or starting—a significant transition, it's common to experience this complex, ever-shifting cocktail of emotions. (Had I not gotten help from a therapist processing my struggles after Kayla's kayaking accident, I doubt I would have discovered how my fears of attachment were holding me back from living a fuller life.) Early in a transition phase, your own perceptions will likely be distorted. It's difficult to make important decisions all on your own during these times.

Sofia might have assumed that she wanted to move away from law to work in nature conversation—but that's not the same as knowing what potential opportunities to proactively pursue. Through conversations with a trusted mentor, she eventually realized it was not law in general that no longer interested her, but corporate law and the specific kind of client issues that come with it. A different friend helped broaden her thinking by asking if she had ever thought about working with Earth Justice, the premier, highly respected, nonprofit, public-interest environmental law organization. (Their tagline: "Because the earth needs a good lawyer.")

Sofia, having never heard of them, studied Earth Justice's

website, and she was able to visualize herself directing her legal skills to nature conservation, which she truly cared about. She happily added that prospect to her expanding list of ideas for future jobs.

Going alone not only constrains your thinking, but we often need input and inspiration from outside our own mental and emotional bubble. Seek out trustworthy friends, family, or colleagues who can serve as sound boards and advisors. Invite these people into your thinking and your process—even though it means letting them in when you're already somewhat off-balance. I also like searching out unusual sources—for direction, or just to make me feel braver and less alone. I've found equally useful insights returning to stories like W. Somerset Maugham's *The Razor's Edge* and Joseph Campbell *The Hero's Journey* and reading authoritative psychologists like Daniel Kahneman, author of *Thinking, Fast and Slow*. When in a significant transition, you are in the middle of an age-old story that applies to all humans leaving a comparatively comfortable but sometimes suboptimal existence for a potentially more meaningful, satisfying future.

In my sixth decade, looking in the rearview mirror, one of the most helpful skills I've acquired is learning how to lean into big life transitions, as unsettling as they seem at first, with the confidence that I will eventually arrive in a better place. I'm still contemplating more adventures and still working on letting go of some of my hard-to-shake habitual ways of thinking that can detract from fully enjoying my life.

That becoming more aware of how transitions can affect you will not mean you can completely avoid all the possible feelings of trepidation or discombobulation. But being clear about why you are having those feelings is helpful. Pursue mastery of these models and tools through constant practice, and you will find yourself considering far more intriguing possibilities for yourself than you've ever imagined.

CHAPTER FOURTEEN

Doubts and Risks

Whether you're simply trying to solve some hard, complicated problems or build a fulfilling life, taking risks is often less risky than playing it safe.

You may be considering starting a new career. You may be stepping into an area where others have far more experience than you. You may be working up the courage to speak a long-held dream or ambition out loud for the very first time.

Why is risk-taking important? There are lots of reasons. For instance, in my experience, when trying to make various things happen, sometimes the safe or conventional approach isn't likely to work in the available time frame, so a riskier option may be worth considering. Recall the time, after looking for bridge funding everywhere we could think, Kayla and I cashed out our kids' college education funds to make a loan to a cash-strapped American Prairie? Had we not risked doing that—with no certainty we'd ever be paid back—American Prairie could have reverted back to what it had been for more than 150 years; a wonderful idea which, so far, no one could figure out how to make happen.

Another reason to take a risk is that without doing so, you may have to settle for something far less than the full dream you have been carrying around for a while. For instance, you may be considering starting a new career in an area in which you have little experience. Even riskier, you may be thinking of leaving a comfortable, well-paying career to do so. If you are thinking of making such a move, you will likely run into new situations that demand different skills—some of which will require even more risk-taking. On the other hand, if you don't take any significant leaps of faith, you may end up stuck in an unsatisfying career and often look back and wish you had tried to make a change.

So, depending on the kind of life you see yourself leading, learning how to take more and better risks may be very useful. I believe that everyone, no matter how much they have avoided uncertainty in the past, can expand and hone their risk-taking skills through deliberate practice. You can learn to consider risks more often, and once you take an action, manage it more effectively toward your desired outcomes.

Taking risks helps accelerate your continuous improvement process. When risk-taking results in a good outcome, you are obviously rewarded. But even when you fail, the risk can be a good learning experience and therefore still a win. As alpine skiing instructors often say, "If you are not falling, you're not learning!"

Occasional failure also helps desensitize you to the negative feelings generally associated with it, which may lead to healthier risk-taking. And knowing the benefits of learning from failure also helps you more graciously and confidently ignore those who say, "See, I told you that wouldn't work." And believe me, people will say that.

The practice of risk-taking builds your confidence over time, and you will need plenty of self-confidence if you are going to take more than a superficial run at trying to change the world for the better.

How does one get on a track of taking more risks and getting better at it over time? What are some useful steps? My first goal when confronting any type of risk is to expand my awareness about why I am even considering it. I ask myself several questions, including, "What exactly am I hoping for here?" "What is it I really want?" and maybe most important, "Why do I want that?" Armed with a better understanding of the what and the why of considering the risk, I then try to lessen the feelings of risk through a variety of means. First, I consciously slow down my thinking and decision-making process. That often involves journaling, because slowly writing things out in long hand helps me become more familiar with how I feel about everything, including actions I am considering. I also talk with others so I can hear myself trying to describe the situation aloud and gather different points of view that are certainly more objective than my own.

MAPPING OUTCOMES

Jim Ewing was a mechanical engineer who worked at TRW Corporation. While in his late thirties, Jim became interested in psychology and took a two-year sabbatical to attend the C. J. Jung Institute in Zurich, Switzerland. Upon his return to TRW, his bosses noticed a pattern: New projects seemed to go better whenever Jim was involved as he had become uncommonly good at evaluating risks. He had a knack for asking the right questions at the right time and in the right sequence. Jim eventually left TRW to become a highly sought-after executive coach. For many years, Jim used his simple, yet surprisingly effective thinking tools to help top leaders navigate risky decisions, including sometimes leaving lucrative careers for more personally meaningful ventures.

I picked up a lot of these tools and ways to use them by studying for years with Jim Ewing and others like him. It's important to acknowledge that some tools and suggestions may seem overly structured and methodical. I'm actually with you: I sometimes recoil from being told to plod carefully through structured approaches to things, but I've (grudgingly) learned that it's often worth it.

One of my favorite tools, called Implemento, was created by Ewing to guide people through assessing and making seemingly risky decisions. Though it takes some time and a lot of thought, its power is in its simplicity.

You begin by describing the risk itself as concisely as possible; keep it to just one or two sentences. Then, you push yourself to list as many details as possible in response to each of the following six questions. That's it. And yes, bullet points are fine.

1. What is the best-case outcome I can imagine?

2. What would I do next if that best-case outcome happens?

3. What is the worst-case outcome I can imagine?

4. If the worst case occurred, how would I recover?

5. What, honestly, is the most likely outcome?

6. How might I augment my actions—in other words, how might I move forward most intelligently with the initial risk—to improve the chances of landing somewhere between the most likely and best-case outcomes?

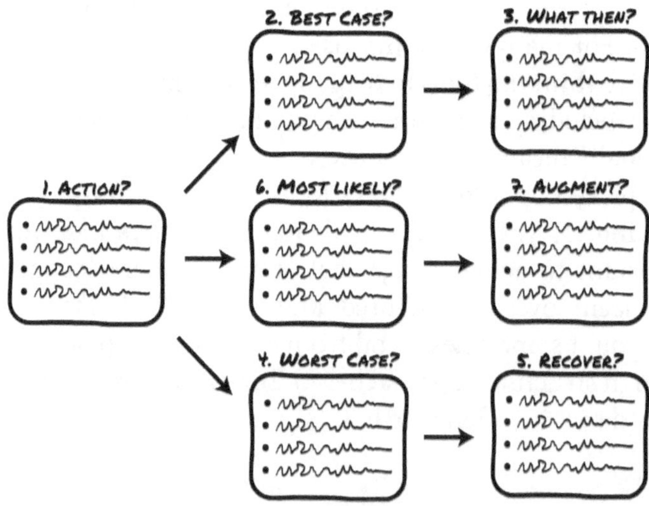

The Implemento template provides a suggested seauence to help visualize your thought process. As you fill in your own answers, you will nearly always find your thinking and your feelings changing about the proposed risk.

Implemento differs from creating a simple list of pros and cons in several important ways. First, it asks you to draw on the pros and cons swirling in your head and to articulate a written and specific best guess at what you think is most likely to happen if you move forward. It also asks you to imagine, with specifics, the worst-case and best-case outcomes, which sets you up to ask: "Now that I see my written answers to these three possible outcomes, does my energy and enthusiasm for taking this risk go up or down?" This helps track how you are feeling about a risk. No matter how well you have calculated your chances of success, you should only go ahead with a risk if it feels right.

The second uncommon aspect of Implemento is that it forces you to think beyond best case, worst case, and most likely. It pulls your attention to the far-right row in the graphic above and demands you think clearly about what you would do given each scenario. Important insights can result from imagining your immediate next steps after each outcome. This helps you reverse-engineer that best-case scenario and determine how to take the initial risk more intelligently, improving your chances of achieving your desired outcome.

The tool actually helps lessen the sense of risk, but equally important, identifies variables that are within your control to increase the chances that you can achieve your imagined best-case outcomes.

Here is an example of a decision that for me held some risk to it. I wrestled with it for months. Back in early 2001, once Kayla was on board with me moving forward with becoming the leader of American Prairie, I sat down with a large sheet of paper and a pencil to start on the Implemento tool. Using the graphic above, I worked on my first task: to summarize a proposed action (the risk I was considering) on the far left.

Here is how I worked my way through the template on and off over the course of three or four days.

1. The Action I am Considering Taking

- Take the helm of what would become the American Prairie project.

- Commit to building and running the organization at least until eventual success seems likely.

- Stay in the role, provided that I enjoy it and feel that I'm still adding unique value.

The sequence of the following six questions is important. The tool makes you first establish your outside parameters by articulating your best hopes, your worst fears, and what you would do if either of them materialized. Then, working toward the middle, you describe your imagined Most Likely Outcome. Myself, I decided to focus my answers on a point in time approximately two and a half years after launching what I loosely estimated to be a twenty-five- to thirty-five-year effort.

2. What is the Best-Case Outcome You Can Imagine?

- I am succeeding in carefully building an early-stage organization of people I enjoy being around, who share and live our organization's values, and who are highly passionate about the product we intend to deliver.

- We are making small but tangible yearly progress and are gaining the confidence of a growing group of supporters, Tribal members, and other local people.

- We have made our first property purchase. It will one day demonstrate to donors and to the public what the much larger reserve will look like.

- I feel that taking this job was the right decision, even though it is highly challenging, and it will take a long time to bring the vision to reality.

- Kayla and I both feel the significant reduction in income is okay because of how rewarding this endeavor feels thus far.

3. If I Achieve the Best-Case, What Would I Do Then?

- Keep carefully building the organization for versatility and strength, filling in specialty roles in finance, fundraising, land buying, and so forth.

- Make and implement plans for immediate initial changes to our first twenty thousand acres to show meaningful habitat and wildlife restoration progress.

- Establish some kind of remote, semimobile camp on the property that allows visitors—especially potential donors—to get inspired through overnight experiences.

- Use the momentum and excitement of successfully acquiring the first property to raise funds for the second one.

- Begin spending more time with the local communities—in particular the Indigenous Tribes—so we can better understand how our work can eventually benefit them.

- Enjoy the fact that I am leading something that, if successful, will have long-lasting value.

I was of course tantalized by Box 2, the Best-Case Outcome, but I was even more interested in Box 3. This is one of Implemento's great advantages: You rarely discover your true goals or subconscious motivations with a simple best-case/

worst-case exercise.

4. What is the Worst-Case Outcome You Can Imagine?

- Fundraising is much harder than expected, and operations funds are too low to proceed at our planned pace, or possibly even to stay in business.

- Not enough people understand the value of our vision or see the need for such a conservation project.

- WWF is proving less helpful with fundraising than I'd expected.

- Our early progress is driving some animosity in the local area.

- Critical agencies that we need as partners, including the Bureau of Land Management, are stating publicly that they do not support our vision.

- My board members are losing faith and are considering leaving the organization.

- The staff—including me—are fatigued by lack of progress, difficulties in fundraising, and the relentless public critique of our efforts.

- Kayla is frustrated that I am spending too much time at work. She is having second thoughts about the prairie project and misses our old lifestyle.

- I feel alone and stressed out.

5. How Would I Recover if the Worst Case Happened?

- Assemble the board more regularly and focus on breaking down the next critical steps of progress into short phases. Determine each phase's financial requirements and together figure out how to secure that funding.

- Establish clear exit criteria with the board to determine what specific conditions would signal it's time to stop the effort and disband the organization.

- Explore and implement ways to secure non-philanthropic operational revenue, such as temporarily leasing some of our lands, or me making operations money some way other than philanthropy.

- Bring the staff together frequently to talk about plans for getting through tough times. Be honest about what worst-case scenarios look like (e.g., not making payroll at times) and how I, as a leader, intend to respond to each one.

- Dial down the aggressiveness of our annual plans to lessen feelings of failure and increase feelings of incremental success.

- Seek Kayla's opinions and advice often.

Putting my pencil down, I tried to first feel, rather than think, what I imagined would be the most likely outcome in Box 6. I knew from experience that the most likely outcome was almost certainly less wonderful than what I'd listed in the best-case box, but not so dire as what I'd listed in the worst-case. I studied the paper and let the most likely scenario slowly settle into my body.

6. What is Your Best Guess at the Most Likely Outcome?

- It was—and still is—a struggle financially, but we've acquired our first piece of land.

- The land purchase has impressed many potential

supporters, demonstrating that we have successfully closed on one deal and are making plans for the next.

- My energy expenditure is intense at times. Kayla and I work as a team to mitigate the downsides. We try to compensate by taking periodic three- and four-day weekends and using every one of my vacation days.

- We have a very small but capable team adeptly handling basic tasks, including bookkeeping, donation tracking, human resources requirements, and so forth.

- Fundraising is much harder and more stressful than I'd anticipated, but we are slowly improving.

- Our vision remains exciting and motivating for me, my family, our staff, the board, and our supporters.

- My many past experiences using this tool had taught me that a go or no-go decision depends heavily on the last question, so I moved to Box 7.

7. Landing Between the Most Likely and Best-Case Outcomes

Using the Catalyst Vision and Alignment process, create a clear picture of where we want to be in increments of six months, one year, eighteen months, two and a half years, and five years. Ensure alignment throughout the staff and board by clearly defining what success looks like at each milestone.

- Schedule twice-monthly calls with my three executive board committee members. Invite them to ask me about anything. Use them as a sounding board. Stay open to their feedback and coaching.

- Go on the road soon with a short, highly visual and inspiring talk about our long-term vision.

Do it repeatedly with small gatherings in board members' homes and other venues to deepen the board and potential donors' understanding and enthusiasm for our vision.

- Work with Kayla to proactively plan fun and rejuvenating family getaways that will remain sacred no matter what is happening at work.

Once finished, I read the contents of the entire template all the way through and once more evaluated my feelings. I felt I could control a great deal of the outcome with my initial list of improvements in Box 7. My recovery actions following a worst-case scenario were tolerable and fairly reasonable, and the answers to what I would do if I got the best-case outcome felt invigorating.

The next step was to ask Kayla to listen to my risk analysis. As always, she pointed out numerous issues that escaped me on the first go-round, and she asked practical questions, suggested ideas for augmenting the action part, and helped make it all clearer, sharper, and more realistic.

AS you know by now, I decided to move forward. A few years later, the result was slightly better than my imagined most likely scenario. A few of my worst-case scenarios actually occurred, especially when it came to fundraising, but I'd put my recovery actions into place even before I needed them. I even ended up with a few of the conditions in my best-case scenario.

Taking the time to examine risks in this holistic manner is helpful no matter what you decide to do afterward. A few years ago, I sat down one afternoon at our kitchen table with my niece, who, in her mid-forties, was contemplating a career change into the world of nonprofit conservation. She had just received an enticing job offer from an organization she was relatively unfamiliar with, and I helped her sketch out her thinking about the situation with the Implemento exercise. An hour or so later, as she sat back and analyzed her own answers, I suggested that she pause and just check in on her emotions.

"When you imagine yourself taking this risk," I asked, "do you feel your energy rise or fall?" The expression on her face, not to mention when she put her forehead down on the table and groaned, said it all. She'd uncovered too many red flags associated with the less-than-attractive company culture at the new job—despite the prestigious role and tempting compensation package.

When she rejected the offer, she did so confidently in her decision and ready to continue her search.

Tips for Making Risk-Taking a More Natural and Frequent Aspect of How You Move Through Life

Remember that achieving the best-case outcome is not necessarily what will excite you the most; it might be what the best-case sets you up for next that matters most. Your thoughts about what you would love to do next are lurking in your subconscious. It pays to take the time to bring them into the light and see how they affect your ideas about how to take that big risk.

Force yourself to write down your worst-case scenarios. (I, for instance, tend to try to bury them in my subconscious so they don't mess up my exciting plans.) This pulls them out of the swirling fears in your mind and sets them on the table in front of you. It is important to face them, all of them. Don't worry about it as you fill the page with your imagined fears and concerns; as is often noted, our very worst fears in life rarely materialize.

Ask yourself, How would I recover if some—or all—of those negative elements were to come true? This helps you access your ability to adapt quickly if things go wrong. Try to expand your list of recovery ideas until you can look at them and say, "I believe these worst-case outcomes are not likely to happen, but if some of them did, I will probably be fine if I execute the actions in my 'How Would I Recover?' box."

The most likely outcome section shows your best guess at what will likely happen if you take the risk. Being clear and informed about what you think is the most likely outcome makes the risk feel less scary and more surmountable.

Box 7 is a creative brainstorming exercise that results in a list of items that may help improve how you take the risk itself. It feeds an entrepreneur's desire to feel more in control of their destiny, which, in turn, increases optimism.

Enlist the help of those who are close to you by taking them all the way through your thinking in the Implemento tool. There is value in hearing yourself trying to articulate how you are framing a risk, and you will often find much value in your sounding board's questions and reactions to your thinking.

Whether it's a day, a week, or six months, make a definite stop time for your decision. Then take walks, write in a journal, do more research, and talk with others. You will use your investigation and vetting time more efficiently if you have a deadline in mind. This helps lessen the chance of consideration fatigue, where you get tired of thinking about and spinning on it endlessly.

Folding is sometimes the wisest move, too. I have decided not to take a risk as often as I've decided to move ahead with one. Using various thinking tools and taking time to revisit your decision process over days, weeks, or months helps you become more fully aware of your headspace while contemplating a risk. Being more aware will help you know when to press on and when to fold. However, people often bail out before they've given their idea a chance to fully develop.

Find the tools that work for you, use them, then use them again. You can stand down from some risks and feel more confident about embracing others. Eventually, you'll experience a reinforcing loop of smart risk-taking and more frequent pursuit of innovations and bold ideas. Taking risks can become second nature—but that doesn't mean it ever feels easy.

—

I wish I had known about imposter syndrome earlier in life. But today, even though I'm aware of when it rears its head and I know how it affects me, it never seems to entirely dissipate. And I have come to understand that it is—at least for me—an unusually strong influence on my thinking when I am considering taking certain kinds of risks.

The definition of "imposter syndrome," first coined in the 1970s by psychologists Suzanne Imes and Pauline Rose Clance, morphed somewhat over the past fifty years until it entered the popular lexicon. It refers to the feelings of uncertainty about one's own abilities, that unsettling sense of unworthiness or self-doubt, that often doesn't align with the more positive impression many others have about you.

I'm guessing you may know exactly what I'm talking about.

These feelings—which can be momentary or stretch on indefinitely—are often accompanied by the fear that you will eventually be outed as a fraud. The more exciting a prospect, the more you stand to lose, or at least it feels that way—until you remind yourself that these feelings are common, natural, and a manifestation of your underlying anxieties.

If you are prone to imposter syndrome like me, know that avoiding it is generally futile. Accepting it and learning to work through it as best you can is helpful. The goal isn't to eliminate any experience of imposter syndrome, the key is how to not let it get in your way or sabotage your enthusiasm and your chances of taking a worthy risk.

If not dealt with effectively, imposter syndrome can cause you to hesitate—leading, in turn, to paralysis and putting the action you've dreamed of taking at risk of not happening at all. And look, I'm not saying you should rejoice every time you feel consumed by doubt. Imposter syndrome is unpleasant at best and, at worst, can manifest as long-term anxiety or depression. But the good news is that these uncomfortable feelings can and will diminish over time if you pay attention to them and work on them consciously.

Experience has taught me that the imposter syndrome is not always confined to doubts about competence: Sometimes these feelings arise when you are pretending to be sincerely interested in whatever you are working on. I have met many people who have discovered this for themselves—in law, medicine, finance, charity work, or political organizing. For a time, they really wanted to like what they had become involved in. They liked being recognized by others for being a part of it, but in quiet moments of honest reflection, it dawned on them that they were not being entirely honest with themselves. They wanted something slightly different, but were worried they'd let people down, afraid to admit it to themselves, or to confidently step toward something more attractive, exciting, or simply a better fit for them.

When you are considering leaving something you currently feel competent at to undertake a new and uncertain adventure, it's possible you will be confronted with this vexing dilemma. Just keep reminding yourself that—at least in the case of nature conservation—if you can somehow navigate this tricky and intimidating juncture in your life, all those wild species at risk of being overrun and possibly outright destroyed by our own species may well benefit from your courageous decision.

I've experienced imposter syndrome myself countless times, including when I first sat down to try to write this book and many times while working on it. It's always been stressful, but in hindsight, I wouldn't trade even one temporarily unnerving experience of it for a chance to take an easier route. In fact, as I scan my memories and my many personal journals, I've learned that imposter feelings, as uncomfortable as they are, are usually a sign that I'm onto something big.

Make Risk-Taking Part of Your Repertoire

In summary, it is always helpful to look at risk from several angles and to use more than one tool. Practice these techniques as often as you can. Practice it when you are considering most anything that feels risky like buying a house, going on a date with someone new, ending a relationship, moving to a new town, taking a new job, or asking for lots more responsibility (or compensation) at your job.

Eventually, taking risks with these tips in mind will become second nature. Artfully using these suggestions will help you stand down from some risks and feel more confident about your path forward. So, begin applying these concepts frequently as you risk moving forward toward what you really want.

You will eventually experience a reinforcing loop of smart risk-taking and more frequent and confident pursuit of innovations and bold ideas.

CHAPTER FIFTEEN

Optimism and Hope

Because of my time spent in the world of wildlife conservation, I often get asked if I am optimistic about humankind doing better in the future than today as far as valuing and preserving our natural environment. I get skeptical looks from some because I say I am absolutely optimistic over the long term—meaning the next twenty-five years or more—assuming certain trends continue.

My optimism is based on my own direct experience. First is the fact that twenty-five years ago, we, as a small group of people, believed we could create a great deal more space for nature in an area that has been almost exclusively devoted to large-scale for-profit agriculture for more than a century. We had little background for doing such a thing, essentially no money, and were met with lot of resistance to our idea, but it's working out anyway. Second, over the years, I've learned about many other people around the world working on similar efforts who are also succeeding, and it is a fact that the total number of such efforts is increasing substantially.

I concur that there are countless trends underway that exacerbate the desecration of our natural environment. It distresses me, particularly since in many cases proven fixes are widely available. With enough political and social will, most fixes seem straightforward to implement, but many factors, including a lack of political courage, innovation, or motivation coupled with fears of leaving behind profits associated with doing things the old way—and fear of change itself—slows forward progress.

Beyond those factors, I believe the greatest hinderance to us realizing a better future for our environment has been the lack of an agreed upon definition of success: Here in the US and as a global society, we simply aren't yet aligned on we want our future relationship to nature to be. If you have been involved in any sort of strategic planning, you know that a lack of collective agreement on your desired end result will confound all discussions on tactics and strategy regarding how to get there.

By 2030, the total mammalian biomass of the earth will likely consist of 97 percent humans and our livestock—and only 3 percent wild mammalian species. This is in contrast to only 150 or so years ago when it was estimated that wild mammals were more than 50 percent of that total biomass. Today some people feel that the 97 percent people and livestock to just 3 percent wild species in 2030 would be an okay ratio. Others, particularly many who work in the nature conservation field, feel that the best we can do is hold the line at today's ratio in 2025—perhaps 93 percent and 7 percent. They define success as preserving the limited fragments of natural areas that are left. Others—including me—feel we should commit to swinging the pendulum back toward the center from where it is now, meaning we should return to a ratio of about 50 percent humans and livestock—including our towns, homes, factories, and roads—and 50 percent of the earth for the estimated 6,400 other species of wild mammals, birds, fishes, and reptiles in the world today. Therin lies the lack of alignment regarding where we are trying to go.

Am I optimistic that as a global society we might, in the near term, completely agree on a clear, multifaceted vision specifying how much room humans should allocate for nature? No, but I am not disheartened by that. When I look around the world today, I see a lot of effective conservation initiatives underway outside the context of such a vision. But more importantly, I'm encouraged because for the first time ever in human history, there are the beginnings of a worldwide discussion about a big, inspiring nature conservation vision.

A 2019, *Scientific Advances* article titled "A Global Deal for Nature: Guiding principles, milestones, and targets" kicked off a global debate about how we might implement the article's recommendations in all countries around the world. The main takeaway from the article is a simple concept called "30x30," which refers to the worldwide initiative for governments to designate 30 percent of the earth's land and ocean surface as "protected" by 2030. First, the good news: 30x30, as a concept, is viewed as the most tangible and ambitious conservation commitment humans have ever attempted. Since December 2022, 190 out of the world's 195 countries have formally signed on to it, meaning that they have publicly committed to do their best to help achieve this goal.

Today many countries are scrambling to identify what already existing protected lands and ocean areas they can count toward their 30 percent contribution. They are also trying to identify what additional land and water areas they could add in the years left until 2030. Progress is occurring, but it's spotty. Gabon, Bhutan, and Canada are setting some impressive examples of protecting biodiversity, reducing deforestation, and preserving carbon-rich ecosystems. Other hopeful examples exist at the province or state levels. California may be making the fastest, most meaningful progress on this idea anywhere in the US, guided by a public document called "California Pathways to 30x30."

Naturally, there have been struggles and setbacks. There is justifiable concern that in many areas Indigenous peoples are not being meaningfully included in strategizing about protecting lands and that many of their ancestral lands could be taken in order to be lumped into the 30 percent protected number.

Some countries who have a lot of highly developed lands in agriculture will have a hard time meeting their commitments by 2030. And currently—depending on who you ask and how they are measuring progress—worldwide, only about 17 percent of land and 8 percent of oceans are solidly protected for nature and biodiversity. There is a long way to go in the next five years. I think it's okay if we don't make it. Here's why:

In his 2016 book, *Half Earth*, the late Dr. Edward O. Wilson proposed saving half the world's land and water areas for biodiversity by 2050. Enthusiasts of Wilson's idea surmised that you could set some useful incremental goals toward that big vision, for instance, protecting 30 percent by 2030, 40 percent by 2040, and 50 percent by 2050. It appears that a growing contingent in the conservation world is in favor of this reframing of the actual long-term goal. So, if we don't quite nail all the goals by 2030, we have time to sharpen our definition of success, improve our execution, to pick up the pace and achieve the much-longer-term goal.

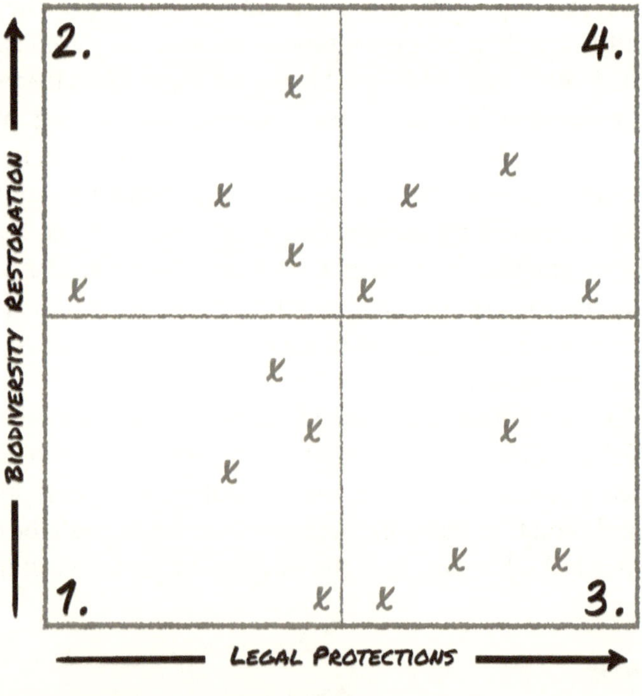

The biggest short-term challenge now is that the 2030, 2040, and 2050 visions are notyet specific enough in one key area to guide effective and coordinated action. They are missing clear, agreed upon criteria regarding what areas of land and water should and will count as suitably protected in the final tally; there is no agreed-upon framework for how to balance biodiversity restoration, legal protections, and other potential human interests. Should we give precedence to areas that have existing legal protections or where biodiversity restoration is already underway? The ongoing debate and lack of agreement about this is taking up time that could be better devoted to action on the ground or on the water, but progress is occurring.

Some people believe a protected area should only count if it meets both requirements: It is deemed to be durably protected legally, and it's clearly a place where maintaining wildlife abundance and thriving biodiversity comes first. In these cases, commercial and recreational interests are a lower priority and are allowed only in limited and sustainable ways, or sometimes not at all. By that criteria that particular protected area would fit squarely in box four in the graphic above.

Others believe a protected area should also count for 30x30 based on its potential, rather than on whether it has been granted initial protections or benefited from any rewilding efforts to date. Commonly in the case of land-based areas, they can be somewhat legally protected from any new roads, homes and factories, the damming of rivers and streams, new airstrips, extraction of minerals, and plowing under native vegetation in order to grow monoculture crops. But it is often the case that livestock grazing, logging, hunting, trapping, and other activities that often have significant detrimental effects on biodiversity are still allowed. And it currently may be missing a substantial amount of native wildlife both in population numbers and variety of species, making it score low on the vertical biodiversity axis.

As one example, the Upper Missouri Breaks National Monument in Montana has somewhat durable legal protections, and yet trapping, extensive hunting and significant livestock grazing, and miles upon miles of barbed wire livestock fencing are all allowed within its borders. Today when you float down the Missouri River through this monument, you will see a lot of fences and cows, but little to no native wildlife such as bison, wolves, elk, grizzly bears, bighorn sheep, etc. Like many National Monuments, a dedicated group of volunteers works through the Friends of the Missouri Breaks Monument organization doing many valuable things like promoting letter-writing to politicians in support of keeping the monument, planting trees to help revive native flora, and producing publications helping the public to enjoy visiting the monument. Things could change in the future, but currently there are no federal government-led plans or actions for making this monument a place where biodiversity clearly comes first and where restoring historical wildlife abundance is a top priority.

In the US, there is precedent for future administrations to roll back federal protections for national monuments in order to allow oil and gas extraction, increased livestock grazing, etc. Upper Missouri Breaks National Monument is vulnerable to such changes by current or future administrations—a vulnerability that would likely result in this monument being appropriately classified below the 30x30 threshold definition of "protected." These debates about what should count in the final tallies continue, and, of course, there is no absolute right answer. Maybe the eventual agreement will be a blend of all these opinions with more flexible criteria. Time will tell.

To me, the questions centered on what should count as protected are like the one posed throughout Robert Pirsig's book, *Zen and the Art of Motorcycle Maintenance*. That question was on the definition of quality, a sometimes-challenging thing to define. As hard as it can be to define quality—such as quality protection for biodiversity—it is critical to get it right if you are going to try to align a large group of people over a long period while they pursue their aspirational goal.

We took significant time to carefully define quality in regard to American Prairie's goals for a multi-million-acre wildlife reserve back in 2001. For instance, it is a place where, in the end, nature and wildlife clearly comes first. It's a place where any human activities including recreation or commercial pursuits have minimal or no detrimental effects on biodiversity richness, wildlife abundance or wildlife behavior. These and other distinct descriptions have made our countless discussions and debates on how best to achieve that quality much more productive ever since.

For those who will devote many, many challenging years pursuing the visions of 2030, 2040, and 2050—coming to agreement on what truly high-quality protection for nature looks like is important. These discussions will likely become loud and emotional, which I think is great. That means they are being handled by people who care. And getting more people to care about and help define our future relationship to nature is a significant part of what this is all about.

As of this writing, 2050 is still twenty-five years into the future. Looking back on American Prairie's beginnings, twenty-five years in the past, I recall so many people telling us that our ambitions were too big, too complex, and required a seemingly impossible amount of coordination to ever work out. But it's working out. That fact reinforces my belief that with persistence and tenacity applied to a detailed and compelling vision, we can get some truly amazing things done in the next twenty-five short years.

It will hardly come as a surprise that I would start by clearly defining a 2050 Vision using the Vision & Alignment template. While a comprehensive vision would include perhaps fourteen to sixteen total goals across multiple categories, my Visionary Goals for 2050 would begin with the following:

- By 2050, the global mindset around our relationship to nature has shifted deeply. We recognize,

and are consistently acting, on our responsibility
to manage ourselves so all species—including
humans—can co-prosper together.

- The transition to clean energy has rendered fossil
  fuels largely obsolete. Renewable power sources
  for our homes, transportation, computing power
  demands, and most all other industries are only
  minimally impacting nature and biodiversity.

- After leveling off, the global human population
  is slowly beginning to decline, moving toward
  a balance that allows wild species and people to
  coexist sustainably.

- The agricultural industry-while annually producing more than enough food for humans— now
  uses far less land, water, and chemicals-much like
  the breakthroughs already seen in ultra-high ag
  production places like the Netherlands—resulting
  in a significantly high percentage of the previous
  total land and marine areas used for agriculture
  being returned to wild nature.

- Rewilding, once a bold experiment, is now a
  global success story. Forests, rivers, grasslands,
  and oceans teem with life once more. Wildlife
  flourishes, restoring ecological balance on a scale
  unseen for centuries.

I hope the efforts related to a 2050 vision steadily attract
more and more people to participate in helping to make it happen. I hope the phenomenon becomes the proverbial genie that
is now out of the bottle and refuses to go back in. I hope this
conversation will not fade away, but instead grow in power and
intensity, and become an unstoppable, long-term movement.
I'm not sure that I will get to see the year 2050, but I would
die happy knowing that, just like with American Prairie, there
is a well-coordinated effort underway centered on every bit of

innovation and ingenuity people can muster to help achieve those end goals.

I also don't worry that we can only make progress under favorable conditions. For instance, American Prairie has existed through four different presidential administrations including those of George W. Bush, Barack Obama, Donald Trump, Joe Biden, and now Donald Trump, again. We have been through four different Secretaries of the Interior, four different Montana governors, and a variety of senators and representatives. Regardless of the administration, we've steadily acquired land, continued to work on growing species like bison, swift fox, beavers, grassland birds and prairie dogs. We've also continued to build relationships with Indigenous nations, government agencies, and other local neighbors, and continuously expanded the ways in which visitors can enjoy the reserve area. My experience has led me to believe that this type of conservation work can—over time—transcend all manner of temporary governmental conditions, which history tells us are all ephemeral.

I get how one can feel dispirited, fatigued, or demoralized when it seems like your efforts to make the world a better place are not moving fast enough and are taking way too long. To help keep my perspective, I often compare the long-term challenges of building the American Prairie project and things like the 2050 global vision idea to other important historical change efforts. One of the most notable to me is the women's suffrage movement in the US. Back in the 1850s, there was a relatively small but growing contingent of people who were adamant that all kinds of rights ought to be afforded to women that they didn't yet have, including the right to vote. But there remained far more people in the county, including many women, who were adamantly against that idea. So, a number of women, and men, got to work pushing for change—even while a completely unified societal vision was still forming. For many years their efforts were uncoordinated and at times at cross purposes. But they eventually got clear on what they wanted and did ultimately prevail. In 1965—by way of the Voting Rights Act—all women, of all races, were finally guaranteed the right to vote throughout the entire US. Remember this: It took roughly 110 years of unwavering effort to get it done. Building the American Prairie or achieving the 50 percent protected by 2050 conservation goals almost seems tame in comparison.

—

I think it is up to each one of us who wants to make a difference, to try to tease out of all the noise, the bright spots of hope related to our natural environment. This does take some work, but when we become aware of enough of those bright spots and how their numbers are growing, we can try to understand the patterns and trends of which they are a part. With better awareness of those trends, we can think more creatively about how to amplify them and contribute to their strength, speed, and momentum. In systems thinking parlance, that is a reinforcing loop—kind of like compound interest in a financial investment account. It is a powerful force that delivers extraordinary outcomes over the long term.

Reports of positive trends that are helping our natural world aren't frequently included in the media. Instead, most news is carefully curated to saturate us with negative stories and inflame our emotions. This follows a familiar news formula: "If it bleeds, it leads." But if you, like me, take the initiative to scour the world for inspiring stories regarding real progress on the environment, you'll find the volume of encouraging patterns and trends almost overwhelming.

CHAPTER SIXTEEN

Trendlines

For many thousands of years, one prominent school of thought—derived from numerous different religious teachings—promoted the idea of humans having dominion over the earth and all its creatures. Depending on the source, some people interpreted that to mean that humans were free to exploit the world's treasures, like damming great rivers, plowing up as much wild habitats as they liked to grow food for people, and managing wild species for mankind's convenience, sport, or profit. Others believed people should minimize that exploitation mindset and instead see themselves as benevolent stewards or overseers of nature versus outright exploiters. Still others—including Hindus, many Indigenous peoples, and others—have felt for centuries that humans should view themselves not as overseers, but as coequals in a very large and complex ecological system. This perspective emphasizes a reciprocal relationship between humans and nature, where all living beings have intrinsic value or inherent worth, and no species has inherent dominance over others.

Today some societies, or portions of them at least, are showing early signs of moving on from the humans-are-dominate view toward humans being one component of a large, complex ecological system, and the belief that we should strive to enable co-prosperity among all beings in that system. As this trend spreads over time, slowly but surely, it should have positive impacts on future government policies at both national and local levels. It should also get us to think more clearly about what we want our relationship to nature to be and help us think about how to create more physical space on the planet for nature than we have now.

The following is a sample of just some additional macro-level trends that I've come to appreciate. One or a small number of them is not enough to drive widespread positive change, but I believe most or all of them in combination can and will make a big difference over the medium to long term.

Over the next few decades, these trends can help contribute to less polluted air, less carbon in the atmosphere and, theoretically, reduced global warming. Indirectly, all of this can end up helping nature and biodiversity.

Like many, I am frustrated with the slowness from some states in the US to fully embrace green energy like solar and wind, but it is true that the adoption of such technology is accelerating faster than expected. In 2024, for the first time in US history, combined electricity generation from wind and solar surpassed that from coal. The United Kingdom—generally thought of as the birthplace of the industrial revolution—as of October 2024, closed down its last coal-fired, electric-power generation plant.

—

Over the past twenty-plus years, I have witnessed a rising public interest in restoring degraded natural environments back to wild nature. These days—as compared to twenty-four years ago, at the start of American Prairie—you can search for "rewilding" or "saving nature" in your favorite podcast platform or search engine and find a rapidly growing suite of offerings citing impressive conservation achievements happening worldwide. They include *The Rewilding Podcast* with James

Shooter, *Rewilding Earth* by The Rewilding Institute, *Forces for Nature* by Crystal DiMiceli, *Rewilding the Planet* by Ben Goldsmith, *The Wild* with Chris Morgan, my own production, *The Answers Are Out There*, and many others.

The number of books being published about the importance of saving nature and biodiversity is also growing. A quarter century ago, conservation biologists often only quoted Aldo Leopold's *A Sand County Almanac* or Rachel Carson's *Silent Spring*. Today it is hard to keep up with the constant publication of well-crafted nature writing by a wide diversity of authors. The opportunity to educate oneself on this topic has grown exponentially in just the past few decades. This in turn is accelerating the discovering, sharing, and implementing of best practices much faster than was common even ten to fifteen years ago. I am noticing that the quality and inventiveness of many conservation efforts is improving more rapidly as a result.

Another trend, assuming it continues, will create more land area for nature—particularly in the American West. As an example, recently the US Bureau of Land Management (BLM) has introduced the concept of Conservation Leasing. As a result, a portion of the BLM's 245 million acres of public land holdings could—in addition to traditional mining, logging and livestock grazing for profit—can theoretically now be leased by private landowners simply to improve nature and wildlife for the health of the natural environment and the public's enjoyment.

After a nationwide public comment period on the concept was completed in mid-2024, the program was published in the Federal Register, making it official. By the time you read this—barring any efforts to block or delay it—the BLM will be processing the first requests from private individuals and organizations to exercise their leases under this new category.

Granted, the BLM is the largest land management entity in the US and this new approach will create lots of questions in the early stages of implementation. It may get held up or even blocked by the US Congress for a time, but I predict it will eventually prevail and become normalized, one way or another, over the next few decades. It will take some years to work out the kinks, but eventually this addition to the BLM's land management policy should allow organizations like American Prairie and other private individual landowners to move more efficiently in their efforts to improve natural areas for everyone, on far more land throughout the American West than most people ever believed was possible.

Across centuries and around the world, Indigenous communities are largely excluded from decision-making processes on local projects that could impact the natural environment. Activities like timber logging, the laying of oil and fiber optic lines, offshore developments can have damaging effects on Indigenous ancestral lands, spiritual history, and local ecosystems. However, a slowly emerging yet promising shift is occurring as Indigenous peoples increasingly lead efforts to restore and protect natural areas.

For instance, the Northern Chumash Tribe has been highly instrumental in establishing the new 4,543-square-mile Chumash Heritage National Marine Sanctuary along California's central coast—the first ever Tribally nominated national marine sanctuary. This initiative integrates traditional knowledge with federal conservation efforts, benefiting species such as the southern sea otter and blue whale. Similarly, the Yurok, Karuk, Hoopa Valley, Klamath, and Shasta Tribes, and Modoc Nation have collectively led the removal of four hydroelectric dams on the Klamath River, marking the largest river restoration project in US history and the largest dam removal project in the world. This already successful endeavor is rehabilitating the river's complex ecosystem and is demonstrating the effectiveness of Indigenous-led environmental initiatives. The US National Park Service's new Bison Shared Stewardship Strategy includes Tribal leaders in the planning and implementing of bison restoration. One of the plan's top strategic priorities is Indigenous ecocultural restoration of bison that goes beyond just a conservation science view of buffalo to incorporate Indigenous cultural and spiritual aspects of restoration as well.

The Tagbanua people of Coron Island in the Philippines successfully manage their marine territories, balancing ecological preservation with sustainable tourism. In Australia, Indigenous Protected Areas (IPAs) now make up over half of the nation's National Reserve System, showcasing Indigenous leadership in conserving vast and biodiverse landscapes.

In Pahang, Malaysia Indigenous Semai women are leading a ranger unit to protect endangered gibbons—defying gender and cultural norms and showing powerful local leadership in biodiversity protection.

Leaders like Nemonte Nenquimo of Waorani Ecuador have used legal strategies to safeguard half a million acres of ancestral forest. Indigenous organizations like Amazon Frontlines and Amazon Conservation Team employ mapping, legal protections, and capacity building to protect vast rainforest territories.

These examples highlight a slowly growing incidence of active Indigenous leadership in nature conservation. I believe progress may likely continue if two trends persist. One is if governments reduce or eliminate the many long-standing systemic impediments to Tribal leadership in conservation-related decision-making. Second is if Indigenous communities continue to proactively seize emerging leadership opportunities across a growing variety of conservation efforts. Indigenous people often live in what is now or used to be some of the most biodiverse places on earth. If the two trends above continue, the total physical area of the world saved for nature and biodiversity should increase.

While searching for stories that are a part of new trends for my podcast, I'm continually surprised to learn about efforts to help wildlife that didn't exist twenty years ago. One such example is the Woods Hole Oceanographic Institution, which, along with others, has been placing robotic buoys in harbors on both coasts of the US where shipping traffic is particularly heavy, and serious injuries or the outright killing of whales by ships strikes are common. The buoys first detect whale songs and then automatically send alerts about the presence of whales to a public website. Federal maritime authorities use that information to make faster local decisions about when to announce and impose temporary "Right Whale Slow Zones." These zones require large ships to reduce their speed while whales are around. Just this one action significantly lessens the incidence of ship-caused whale injuries in busy harbors and shipping lanes.

These and other practices are spreading to places such as the island country of Dominica, where the largest marine protected reserve in the Caribbean is now being assembled to protect sperm whales. Ship speed and route restrictions coming in and out of the main harbor are part of that protected area's multifaceted strategy for helping more sperm whales survive. A growing number of similar efforts around the world—most of which the broader public is not aware—help migrating birds, large predators, reptiles, and other species as well.

Each day in the US roughly one million vertebrate animals are killed on American highways, amounting to 350 million wild vertebrates being killed on our roads each year. West Virginia usually has the most roadkill. Montana usually holds the number two spot. Meanwhile, approximately five thousand people are injured in the US each year in collisions between vehicles and wildlife, resulting in two hundred to four hundred human deaths.

More and more countries, including the US, are working to retrofit roads with specially designed underpasses and overpasses, connecting critical habitats and significantly decreasing wildlife deaths from road accidents. These structures allow for safe passage of wild species, from reptiles to tigers to grizzly bears.

The Wallis Annenberg Wildlife Crossing at California's Liberty Canyon is proof that people value this movement. When completed in 2026, the crossing will span ten lanes of traffic and connect two critical areas of habitat for mountain lions and other wildlife. The project's total cost is estimated to be around $87 million—a level of money usually associated with performing arts centers and university buildings—and roughly 60 percent has been contributed by individuals, foundations, and corporations, rather than the government.

The net effect of these wildlife crossings over or under roadways is more effective connections between wild habitats and thereby increasing the overall amount of land available for nature around the world.

Lastly, as an example of occasional convergence with some of these trends, the Conservation Leasing Initiative in the Bureau of Land Management states, as part of its purpose, the intention to help create better corridors and connectivity between protected areas for wildlife. These criteria have never before been spelled out in any leasing program in the BLM's history.

In many parts of the world, barbed wire fence has been a standard technique for containing livestock since the late 1800s. Back then it was an initially expensive but practical way to keep cows, sheep, and horses where you wanted them. In addition, the more fence you had, the less employees you needed on the payroll to keep track of wandering livestock. However, as fencing became ubiquitous in the American West, Australia, many African countries, and elsewhere, it also disrupted wildlife movements, including the long migration routes of species like pronghorn, wildebeests, and oryx. Many of these annual migration routes had been used by wild species for thousands of years.

Another downside of physical fencing is that once it is put

in place, the costs to move it are generally prohibitive. Just one mile of new fence today in Montana can cost in excess of $10,000 per mile, so the fencing often remains in place for decades. Many a rancher might like to move one or more of his or her old fences to better utilize their land base, if they had a magic wand to do so. Today that magic wand exists.

In 1973, Richard Peck launched the Invisible Fence to give dog owners a way to keep their pets in a yard without using physical fences. The system originally relied on buried wires to trigger a series of beeps on the pet's collar, warning them away when they got too close to the yard's boundaries. The now-wireless system has evolved to include a mild-but-surprising shock if the dog ignores the warning beeps. Most animals learn the property boundaries after just a few static electricity-like shocks and stay safely within the beep-boundaries of their yard.

After more than forty years in service, this virtual fence technology has caught the attention of the livestock world. A growing number of companies from Norway, the US, New Zealand, and Australia are supplying these animal containment systems primarily to cattle producers.

The systems consist of a series of small radio towers placed across one's livestock ranch and collars for every cow in the herd. A rancher can look at her or his virtual fence system for even a thirty-thousand-plus-acre ranch and change the layout of their pastures every day. They do this using their phone, tablet, or laptop from basically anywhere. This ability to constantly learn, adapt and improve grazing strategies is becoming a key tool in the growing area of precision agriculture.

There is significant cost for the original setup, but overtime virtual fence pays for itself in a number of ways. There are no costly, labor-intensive repairs needed as there are with a physical fence that has been damaged by heavy snow loads, prairie or forest fires, or from wild species like elk or kudu that can sometimes damage the fence when trying to go through or over it.

When ranchers want to move an existing virtual fence, add additional lengths of fencing, or change the geometric shape of a pasture—operational costs are reduced because no additional employees are needed to help with this task. The new fence is repositioned on the landscape virtually. As soon as the rancher switches on the new fence using their device, the invisible fences begin emitting a signal to the livestock when they get near. That is the magic wand in action.

The good news for wildlife is that while the cows must stay where the rancher wants them, all wildlife species can roam in ways they may not have been able to for more than a century. And wild species can once again follow old migration routes across what were, for a time, highly fragmented landscapes.

Just like with electric cars and trucks, it will be a while before e-fence is solidly the new standard for livestock containment, but its use is expanding. I predict in a few years many thousands of miles of physical fence that has long impeded the free movement of wildlife will have been removed across eleven western US states. In perhaps ten years or more, hundreds of thousands of miles fencing will have been permanently removed which—while improving efficiency and dramatically lessening overhead costs for livestock producers—will also benefit all manner of wildlife and wild habitats in many ways.

—

Many decades ago, when I was in public school, students learned about wild species one at a time. As we made our way through birds, deer, elk, coyotes, and bears, little time was spent on learning about the nuanced interdependency between these species and their habitats. It wasn't until the early 1980s, while Kayla and I were traveling in Mexico, the Caribbean, and Southeast Asia, that I learned to see things differently. Those mind-expanding experiences continued while living right next to and learning about the Monterey Bay ecosystem in Santa

Cruz, California, from the mid-1980s through the mid-1990s. Later, after starting American Prairie in the early 2000s, I learned more through endless conversations with conservation biologists and reading many articles and books on the subject. During these thirty-plus years, I was slowly swapping out the lens I had been taught to look through in my public school education for one that caused me to see the natural world in a different, more complex, and far more interesting way.

Today, the notions of whole systems ecology and the idea of intact ecosystems are becoming mainstream. In many countries people in their teens, twenties, and early thirties are much better educated about these concepts than people of my generation. As a result, the younger generations are increasingly becoming involved in new conservation projects with the intactness concept at the forefront. Similar to their adeptness with technology as compared to those of us in older generations, grasping the importance of establishing large core areas for nature and connecting them with effective corridors, comes more naturally to them. As this education trend continues and younger generations take over positions in politics, business, academia and elsewhere, our societal decision making about how to do better for our natural environment should improve.

Until fairly recently, the field of conservation biology was primarily the domain of white males. This is changing rapidly, and I believe it will continue to drive positive changes in the effectiveness of nature-saving activities. People of color and all ethnicities are also entering the field, but the differences I notice with more women becoming involved seem—for the moment—the most pronounced.

As compared to even a few decades ago, today it is not uncommon for women to make up more than 50 percent of the employees at a conservation organization (as is the case at American Prairie) and they are spread throughout all roles and all levels. The presence of women is adding diversity of thought and richness to team dynamics in organizations, which positively impacts creativity and innovation. Those who have joined the conservation movement so far are helping to dilute, proportionally, the white male culture (of which I am a part). This in turn is making it easier for still other women to join these evolving organizations and to feel like they fit and are valued from the get-go. In addition to improving the quality of thought and execution in this field, due to the increasing inclusion of many more women, the overall capacity of the nature conservation industry is now expanding faster than I'd witnessed twenty-five years ago.

—

For as long as there has been Homo sapiens on earth—current estimates are around three hundred thousand years—women, traditionally and culturally, have generally had far fewer real choices than men in how to lead their own lives. But in the past few decades, an accelerated rate of change has been underway in that situation. Progress definitely remains unequal across geographies and local cultures, but in general, the empowerment of women and them feeling increasingly free of cultural pressures when deciding how they want to live their lives, is spreading throughout many parts of the world faster than ever in history. Of course, these changes should have happened for women a very long time ago, and today they are still not happening nearly as fast as they should. But the fact is that the current pace of change in favor of women's empowerment and expanding opportunities to design their own life trajectories is unprecedented.

One specific outcome of this trend that could benefit nature and biodiversity is a growing percentage of women are deciding to have fewer children—or no children at all—as compared to previous generations. There are a myriad of reasons cited for this trend. But one thing is certain, women choosing to have fewer children means the global human population growth rate is slowing down measurably and earlier than experts have predicted.

If this trend continues for the next thirty to forty years, demand for housing, goods and services, bigger highways for auto and truck transport, wood products, new factories, shipping and even agricultural products should lessen over time. That suggests the significant negative environmental impacts often associated with all those things should subside as well.

There are many who worry about global population decline. They believe capitalist economies require constant growth and expansion to ensure demand for goods and services. Less population growth, no growth, or a decline in human population translates into fewer consumers. Some people believe that having fewer consumers will inevitably lead to economic stagnation and somehow, eventual human suffering.

The bottom line is, this trend is real and, while there are always downsides to any big change, I think humans can and will adjust just fine to a leveling off, and later the eventual, gradual long-term decline, in human population. In my opinion, while adjustments will be needed to mitigate potential downsides, I think there are many exciting environmental benefits to this change. A slowly declining human population could help in righting many of the extraordinary wrongs we as a species have inflicted on nature over the past four hundred or so years.

CHAPTER SEVENTEEN

Feeding the World's Humans

Over the past ten years or so, I've learned there is much good news emerging from the agricultural industry that could eventually help nature and wildlife. Specifically, innovative techniques for raising more food for humans on far smaller parcels of land are slowly being put into practice in many areas of the world.

While our continued encroachment into natural areas with our roads, factories, homes, timber logging, and airports all contribute to loss of native habitat, it is widely accepted that our current farming and ranching techniques—and conversion of more wild lands to agriculture—are responsible for the majority of wild habitat destruction. The good news is that increased efficiencies in global agriculture practices are showing promise that food production activities could one day use at least 60 percent less land than is used today, while still producing ample profits for producers and ample healthy food for humans.

Regenerative agriculture is an increasingly common term which originally referred to farming techniques geared toward improving soil quality. The term has morphed into a planet-friendly set of practices that includes adaptive grazing, no-till planting, and limited or sometime no use of pesticides or fertilizers. Thus far in the US, it's estimated that 2 to

4 percent of farmers are practicing the concept. Awareness about it is increasing, as is support by corporations like General Mills and Nestlé. Some new policy incentives are slowly coming online for it by way of subsidies, grants, and carbon credit programs, so expanded adoption of the practices seems likely. However, even if 90 percent of farmers eventually operate within the principles of regenerative agriculture, it is not enough of a change to traditional ag practices to create far more room on the planet for nature by 2030, 2040, and 2050.

Sustainable intensification is the agricultural sector's term for growing more food than traditional ag practices while producing fewer negative impacts on the environment, including using less physical space, therefore providing more room for nature. A growing component of sustainable intensification is called Controlled-Environment Agriculture (or CEA). CEA seeks to lessen or eliminate the use of pesticides and herbicides, to save water, and to protect crops from hail, wind and other sources of damage, including wildlife. One key strategy of CEA is to grow food crops and raise livestock indoors. Most pertinent to the topic of creating more protected space on earth for nature, CEA can significantly reduce the land area needed to produce food from both plants and livestock when compared to traditional agricultural practices.

Initial resistance to or hesitancy about sustainable intensification agriculture often centers on two assumptions: That this technique cannot grow enough food for a projected peak world population of ten billion people; and that even if it could grow enough food, overhead costs would be too high for agriculturists to make a profit and stay in business.

One example to address those concerns—in addition to Demark, South Korea, and other longtime successful ag innovators—is the tiny country of the Netherlands. The following comparison helps illuminate how our American ag industry might benefit from more widespread adoption of the think far smaller, while producing far more ideas.

My home state of Montana consists of roughly 147,000 square miles. The entire country of the Netherlands is just over 16,000 square miles. Therefore, you could fit nine Netherlands inside Montana.

Montana, with good reason, is viewed as an agricultural leader—at least by US standards—from a production standpoint. The state has a total annual agricultural output (crops and livestock) that usually averages between four and five billion US dollars.

The Netherlands—one ninth the size of Montana—has an annual average agricultural output between $38 and $45 billion in farm-gate value. In 2025, the relatively tiny Netherlands is currently ranked as the second largest agricultural exporter in the entire world, after the US.

To restate the above, the Netherlands—which compared to Montana is fairly crowded with people—each year achieves roughly five times the gross revenue of Montana's agricultural sector. And they do this on one-ninth of Montana's land mass.

More important to preserving nature than Netherlands high level of production and profitability is that they produce so much food and monetary value using far less land than does Montana. To produce four to five billion dollars in ag value, Montana currently requires approximately fifty-seven million acres of land devoted to agriculture. The Netherlands produces its $38 to $45 billion annually using only an approximate *eleven million* acres for crops and livestock—an extraordinary difference in acre to acre efficiency and overall productivity

Of note, while producing this much food for the world, the Netherlands has not sacrificed nature and wildlife; instead, the country is home to a diverse range of wild species supported by unique landscapes, including costal dunes, wetlands, forests, heathlands, and river deltas.

As one example of their ability to coexist with nature and wildlife, after an approximate two-hundred-year absence, wolves have made their way back to the Netherlands. There are now nine breeding pairs in the wild that last year produced thirty-nine pups. Seven wolf packs are in the Veluwe region, two in the Drenthe, and two on the border between Drenthe and Friesland. A country that is one ninth the size of Montana, and is a global powerhouse in terms of food production, is also prioritizing saving nature and wildlife, including embracing the return of a top predator that has been absent for two centuries.

The Netherlands—along with countries like Denmark, South Korea, and others—has always been a small country with very limited arable land and a cold winter climate. They've had to, out of necessity, continuously seek the best ways to produce food given those parameters. They discovered that by committing to nonstop, continuous improvement and aggressive innovation in their ag practices, there could be virtually no end to finding new ways to grow more food using less land.

This reminds me of Moore's law regarding computer chips. In 1965 Gordon Moore, who later cofounded the Intel Corporation, theorized that the number of transistors that will fit on a microchip without making the chip bigger will double roughly every two years. At the time few people believed his prediction. But sixty years later—while the pace of that doubling is beginning to slow somewhat—his foresight remains largely accurate. Computer chips continue to get smaller and more powerful. Key to Moore's theory was his overt and unwavering belief in a mindset: a relentless, obsessive commitment to the core values of innovation and continuous improvement.

Another key factor to the Netherlands's track record for ag innovation is its relationship to Wageningen University, whose influence on the region is similar to Stanford University's on Silicon Valley in California. Like those interested in technology who beat a path to Stanford U's door, budding agriculturalists from around the world who want to learn the very latest innovations in sustainable intensification agriculture, most often choose Wageningen University out of all ag-focused universities around the world, including those in the US.

In contrast to the Netherlands and other small countries, the US has an abundance of land. Many US agriculturists who want to produce more product, first opt to put more of their own private land under cultivation or into livestock grazing, or lease or purchase more land for that purpose. The result of this mindset creates conditions where producing food for humans is first priority, and thereby further shrinks the area of the earth's surface that is available for nature and wildlife.

The Netherlands regularly outperforms the US enormously in an acre-to-acre comparison with many food products like onions, potatoes, tomatoes, dairy, pork and beef, and many more. Given that, the solutions we need in agriculture—assuming we are curious about how to be more productive while making more room for nature—are sitting in plain sight.

Sustainable intensification ag practices like CEA are indeed transferable to other parts of the world. Today some US-based farmers and ranchers are starting to use Netherlands-type techniques. They are demonstrating that it can be done successfully—meaning profitably—in the US, even where land is expensive, winters can be long and cold, and where aridity can make getting enough water a challenge.

Just one such example is Paul Sellew, CEO of US-based Little Leaf Farms. Sellew was first exposed to the Netherlands farming techniques many years ago while he was playing pro basketball in the European league. Paul combined the controlled environment ag practices he learned there with others from around the world and started his own produce company in the American Northeast. Now, using what he calls the most technologically advanced greenhouses in the world to practice high quality CEA, his team grows on average, the same amount of produce on just ten acres as do the one hundred-acre farms nearby that are producing the exact same food crops outdoors. That's a 90 percent reduction in land dedicated to growing the same volume of food as an outdoor farm. His company also uses one-tenth of the water as compared to neighboring outdoor farms. And they use zero pesticides or herbicides because harmful bugs and weeds are non-issues inside his greenhouses.

Importantly, Little Leaf Farms is profitable, even after factoring in the start-up costs of building and running the greenhouses, which also have ultra-low electricity demands as they are powered by solar energy. Each year, Paul and a growing number of others who are putting these techniques into practice are proving that nutritious, high-quality food for humans can be grown on as little as a tenth of the land and using far fewer resources and harmful inputs than we do now in the US.

In regard to the question of how to produce enough food for a future human population of ten-plus billion, most food security experts suggest there are two key issues that, if solved, could largely eliminate concerns about food scarcity.

The first issue is that there is general agreement that it is not a shortage of food that is our problem; it is most often the affordability of the food and access to existing food stocks that is the problem. The second issue is that it's estimated that between 30 and 40 percent of all food produced—including within the US—is wasted before it reaches the consumer through spoilage during transport, while waiting in storage, rejection by store managers at the retail level for aesthetic reasons, and other factors. Given those issues, from a systems thinking mindset, "How do we grow more food for a population of ten or so billion people?" is the wrong question. Looking forward—with an eye toward borrowing existing best practices and creating more space for nature—a helpful question would be, "How can we help agriculturists around the world adopt myriad existing food production techniques that dependably produce more broadly affordable food on far less land than we are doing now?"

As just one idea, there is plenty of data suggesting that agriculturists—just like many of us—will respond to financial incentives. Currently a substantial portion of the nineteen-billion-dollar US Farm Bill budget goes to heavily subsidizing for-profit agricultural operations for decades old agricultural techniques. With the right kind of political leadership, there could be a repurposing of those subsidies to help individuals convert to more productive techniques like using CEA infrastructure. They could also offset costs to install virtual fencing (which can help raise more livestock on less land while improving habitat for wildlife) and encourage more participation in the regenerative ag space. The cost to taxpayers for these subsidies could be offset by an equal reduction or elimination of current Farm Bill subsidies that support much less efficient, and far less nature-friendly approaches to producing food. If the incentives were well designed, over time this could portend a significant change in the culture and mindset of American agriculture industry to one that is somewhat equivalent to Moore's law with computer chips:

Can we really make these needed big changes in agriculture? Well, consider other sweeping changes that are occurring today. For instance, my now pre-school-aged grandchildren may get their drivers licenses in 2036 and 2038. I am guessing they will likely never drive an internal-combustion-engine car. After 130 years of dominance in the car market, the transition away from fossil-fuel-burning vehicles is underway. Coal, as fuel to burn in coal-fired power plants, is phasing out rapidly. And consider the variety of positive trends concerning the empowerment of women, improvements in environmental education, changes to how agriculture is being done in many other countries, and many others I don't have room to list.

I believe it is important to free our minds from our traditional approaches to producing food for ourselves and livestock, let our imaginations run and begin to visualize this idea of creating far more room for nature. Once we clearly understand, and later fall in love with that vision, we will create a path of least resistance toward it and things will begin to flow in that direction. Choose to not be like the countless people who told me and my fledging, poorly funded team back in 2001, that the American Prairie dream was too big, too complicated, too expensive, and too controversial. Take a few moments to peruse American Prairie's website and check out what has been accomplished since then. And then choose not to be cynical and to not sound like those people, many of whom specialize in sitting on the sidelines throwing rocks (in the form of criticism) at those who are trying to make big things happen. Instead, choose to be optimistic *and bold.*

I am suggesting we enthusiastically join this not-yet-completely-crystalized global vision for 2050, right here, right now. And I am suggesting this is the best time to start working on making it clearer, more understandable, and more compelling—and to pursue it much more aggressively.

The next time you drive through the central valley of California, which has roughly seven million acres of land under cultivation—or somewhere similar elsewhere in the world— imagine all of those strawberries, leafy greens, rice, artichokes, carrots, onions, garlic, and more, using upwards of 50 to 75 percent less land, water, pesticides and herbicides, as compared to today; like Little Leaf Farms. And picture those agriculture producers still there, still in business and creating the quality food that we need and still making profits for themselves.

And imagine seeing various forms of wildlife on the enormous areas of newly freed up land—perhaps even grizzly bears, prominent on California's state flag given they used to be everywhere in the region. This can absolutely be done if, as we look toward what we are doing today to benefit future generations, we believe nature is important. We have to imagine. Like the American Prairie effort that seemed so far-fetched twenty-four years ago—it starts with a compelling vision, followed by enough people choosing to act.

CHAPTER EIGHTEEN

Onward

My time with American Prairie has changed my belief about who is responsible for protecting habitats and wildlife. I once thought it was primarily the job of governments or large global conservation-focused NGOs. I now believe our best hope for supporting or accelerating some of the positive trends I have noted in the near term, is the addition of a third force in conservation: The work of small groups of people—few of whom are wealthy, well-connected, or possess advanced degrees in areas like conservation biology—coming together, getting laser-focused on an exhilarating vision to make the world better, and then getting to work. That is how American Prairie began.

As noted, this is already happening around the world in growing volume and with remarkable results with people acting in accordance with a sixty-year-old quote attributed to Eldridge Cleaver: "There is no more neutrality in the world. You either have to be part of the solution, or you're going to be part of the problem." These people are part of the solution. Here are just a few examples:

Violet Sage Walker, Chairwoman of Northern Chumash Tribal Council, helped lead a twenty-year effort to create a 4,543-square-mile marine sanctuary along Californias central coast. Officially designated in 2024, the Chumash Heritage

National Marine Sanctuary now protects marine biodiversity, sustainable fishing practices and indigenous heritage, while also retiring thirty-three oil and gas leases and rerouting cargo and cruise ship lanes to safeguard whales and reduce pollution in the sanctuary.

In Tanzania, Laly Lichtenfeld and Paul Trout cofounded African People & Wildlife in 2005. To date, they have constructed more than 1,600 natural "living walls" that protect livestock from wild predators across more than fifty local communities. Hundreds of lions' lives have been saved as a result. Their innovations and approaches to human/wildlife coexistence are also helping to save other wild species and are being replicated now, even beyond Tanzania.

Australian military veteran Damien Mander redirected his expertise toward conservation, founding Akashinga in 2009. His all-female ranger force now protects over twenty million acres of African wildlife habitat from poaching, demonstrating how determined individuals can make an extraordinary impact.

Ecologist Dominique Gonçalves manages the elephant ecology program at the 2,500-square-mile Gorongosa National Park, in Mozambique's Great Rift Valley. Dominique strives to integrate the needs of wildlife, people, community, and sustainable tourism. During the fifteen-year Mozambique civil war, the elephant population there dropped from and estimated fifty thousand to just three hundred by the early 2000s. One of Dominique's many elegant solutions to lessen human conflicts with elephants was to borrowed from other areas like Tanzania. Local farmers now hang beehives along their farm fences: When the elephants—who are famously afraid of bees—bump the wires on which the hives hang, the bees emerge quite upset. The elephants quickly retreat, and fragile farm crops are saved. Thanks to the work of Dominique and her colleagues, the elephant population at Gorongosa recently reached five hundred.

In northern Mexico, the Northern Jaguar Project (NJP), cofounded by Diana Hadley, Peter Warshall, and Rick Williams, has grown to seventy-five thousand acres of protected jaguar habitat. NJP is working with surrounding ranchers who, after receiving help in implementing new wildlife friendly ranching practices, agree not to harm any of the four major felines: jaguars, mountain lions, ocelots, and bobcats. Populations of all of those species are improving as a result.

These are just a few of the countless, once-small efforts, usually started by only a handful of people, that now have big impacts creating more room for nature though most people have never heard of them. If a few hundred thousand, or maybe a few million more of the world's eight billion-plus people, decided to take similar actions and become involved in similar efforts, the pace of achieving positive effects for nature could speed up considerably.

Last Thoughts That May Pertain to You.

Maybe as you are reading this book, you are considering joining the world of nature conservation either as a paid vocation or as a consistent volunteer, or some hybrid between the two. I can only speak from my own experience, but here are a few last thoughts as you weigh your options and explore possibilities.

Deciding to Be Optimistic

I continue to encounter people who have largely lost hope for our planet and the natural world. They feel we are too late to adjust our course. Climate nihilism, which afflicts a number of young people, is just one example. They worry that today's leaders in government, industry, academia and elsewhere are not going to step up and act boldly for nature any time soon. Yet for all the reasons I've mentioned, I remain optimistic when contemplating the long view. Deliberately seeking out good news about the planet's prospects rather than always letting someone else curate my news for me improves my outlook. I continue to learn about both the good and the bad happening out there regarding our environment, and I actively decide to stay optimistic, doing what I can to be part of the solution, no matter how small my individual actions might seem in the greater scheme of things.

The well-known theologian and author Matthew Fox has pondered in his writings how we might best acquire the skills and experiences needed to craft a continuously improving society. Fox theorizes that perhaps the single most helpful thing might be to work together on preserving nature at a large scale. He reasons that in order to do so, everyone involved would have to try to understand nature at a deep level. This means learning about interdependencies within and between complex systems, appreciating the ever-changing, dynamic aspects of those systems. It means being willing to be persistent, open-minded, and prepared to change our own long-held assumptions to help find the long-term solutions required to protect nature. By doing all of that, he theorizes, we would learn the generic fundamentals and mindset required to effectively make myriad other societal improvements as well. I think Fox is right. I've found that working on land conservation issues that will benefit wildlife and people pushes us to operate out of our best selves, to think much further into the future than other topics might demand of us, and to stay true to our goals while accommodating other's motivations as well.

I had to learn, and change, a great deal to understand and address the challenges we had in front of us at American Prairie. I had to let go of many initial assumptions about how we would get things done while pursuing our vision. I am not sure what other job would have pushed me as much to examine my own limitations and to incorporate new ways of thinking about things that contradicted what I'd thought was normal or true.

As I changed, so did many of my colleagues, and therefore we as an organization. The result: Every year—even though I am no longer the leader there—American Prairie gets better at what it does, at executing in general, and at finding and implementing lasting solutions that the majority of stakeholders feel are fair and workable.

Given the trends I am watching and the people with whom I am privileged to speak and who are part of driving those trends, I honestly believe the long-term looks promising for my pre-school-aged grandchildren. I really do believe that, when they are middle-aged adults, they will see and experience much cleaner air, far more intelligent and thoughtful approaches to agriculture, far more small and large parks and protected areas having been dedicated as wildlife sanctuaries, better protected wildlife populations in the oceans and terrestrial places, and less pollution overall than existed way back in 2025.

Keep in mind that no matter what kind of project you undertake, making a profound impact in nature conservation can take quite a long time. Like most people, I love the feeling of finishing a job. But I have learned through experience that signing up for the long haul in conservation is usually a requirement if your results are going to be both meaningful and long-lasting.

American Prairie is an example of this mindset made real. Now in its third decade, the current trajectory of our grassland rewilding effort is a pleasure to follow. As of 2025, American Prairie is already larger, in total acres, than forty-one of the sixty-two US national parks—and it continues to grow every year. A steadily increasing number of local people hold a favorable opinion of American Prairie and our goals. Money raised thus far exceeds that of any other US wildlife reserve-building effort in recent times. Small but growing populations of previously eradicated species, such as swift fox and bison, and now even grizzly bears, are back and growing. The number of annual visitors from around the globe rises each year, as does the number of donors and volunteers. And yet there is still much work to do to realize the ultimate vision.

Such a life-changing commitment to helping nature may not be for everyone. But it, or something like it, might be just right for you. And if you think it is, then ask yourself, "Is this the right time for a big, bold move?" I hope it is. Nature is waiting.

Yes, maybe the best time to become involved in enhancing and preserving nature for you, and for all of us, was many years ago—but the second-best time is now.

Afterword: An Invitation

GEORGE HORSE CAPTURE, JR

For years, my people prayed to bring back not just the buffalo, but everything. Wanting buffalo to come back, wanting things to be set right again—for a long time, it was just a thought. When I was younger, I couldn't figure out what it meant, or how to go about it. Was this destined to just be a want? Just be a prayer?

I've always looked at it as a way for others to learn more about the place, about the prairie, and about my people. Thanks to this endeavor, we're pushing aside barriers, imagining what this work could mean to others.

The prairie is the oldest Grandmother in existence, and despite everything, she is still willing to work with us. She has gifts that she wants to give if we're there showing an interest. It takes more than just money to make this a reality: it takes love and compassion, not just for other humans or for the buffalo, but for Grandmother in general.

How can we light a candle so that people can find this place to be a part of? Go out there and have your own experience; it's a gift to you, it's one you can go back and share with your own grandkids. In this place, you can walk with the with the Tribes, homesteaders; with the buffalo, you walk with three-toed sloths. You're walking where so many have walked before, and you become part of that. Even a footprint becomes a part of the landscape.

It takes a lot of courage to act on a dream. So often we're out there setting up our own little kingdoms.

There's so much hope out there, on prairies, on mountain-tops. It's well worth while—it's a good thing. Come and see.

GEORGE HORSE CAPTURE, JR. *Aaniiih (Gros Ventre) elder, former Fort Belknap Indian Community Tribal Council Vice-President, Director of Aaniiih Nakoda Tours, and your friend on the prairie*

Acknowledgments

This is my first attempt at writing a book. I realized very early on that it was kind of like American Prairie: If I tried to do it on my own, it would never get finished. I owe heartfelt thanks to many people who each in their own way helped make it better and helped keep it moving toward completion.

A thank you goes to Gene Stone for his editing skill, his remarkable patience over three years dealing with me as a first-time author, his endless mentoring, suggestions on the book's structure, his candidness when my work was not hitting the mark, and his valuable praise when it did. His experience was evident and highly appreciated the entire way through.

To Will Neville-Rehbehn, Kirsten Johanna Allen, and the impressive Torrey House Press team both for wanting this book and for expertly guiding it through its final stages. To Betsy Gaines Quammen for introducing me to Torrey House Press.

To Lisa Thomas at National Geographic Books, whose initial spark convinced me to embark on this endeavor. To Nick Bromley for his expert editing and steady encouragement. To Steve Cousins, who, early on when I was wavering, encouraged me to pursue this project. To David Quammen who—when I was not at all sure—affirmed the viability of my book idea.

To Clyde Aspevig, who listened to my misgivings over the years and kept encouraging me to simply tell the story as I'd experienced it. To Bill Gunn and Mark Cool for their thorough readings of the entire book and their valuable feedback. To Alison Fox, CEO of American Prairie, for her comprehensive review and helpful suggestions. To Dakota Meeks for helping me navigate some challenging topics.

To Dan Flores, who coached me through the daunting middle stages when the end seemed so far away and offered advice on working with editors. To Curt Freese for answering many questions along the way that ensured factual accuracy. To Simon Reeve for sharing his book-writing experiences and responding enthusiastically to my structural concepts.

My sincere appreciation to Ken Burns for his generous foreword.

To George Horse Capture Jr. for our two decades of friendship, and for our many conversations as he thought through what messages he would like to leave for readers in his afterward.

To my daughter, Siri, for her thoughtful feedback from a younger generation's perspective.

To the combined staff, trustees, emeritus board, advisors, and cherished supporters of the American Prairie project, Without you, there would be no story to tell.

To my son, Dylan, for his three years of ceaseless encouragement to keep going, even on my most doubt-filled and challenging writing days.

And to my extraordinary wife, Kayla, for her countless readings and insightful suggestions on this project, and her partnership and adventuresome spirit in all things throughout our forty-five years together.

—

A portion of the proceeds from sales of *Wild on Purpose* will be donated by the author to Life's Language Lodge, a Nakoda and Aaniiih language nest on the Fort Belknap Indian Reservation in North Eastern Montana. To learn more, visit fort-belknapcedc.org/initiatives.

Suggested Further Resources

The following recommendations include some classics, some academic works, and some literary titles that introduce different topic areas. I have found that reading eight to ten books in a subject area, with their overlapping and repeating themes, invited new insights and ideas for application.

General History of Wildlife in North America

Flores, Dan. *Wild New World: The Epic Story of Animals and People in America*. Firsted, 2022.

Flores, Dan. *American Serengeti: The Last Big Animals of the Great Plains*. University Press of Kansas, 2016.

Nijhuis, Michelle. *Beloved Beasts: Fighting for Life in an Age of Extinction*. W. W. Norton & Company, 2021.

Leopold, Aldo. *A Sand County Almanac: And Sketches Here and There*. Oxford University Press, 2020.

Carson, Rachel. *Silent Spring*. Houghton Mifflin, 2022.

Grasslands Ecology and Wildlife:

Manning, Richard. *Grassland: The History, Biology, Politics, and Promise of the American Prairie*. Viking, 1995.

Freese, Curtis. *Back from the Collapse: American Prairie and the Restoration of Great Plains Wildlife*. University of Nebraska Press, 2023.

Lott, Dale F. *American Bison: A Natural History*. University of California Press, 2002.

Byers, John A. *Built for Speed: A Year in the Life of Pronghorn*. Harvard University Press, 2003.

Schullery, Paul. *Lewis and Clark among the Grizzlies Leg-

end and Legacy in the American West. TwoDot, 2002.

Hampton, H. Duane, ed. *Life and Death at the Mouth of the Musselshell.* Stoneydale Press, 2011.

Garcia, Andrew. *Tough Trip Through Paradise 1878–1879.* University of Idaho Press, 1967.

American Prairie. YouTube channel. https://www.youtube.com/user/AmericanPrairie.

Indigenous History on the Northen Great Plains:

Lame Deer, John (Fire), and Erdoes, Richard. *Lame Deer, Seeker of Visions.* Simon & Schuster, 1994.

Grann, David. *Killers of the Flower Moon: The Osage Murders and the Birth of the FBI.* Doubleday, 2017.

Welch, James. *Fools Crow.* Penguin Books, 1987.

Momaday, N. Scott. *House Made of Dawn.* Harper Perennial Modern Classics, 2010.

Welch, James, and Stekler, Paul. *Killing Custer: The Battle of Little Big Horn and the Fate of the Plains Indians.* Penguin Books, 1995.

Storm, Hyemeyohsts. *Seven Arrows.* Ballantine Books, 1972.

Leadership and Building Quality Organizations:

Kotter, John P. *John P. Kotter on What Leaders Really Do.* Harvard Business Review Press, 1999.

Kotter, John P. "Leading Change: Why Transformation Efforts Fail." *Harvard Business Review* 73, no. 2 (1995): 59–67.

Senge, Peter M. *The Fifth Discipline: The Art & Practice of the Learning Organization.* Crown Currency, 2006.

Bradford, David L., and Cohen, Allan R. *Managing for Excellence: The Guide to Developing High Performance in Contemporary Organizations.* Wiley, 1997.

Kouzes, James M., and Posner, Barry Z. *The Leadership Challenge: How to Make Extraordinary Things Happen in Organizations.* Jossey-Bass, 2012.

Sinek, Simon. *Leaders Eat Last: Why Some Teams Pull Together and Others Don't*. Portfolio, 2017.

De Pree, Max. *Leadership Is an Art*. Crown Currency, 2004.

Collins, Jim. *Good to Great: Why Some Companies Make the Leap...And Others Don't*. Harper Business, 2001.

Lencioni, Patrick M. *The Five Dysfunctions of a Team: A Leadership Fable*. Jossey-Bass, 2002.

Personal Purpose, Values, Transitions and Visioning:

Bridges, William, and Bridges, Susan. *Transitions: Making Sense of Life's Changes*. Balance, 2019.

Fritz, Robert. *The Path of Least Resistance: Learning to Become the Creative Force in Your Own Life*. Ballantine Books, 1989.

Cameron, Julia. *The Artist's Way: Spiritual Path to Higher Creativity*. Tarcher, 2016.

Gerrity, Sean, host, *The Answers Are Out There*, podcast, "Personal Vision and Strategy," https://www.theanswersare-outtherepodcast.net/podcast.

Ferrucci, Piero. *What We May Be: Techniques for Psychological and Spiritual Growth Through Psychosynthesis*. Tarcher, 2009.

Kafka, Franz. *The Metamorphosis*. Simon & Schuster, 2009.

Castaneda, Carlos. *Journey to Ixtlan: The Lessons of Don Juan*. Washington Square Press, 1991.

Doty, James R. *Mind Magic: The Neuroscience of Manifestation and How It Changes Everything*. Avery, 2024.

Chestnu, Beatrice. *The Complete Enneagram: 27 Paths to Greater Self-Knowledge*. She Writes Press, 2013.

André, Christophe. *Looking at Mindfulness: Twenty-five Paintings to Change the Way You Live*. Blue Rider Press, 2016.

The Future of Conservation:

Klein, Ezra, and Thompson, Derek. *Abundance*. Avid Reader Press, 2025.

Attenborough, David, and Hughes, Jonnie. *A Life on Our Planet: My Witness Statement and a Vision for the Future.* Grand Central Publishing, 2020.

Wilson, Edward O. *The Future of Life: ALA Notable Books for Adults.* Vintage, 2002.

Wilson, Edward O. Half-Earth: *Our Planet's Fight for Life.* Liveright, 2017.

Martin, Laura J. *Wild by Design: The Rise of Ecological Restoration.* Harvard University Press, 2025.

Fothergill, Alastair, producer. Planet Earth. BBC Natural History Unit, 2006, https://www.bbcearth.com/shows/planet-earth.

Fothergill, Alastair, and Scholey, Keith, producers. *Our Planet.* Silverback Films, 2019, https://www.ourplanet.com/en/explore/one-planet.

Wright, Matthew, producer. *Asia.* BBC Studios Natural History Unit, 2024, https://www.bbcearth.com/shows/asia.

Joffe, Abraham, Lyon, Nick, and Tuck, Joe et al., directors, *Our Oceans,* 2024, https://www.netflix.com/title/81139969.

ABOUT THE AUTHOR

Sean Gerrity is the founder of American Prairie, a Montana-based conservation organization dedicated to creating one of the largest wildlife reserves ever assembled in the Lower 48. A National Geographic Explorer, Gerrity serves on multiple advisory boards focused on global conservation, including African People and Wildlife and the Kratt Brothers Creature Hero Foundation. Raised primarily in Great Falls, Montana, he now lives in Bozeman with his wife, Kayla Gerrity.

ABOUT THE COVER ART

"The glaciated plains of northern Montana represent one of the few remaining ecosystems of its kind left in the world today. This beguiling landscape with its harsh weather, silhouettes of distant mountain ranges on never-ending horizons, and big dramatic skies, is where I grew up."

—Clyde Aspevig

Common Ground, a six foot by ten foot oil on canvas by artist Clyde Aspevig, can be viewed at American Prairie's National Discovery Center in Lewistown, Montana. Aspevig lives in Montana with his wife and fellow artist, Carolina Guzman.

ABOUT TORREY HOUSE PRESS

Torrey House Press exists at the intersection of the literary arts and environmental advocacy. THP publishes books that elevate diverse perspectives, explore relationships with place, and deepen our connections to the natural world and to each other. THP inspires ideas, conversation, and action on issues that link the American West to the past, present, and future of the ever-changing Earth.

As a 501(c)(3) nonprofit publisher, our work is made possible by generous donations from readers like you.

Visit www.torreyhouse.org for reading group discussion guides, author interviews, and more.

SPECIAL THANKS

Wild on Purpose was made possible by the generous support of Furthermore, a program of the J. M. Kaplan Fund. Torrey House Press is supported by the King's English Bookshop, Maria's Bookshop, the Jeffrey S. & Helen H. Cardon Foundation, the Sam & Diane Stewart Family Foundation, the Barker Foundation, the George S. and Dolores Doré Eccles Foundation, Diana Allison, Klaus Bielefeldt, Joe Breddan, Karen Edgley, Laurie Hilyer, Susan Markley, Marion S. Robinson, Kitty Swenson, Shelby Tisdale, Kirtly Parker Jones, Robert Aagard & Camille Bailey Aagard, Kif Augustine Adams & Stirling Adams, Rose Chilcoat & Mark Franklin, Jerome Cooney & Laura Storjohann, Linc Cornell & Lois Cornell, Susan Cushman & Charlie Quimby, Kathleen Metcalf, Betsy Gaines Quammen & David Quammen, the Utah Division of Arts & Museums, Utah Humanities, the National Endowment for the Humanities, the National Endowment for the Arts, the Salt Lake City Arts Council, the Utah Governor's Office of Economic Development, and Salt Lake County Zoo, Arts & Parks. Our thanks to our readers, donors, members, and the Torrey House Press Board of Directors for their valued support.

Join the Torrey House Press family and give today at www.torreyhouse.org/give.

www.ingramcontent.com/pod-product-compliance
Lightning Source LLC
Chambersburg PA
CBHW021151260726
48656CB00025B/2381